ICONS 2021

The Sixteenth International Conference on Systems

April 18 - 22, 2021

ICONS 2021 Editors

Ramakrishnan Raman, Honeywell Technology Solutions, India

Chung-Ta King, National Tsing Hua University, 台灣

Ali K Raz, George Mason University, USA

Cosmin Dini, IARIA, EU/USA

Printed from e-media with permission by:

Curran Associates, Inc.
57 Morehouse Lane
Red Hook, NY 12571

Some format issues inherent in the e-media version may also appear in this print version.

Printed with permission by Curran Associates, Inc. (2023)

International Academy, Research, and Industry Association (IARIA)
412 Derby Way
Wilmington, DE 19810

Phone: (408) 893-6407
Fax: (408) 527-6351

petre@iaria.org

Additional copies of this publication are available from:

Curran Associates, Inc.
57 Morehouse Lane
Red Hook, NY 12571 USA
Phone: 845-758-0400
Fax: 845-758-2633
Email: curran@proceedings.com
Web: www.proceedings.com

Table of Contents

ICONS 2021

Forward

The Sixteenth International Conference on Systems (ICONS 2021) continued a series of events covering a broad spectrum of topics. The conference covered fundamentals on designing, implementing, testing, validating and maintaining various kinds of software and hardware systems.

In the last years, new system concepts have been promoted and partially embedded in new deployments. Anticipative systems, autonomic and autonomous systems, self-adapting systems, or on-demand systems are systems exposing advanced features. These features demand special requirements specification mechanisms, advanced behavioral design patterns, special interaction protocols, and flexible implementation platforms. Additionally, they require new monitoring and management paradigms, as self-protection, self-diagnosing, self-maintenance become core design features.

The design of application-oriented systems is driven by application-specific requirements that have a very large spectrum. Despite the adoption of uniform frameworks and system design methodologies supported by appropriate models and system specification languages, the deployment of application-oriented systems raises critical problems. Specific requirements in terms of scalability, real-time, security, performance, accuracy, distribution, and user interaction drive the design decisions and implementations.

This leads to the need for gathering application-specific knowledge and develop particular design and implementation skills that can be reused in developing similar systems.

Validation and verification of safety requirements for complex systems containing hardware, software and human subsystems must be considered from early design phases. There is a need for rigorous analysis on the role of people and process causing hazards within safety-related systems; however, these claims are often made without a rigorous analysis of the human factors involved. Accurate identification and implementation of safety requirements for all elements of a system, including people and procedures become crucial in complex and critical systems, especially in safety-related projects from the civil aviation, defense health, and transport sectors.

Fundamentals on safety-related systems concern both positive (desired properties) and negative (undesired properties) aspects. Safety requirements are expressed at the individual equipment level and at the operational-environment level. However, ambiguity in safety requirements may lead to reliable unsafe systems. Additionally, the distribution of safety requirements between people and machines makes difficult automated proofs of system safety. This is somehow obscured by the difficulty of applying formal techniques (usually used for equipment-related safety requirements) to derivation and satisfaction of human-related safety requirements (usually, human factor techniques are used).

We take here the opportunity to warmly thank all the members of the ICONS 2021 technical program committee, as well as all the reviewers. The creation of such a high quality conference program would not have been possible without their involvement. We also kindly thank all the authors who dedicated much of their time and effort to contribute to ICONS 2021. We truly believe that, thanks to all these efforts, the final conference program consisted of top quality contributions. We also thank the members of the ICONS 2021 organizing committee for their help in handling the logistics of this event.

ICONS 2021 Chairs

ICONS 2021 Steering Committee

David Inkermann, Technische Universität Clausthal, Institute of Mechanical Engineering, Germany
Christoph Knieke, Technische Universität Clausthal, Institute for Software and Systems Engineering, Germany
Giulio Telleschi, MBDA, Italy
Mo Mansouri, Stevens Institute of Technology, USA
Mark Austin, University Of Maryland, USA

ICONS 2021 Advisory Committee

Marko Jäntti, University of Eastern Finland, Finland
Zoubir Mammeri, IRIT - Paul Sabatier University, France
Raimund Ege, Northern Illinois University, USA

ICONS 2021 Publicity Chairs

Lorena Parra, Universitat Politecnica de Valencia, Spain
Jose Luis García, Universitat Politecnica de Valencia, Spain

ICONS 2021

Committee

ICONS 2021 Steering Committee

David Inkermann, Technische Universität Clausthal, Institute of Mechanical Engineering, Germany
Christoph Knieke, Technische Universität Clausthal, Institute for Software and Systems Engineering, Germany
Giulio Telleschi, MBDA, Italy
Mo Mansouri, Stevens Institute of Technology, USA
Mark Austin, University Of Maryland, USA

ICONS 2021 Advisory Committee

Marko Jäntti, University of Eastern Finland, Finland
Zoubir Mammeri, IRIT - Paul Sabatier University, France
Raimund Ege, Northern Illinois University, USA

ICONS 2021 Publicity Chairs

Lorena Parra, Universitat Politecnica de Valencia, Spain
Jose Luis García, Universitat Politecnica de Valencia, Spain

ICONS 2021 Technical Program Committee

Qammer H. Abbasi, University of Glasgow, Scotland, UK
Mohamed A. Abd El Ghany, German University in Cairo, Egypt
Witold Abramowicz, Poznan University of Economics, Poland
Afaq Ahmad, Sultan Qaboos University, Oman
Abdelouhab Aitouche, YNCREA/HEI | University of Lille, France
Ali Al-Humairi, German University of Technology (GUtech), Oman
Walid Al-Hussaibi, Southern Technical University (STU), Iraq
Mohammed Al-Khafajiy, University of Reading, UK
Saloua Bel Hadj Ali, University of Tunis-El Manar / University of Gabès, Tunisia
Mark Austin, University Of Maryland, USA
Muhammed Ali Aydin, Istanbul University-Cerrahpasa, Turkey
Snježana Babić, Juraj DobrilaUniversityofPula, Croatia
Lubomir Bakule, Institute of Information Theory and Automation, Czech Republic
Janibul Bashir, National Institute of Technology, Srinagar, India
Suvadip Batabyal, BITS Pilani, Hyderabad Campus, India
Pankaj Bhowmik, University of Florida, USA
Alejandro J. Bianchi, LIVEWARE S.A. / Universidad Catolica Argentina, Argentina
Francesco Bianconi, Università degli Studi di Perugia, Italy
Birthe Boehm, Siemens AG, Germany
Sander Bohte, Machine Learning group - CWI, Amsterdam, The Netherlands

Christoph Knieke, Technische Universität Clausthal, Institute for Software and Systems Engineering, Germany
Kwangman Ko, Sang-Ji University, Korea
Andreas Koch, University of Salzburg, Austria
Ramin Tavakoli Kolagari, Technische Hochschule Nürnberg, Germany
André Koscianski, UTFPR - Federal Technological University of Paraná, Brazil
Dragana Krstic, University of Niš, Serbia
Shahar Kvatinsky, Technion - Israel Institute of Technology, Israel
Sara Laafar, Cadi Ayyad University, Marrakech, Morocco
Sándor Laki, ELTE Eötvös Loránd University, Budapest, Hungary
Robert S. Laramee, Swansea University, UK
Hoang D. Le, University of Aizu, Japan
Tao Li, Nankai University, China
Martin Lukac, Nazarbayev University, Kazakhstan
Ivan Luković, University of Novi Sad, Serbia
Jia-Ning Luo, Ming Chuan University, Taiwan
Asmaa Maali, Cadi Ayyad University, Marrakech, Morocco
Vuong Mai, KAIST, Korea
Zoubir Mammeri, IRIT - Paul Sabatier University, Toulouse, France
D. Manivannan, University of Kentucky, USA
Mo Mansouri, Stevens Institute of Technology, USA
Alberto Marchisio, Technische Universität Wien (TU Wien), Vienna, Austria
Olivier Maurice, ArianeGroup, France
Bruce R. Maxim, University of Michigan-Dearborn, USA
Michele Melchiori, Università degli Studi di Brescia, Italy
Nadhir Messai, Université de Reims Champagne-Ardenne, France
Zelalem Mihret, KAIST, Korea
Paulo E. Miyagi, University of Sao Paulo, Brazil
Fernando Moreira, Universidade Portucalense, Portugal
John Moscholios, University of Peloponnese, Greece
Anway Mukherjee, Lucid Motors, USA
Tarak Nandy, University of Malaya, Malaysia
Rohit Negi, Indian Institute of Technology, Kanpur, India
Nga Nguyen, ETIS Laboratory | EISTI, Cergy, France
Joanna Isabelle Olszewska, University of West of Scotland, UK
Tim O'Neil, University of Akron, USA
Maurizio Palesi, University of Catania, Italy
Francesca Palumbo, Università degli Studi di Sassari, Italy
Samuel Pastva, Masaryk University in Brno, Czech Republic
Szczepan Paszkiel, Opole University of Technology, Poland
Davide Patti, University of Catania, Italy
George Perry, University of Texas at San Antonio, USA
Safanah M. Raafat, University of Technology, Baghdad, Iraq
Sujan Rajbhandari, Coventry University, UK
Ramakrishnan Raman, Honeywell Technology Solutions, Bangalore, India
Grzegorz Redlarski, Gdańsk University of Technology, Poland
Piotr Remlein, Poznan University of Technology, Poland
José Ignacio Rojas-Sola, University of Jaén, Spain

Juha Röning, University of Oulu, Finland
Somayeh Sadeghi-Kohan, Paderborn University, Germany
Francesca Saglietti, University of Erlangen-Nuremberg, Germany
Souhir Sallem, National School of Engineering of Sfax, Tunisia
Christophe Sauvey, Universite de Lorraine, France
Tomas Schweigert, Expleo, Germany
Avi Shaked, Tel Aviv University, Israel
Yilun Shang, Northumbria University, UK
Charlie Y. Shim, Kutztown University of Pennsylvania, USA
Yong-Sang Shim, Kutztown University of Pennsylvania, USA
Seyit Ahmet Sis, Balikesir University / BİLGEM-TÜBİTAK (The Scientific and Technological Research Council of Turkey), Turkey
Pedro Sousa, University of Minho, Portugal
Olarik Surinta, Mahasarakham University, Thailand
Elisabet Syverud, University of South-Eastern Norway, Kongsberg, Norway
Sajjad Taheri, University of California, Irvine, USA
Shahab Tayeb, California State University, USA
Bedir Tekinerdogan, Wageningen University, Netherlands
Giulio Telleschi, MBDA, Italy
Ahmed Toumi, Sfax University, Tunisia
Carlos M. Travieso-González, University of Las Palmas de Gran Canaria (ULPGC), Spain
Denis Trček, University of Ljubljana, Slovenia
Snow H. Tseng, National Taiwan University, Taiwan
Penka Valkova Georgieva, Burgas Free University, Bulgaria
Irena Valova, University of Ruse, Bulgaria
Tom van Dijk, University of Twente, Enschede, Netherlands
Wenxi Wang, University of Texas at Austin, USA
Natalia Wawrzyniak, Maritime University of Szczecin, Poland
Katarzyna Wegrzyn-Wolska, AlliansTIC Laboratory | EFREI PARIS, France
Yair Wiseman, Bar-Ilan University, Israel
Kuan Yew Wong, Universiti Teknologi Malaysia (UTM), Malaysia
Mudasser F. Wyne, National University, San Diego, USA
Linda Yang, University of Portsmouth, UK
Jian Yu, Auckland University of Technology, New Zealand
Sherali Zeadally, University of Kentucky, USA
Jovana Zoroja, University of Zagreb, Croatia

Copyright Information

Extending System Engineering Methodology into the Era of Artificial Intelligence

Hany Fawzy
Space Utilization, Canadian Space Agency
Longueuil, Canada
e-mail: Hany.Fawzy@canada.ca

Abstract - **The world is on the footsteps of a time when the advances of technology supported by Artificial Intelligence (AI) will force all stakeholders to re-examine their traditional methods for designing and engineering of all future intelligent and autonomous systems. These systems would have the advantages of: Self-awareness, Self-control, Self-improvement through learning and could be Self-sufficient. We believe that AI and Autonomy shall go hand in hand in all future engineering applications. Modelling of applications, whether for Earth or Space, are lacking the capacity to model AI and autonomous systems lifecycle management. In this paper, we are defining the main guidelines that are needed to extend system modelling languages to cope with the future. This is while questioning, what a future engineering and planning lifecycles that support the migration from traditional systems to intelligent and autonomous ones, should look alike.**

Keywords- AI; Machine Learning; SysML; System Engineering; Advanced Technologies; System of Systems; Methodology.

I. INTRODUCTION

We live in an era when the increasing demand for more intelligent and autonomous technologies that can accommodate growing Terrestrial and Space applications from self-driven cars to space robotics, should influence the traditionally used engineering methodologies.

The state of the art in System Engineering is based on the capacity to model and define the system under design, that means, the capacity to accurately define the different systems' states using a well-structured modelling language and interfaces. Consequently, it has the capability to define system behaviour and influence actors. Albeit how a system model is qualified as of high fidelity, it cannot guarantee the designed system representation in a real world or cover its whole solution domain. There is a wide range of definitions for such intelligent autonomous applications. Some of them are more restrictive than others. However, the simplest one would have the capacity to emulate and simulate human intelligence operating a machine using learning, reasoning and interacting with a dynamic world environment.

That is why, system modelling languages and other techniques start adding more extensions to the languages to define space applications or provide more accuracy to problem resolution. Nevertheless, they are still lagging in their capacity to model accurately a dynamic system and better identify its behaviour and the dynamic world around it. This is the current state of our applications which we describe as intelligent, advanced and characterize them as autonomous.

In fact, such lagging is a result of the human trust and capability to validate and verify the presence of such requirements in our engineering documentation. We are not able to model, define, audit and verify requirements that should be in an intelligent autonomous system.

This paper discusses the principles to extend or add a new toolbox to model base system engineering principles. These principles are: self-awareness and discovery, self-control, self-improvement through learning and Machine to Machine connectivity and cyber security.

The paper is structured as follows. In Section II, we present the modelling guidelines that any AI or Autonomous (self-control) system design must comply with. Section III addresses a plan to handle and build on an organization knowledge and resources to address AI and Autonomy applications. Section IV presents our implementation. We conclude the paper with Section V where we present the conclusion and the future work to complete such research.

II. PRINCIPLES

Hereby, we are proposing the modelling guidelines that any AI or Autonomous (self-control) system design must comply with. Model Based System Engineering (MBSE) is the methodology of choice for most of the engineering designs. The Systems Modelling Language (SysML) was proposed by the Object Management Group (OMG) to address the challenges and needs in model-based system engineering [8]. SysML is a modelling language used to add powerful capacity to model a wide range of system engineering problems.

This section describes the extension proposal for SysML [5]. It presents the domain model of the extension and a proposal for the profile extending SysML for different AI & Autonomous systems modelling.

In this phase of our research, we based the extension definition to the following principles used in SysML: a domain model, a profile and a syntax [5].

A. Self-awareness

Living in a future engineering world application based on AI, there is a need to make sure that these applications have the capacity to understand and be aware of their environment [5].

In SysML, to be able to model self-awareness [7] for intelligent autonomous systems, we need a definition of awareness. Consequently, awareness would be the capacity to *recognize and understand the dynamic world model interactions with the system.*

B. Dynamic world modelling

In order to benefit from the self-awareness principle, the world model should also have the capacity to *dynamically model the world* where the engineering system would function. Dynamically modelling would provide the capacity of the first principle to be able and implement awareness.

In this paragraph we will not discuss the fidelity of the world model currently used or if it is dynamic or not. A world model, in our study, *must be able to discover and introduce new elements when necessary to the world it represents.*

C. System of Systems Modelling

To fulfil the dynamic world modelling in which a system would operate or function, this requires the capacity to model it from a System of Systems (SoS) view [2]. In fact, if we are modelling the design of a health system that allows vaccination in the current pandemic, among others, we must be able to model the socioeconomic reality of its world. In fact, such principle would allow the model *growth.* It also supports the understanding of the *dynamic behavior,* especially in complex systems. In this phase of research, we would start by the following inputs as an approach to define a dynamic System of Systems (SoS) world model [1] (paragraphs 2.2 and 2.3) [6]:

- Casual Loops;
- Stock and flow diagram;
- Equations;
- Equations in continuous time;
- Equations in discrete time; and
- Dynamic simulation results.

D. Machine-to-Machine Communication

Communication is an important aspect of our model. This principle, in addition to others mentioned, will support the understanding of the system model input and output. It will support the definition of required input to the model, how much the input is *trustworthy* and whether it *comes from a machine or not (discovery).*

E. Self-improvement Through Learning

Machine Learning (ML) is the main new science of AI. The need to train the AI is becoming a major element in the success of any AI application design. Also, the fact that there is a Big Data repository that supports such ML approach. However, future designs, especially in the space industry, know a limit in space and time (RAM and CPU power). Consequently, *training and retraining* of the engineering systems is important. The state-of-the-art references multiple techniques, among which, the nearest neighbor algorithms that do not have a training phase and Naïve Bayes methods.

F. Autonomy (Self-control, and could be Self-sufficient)

Autonomy is another important principle whose modelling would be required. It would support the definition and the capacity of the system to *trust its output, control its inputs and outputs, request of support.* Support could come from another machine or from a human actor. A system might need maintenance training with new data down the road, and training is likely a continuous need.

G. Trust and Data Sets

In traditional systems design, especially in software (SW), configuration management is used to define a *data and system baseline.* However, we will need to handle *data and metadata configuration management.* This is new to the engineering methodology. Also, data need to be clean: complete and representative of the operation environment. Human-on-the-Loop actors might be required at early stages of the design to verify that data are relevant and behaviours are appropriate in response to the training [6].

H. Verification and Validation

There is no well agreed upon approach to test and this is Verify and Validate (V&V). Some researchers consider AI and ML systems have a black box approach to validate and verify the different systems requirements. There must be a capacity to model V&V of the system.

Consequently, this would contribute to increase the trust and confidence in the system. Also, it would allow the capability for test engineers to demonstrate the system compliance to requirements statements and requirements traceability.

III. Planning for AI and Autonomy

As stated, AI and autonomy are part of engineering applications future. Currently, most countries are building towards such future. The domain of AI and autonomy will experience strong world competition in the coming decades after the knowledge era. Governments started by establishing strategic plans in order to be ready and enter such augmented knowledge era. We believe that organizations should do the same. In fact, the burden in that age would fall on academia, industry, public and organizations addressing advanced technology more than any level of government.

Consequently, the state of the art including this paper proposed a plan to handle and build on an organization knowledge and resources to address AI and Autonomy applications. The section below presents a summary of the state of art as well as our own implementation plan.

The plan has to address the organization's needs, goals and objectives. It aims at identifying the objectives and priorities of adopting artificial intelligence and promoting autonomous operations in their respective industry, science or research. This is in addition to identifying opportunities and gaps that should be addressed, as well as outlining desired outcomes for this organization. Finally, this plan will describe the needed management and technical approaches and expected economic gains.

A. Autonomy and AI Strategy for the program

Define *what* are the AI and autonomy needs, objectives and goals and how they are linked to the organization's overall strategy.

B. Application Area Identification

This section defines the potential ways in which autonomy and AI capabilities can be added to the organization's activities. This section will also assess the extent to which Autonomy and AI can be feasibly applied to meet a minimum set of goals. The section will conclude with the results of *why* Autonomy and AI can be used, rationale behind that conclusion and, if needed, a priority of implementation.

C. Planning Section

The plan has to outline when AI and autonomy shall be integrated at the different levels of products, operations, economic activities, etc. It will consider the different alternatives of building and buying Autonomy and AI solution to a specific problem as identified on Application Area Identification.

D. Implementation Section

In this section, the plan will explain how the Autonomy and AI will be best integrated within the program, including the possibility of the hardware being in space prior to the software being completed. It will also address how the ground segment can be designed to support data science and ongoing analysis results.

E. Technology Aspects

In this section, we will identify, what technology is required to achieve our Autonomy and AI priorities. Does the program have the right technology in place already? If not, what technology development do we need to put in place?

F. What Is Next

This section will detail the change management process and the key next steps. This section will be as a result of identifying a subsystem, a function or a technology that is targeted to be automated or a candidate to introduce AI.

IV. IMPLEMENTATION

Inspired by [4] we developed the following extension to adapt to our principles and extend the SYSML to accommodate AI and Autonomy applications.

Figure 1 shows the proposed domain model defined as a meta-model. This represents the syntax that can be used to describe the above mentioned principles.

Figure 2 offers a high-level view of the organization of the SysML profile. This SysML is proposed in order to extend SysML with constructs for AI and Autonomy principles' modeling. Similar to [4], the profile is organized into two top-level packages: the Ai-Autonomy Library and SysML. The first is an UML Model Library which defines datatypes and reusable concepts, while the other will contain the concepts of AI-autonomy data.

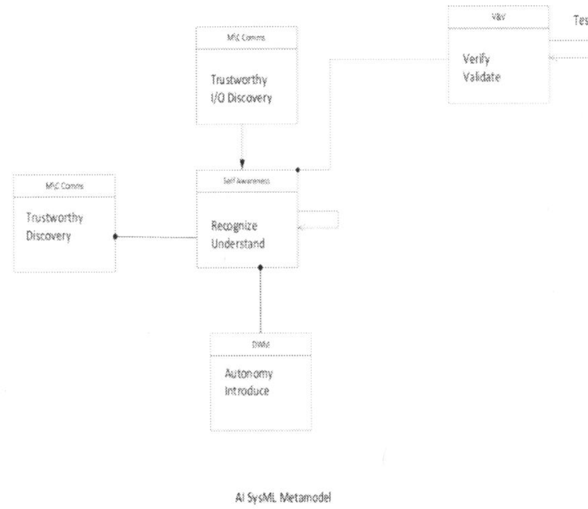

Figure 1. AI SysMl Metamodel.

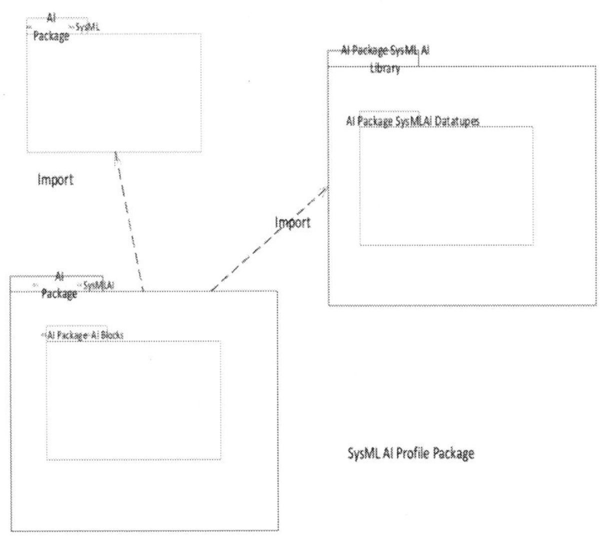

Figure 2. SysML AI Package

V. CONCLUSION AND FUTURE WORK

We started to implement the principles 2.1 to 2.4 as extension to SysML. There will be ongoing work to define the remaining ones.

We will also be studying additional principles such as Testing, Cyber Security due to the increased threat surface as a result of introducing AI-based systems. Also, the modelling of AI-based system standardization and certification.

We have also identified multiple challenges that we are working on as part of this research:

- Human role;

- Lack of human role to review and assume responsibility;
- Human factors (HMI, etc.); and
- User's acceptance.

- Learning and Big Data
    - Learning would require huge and continuous data, in fact, Self-improvement might require continuous source of huge amount of data.
- Self-awareness
    - Sensory input and lack of;
    - Knowledge base and the ability to reason about abstract concepts; and
    - Decision-making capability and legal social context.
- Computing power and the public trust in AI
- Would there be an AI standard or international global use rules?

This paper described an important aspect of our modeling of future AI and Autonomous applications. The traditional MBSE and systems engineering approaches and methodologies are well adapted to accommodate the advanced nature of those advanced technologies as represented by AI. The paper discussed multiple principles that MBSE tools based on SysML has to adopt in order to cope with the rapid AI based applications development. The paper presented in Section II a set of principles that would allow the current System Engineering approaches based on MBSE to model AI and autonomous systems. In fact, we extended the modelling of AI and autonomous systems to include SoS aspects. We provided a possible SysML extension based on the OMG work [8]. We are also investigating future work to improve our modelling approach.

Acknowledgment

I would like to extend my thanks to CSA executive and technical management especially the Space Utilization sector for their continuous support. I also extend my thanks to Dr. R. Raman for his cooperation with me in this domain and allowing me the opportunity to participate in the conference.

References

[1] M. Haussesse, SOS for SoS: A new paradigm for the system of systems modelling, IEEE Aerospace Conf, 2014.

[2] OMG, SoS Modelling needs, MBSE For SoS IW 2015.

[3] M. Chami, C. Zogbi and JM Bruel, A First Step towards AI for MBSE: Generating a Part of SysML Models from Text Using AI, NCOSE Artificial Intelligence for Systems Engineering: 2019 Conference Proceedings (pp.123-136).

[4] J. Cabot, SysML extension for ECAD (Electrical Computer-aided Design), DSLs, Model-driven Engineering, project, 2018.

[5] J. D. Sterman, Business Dynamics: Systems Thinking and Modelling for a Complex World. Boston: McGraw-Hill, 2000.

[6] A. Gonfalonieri, 5 Ways to Deal with the lack of Data in Machine Learning, KDnuggets, 2019.

[7] M. Myrtveit, The World Model Controversy, The SDG, University of Bergen, 2005.

[8] OMG, SysML.org website.

Reinforcement Learning for Emergent Behavior Evolution in Complex System-of-Systems

Anitha Murugesan
Honeywell Aerospace
Plymouth, Minnesota, USA
email: anitha.murugesan@honeywell.com

Ramakrishnan Raman
Honeywell Technology Solutions Lab
Bangalore, Karnataka, India
email: ramakrishnan.raman@honeywell.com

Abstract—**The ease of inter-connectivity among modern systems is permeating numerous System-Of-Systems (SoS), wherein multiple, independent systems interact and collaborate to achieve unparalleled levels of functionality that are otherwise unachievable by the constituent systems in isolation. This has resulted in exponential increase in complexity associated with modern systems and SoS. Complex SoS are characterized by emergent behavior which is very difficult, if not impossible, to anticipate just from knowledge of constituent systems. The emergent behavior manifests at the boundary of the SoS and impacts the Measures of Effectiveness (MOEs) of the SoS. In the context of SoS, each constituent system has its own MOEs, while the SoS has its own MOEs. Constituent systems collaborate and interact with each other, towards achieving the desired functionality and behavior at SoS level. Recently, there is an explosion in the adoption of Machine Learning techniques and models in various systems, and these techniques are increasingly being used to control many physical systems, such as cars and drones. Reinforcement Learning is a type of machine learning approach that allows agents to optimally learn strategies through interactions with its environment. This paper presents a novel approach towards using reinforcement learning models and techniques for evolving MOEs of the constituent systems and SoS towards addressing emergent behavior. The proposed approach, through SoS-Constituent System MOE Relationship, enables constituent systems to learn and adapt their behaviors in tandem with the evolution of emergent behavior at SoS level.**

Keywords—Systems of Systems; Emergent Behavior; Measures of Effectiveness; Reinforcement Learning; Complexity.

I. INTRODUCTION

Advances in machine learning have enabled the development of sophisticated autonomous systems such as self-driving vehicles, and drones. Though developed independently, these systems are expected to be brought together as System-of-Systems (SoS) and operate in a real-world environment. This demands integration of the heterogeneous and inter-operable systems to provide superior levels of functionality.However, to operate in SoS context the systems should be able to achieve their objectives as well as adapt based on SoS-level objectives– that are typically defined as system-level and SoS level Measures of Effectiveness (MOE). For example, consider a self-driving truck planning a shortest path (truck MOE) through the city using its own navigational aids. However, if certain roads in the city (SoS context) have to be used for other high-priority purposes (SoS MOE), the truck is expected to alter its path to respect the city-level constraint. While the new path may not be optimal for the truck, it is expected to near-optimally meet the MOEs at both SoS and system levels. Conventional approaches involve human intelligence in understanding such relationships between constituent systems MOEs and SoS MOEs, towards addressing emergent behavior and MOE evolution. However, with the recent evolution of autonomous systems, there is compelling need and interest to explore approaches that enable systems to automatically learn the implications at SoS level.

In this paper, we propose the use of Reinforcement Learning (RL) approaches to enable a system to learn optimal policies in SoS-context. Our approach trains non-collaborative, independent agents whose rewards are uniquely designed to balance system-level and SoS-level goals. Our approach leverages the SoS-Constituent System MOE Relationship to uniquely design the reward structure of each system (embedded with an intelligent agent). This enables constituent systems to learn policies respecting the SoS and system-level MOE towards addressing evolving emergent behavior.

The rest of the paper is organized as follows: Section II discusses complexity, emergence and MOE evolution in the context of SoS, and briefly introduces reinforcement learning. Section III illustrates the proposed approach, while Section IV describes the simulation of the proposed approach, and the experimental results. Finally, Section V has the conclusion.

II. BACKGROUND & RELATED WORK

A. *Systems and SoS*

A system can be considered as an integrated and interacting combination of elements and/or subsystems to accomplish a defined objective [1]. These elements may include hardware, software, firmware and other support. SoSs are systems of interest whose system elements are themselves systems [2]. SoS has evinced keen interest among the systems engineering community, and there has been significant research pertaining to principles and practices on the architecture design, development, deployment, operation and evolution of SoS [3]-[6]. Applications of SoS principles and practices span many domains, including electrical power distribution, and Internet-of-Things. SoS characteristics discussed in literature include operational/ managerial independence, emergent behavior and evolutionary development.

B. *Complexity and Emergence*

In a general sense, the adjective "complex" describes a system or component that by design or function or both is difficult to understand and verify. There are different types of complexity measures discussed from different perspectives [7]. Emergence, hierarchical organization and numerosity are some of the characteristics of complex systems [8]. Emergence refers to the ability of a system to produce a highly-structured collective behavior over time, from the interaction of individual subsystems [7]. Common examples include a flock of birds flying in a V-formation, and ants forming societies of different classes of individual ants, wherein these patterns are not induced by a central authority. For a system, emergent behavior refers to all that arises from the set of interactions among its subsystems and components. Complex systems and SoS are expressed by the emergence of global properties which are very difficult, if not impossible, to anticipate just from a complete knowledge of component or subsystem behaviors [9][10]. Emergent behavior can be characterized as positive or negative, depending on the impact on the MOEs. The challenge for complex SoS is that there is inadequate knowledge on combination of events that would result in a negative emergent behavior. Specifically, for complex SoS, the "stringing" together of the constituent systems results in unique functionality and emergent behavior being exhibited at the SoS level that is very difficult to envision and predict, and cannot be attributed to any of the constituent systems individually.

C. MOEs in SoS

MOEs are the operational measures of success that are closely related to the achievement of the objective of the system of interest, in the intended operational environment under a specified set of conditions [1]. MOEs are measures designed to correspond to accomplishment of mission objectives and achievement of desired results. MOEs provide quantifiable benchmarks against which the system concept and implementation can be compared. It reflects the overall customer and user satisfaction, and it manifests at the boundary of the system. MOEs are independent of the specific solution. Example of MOEs include service life of satellite, search area coverage and survivability. Failure of the system to meet an MOE implies that the system does not meet its purpose and objectives [11].

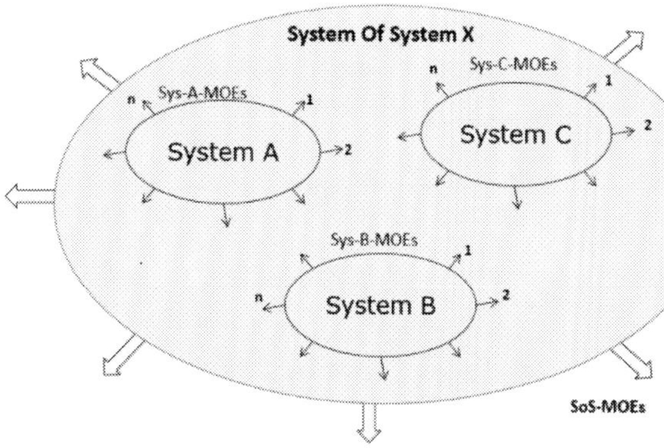

Figure 1. SoS-Constituent System

Understanding MOEs is critical to analyze the impact of the emergent behavior at SoS level. In the context of SoS, each constituent system of the SoS has its own MOEs. The MOEs for a constituent system can be independently measured to assess its success. MOEs of the SoS are the operational measures of success for the SoS as a whole. Figure 1 illustrates SoS MOEs versus constituent system MOEs. System A can have MOEs: SysA-MOE-1, SysA-MOE-2 and SysA-MOE-3. The MOEs of System-A represent the measures of success for System-A as an independent system, and the MOEs for System-A can be independently measured to assess the success of System-A. In addition to each constituent system having its own MOEs, MOEs are also relevant at the SoS level, i.e., SoSx would also have its own MOEs. The MOEs at the SoS level represent the measures of success for the SoS as a whole. Figure 2 further illustrates the impacts on MOEs at system level and at SoS level. The MOEs of the system are impacted by the behaviors exhibited by the system. Similarly, the MOEs of the SoS are impacted by the behaviors exhibited at SoS level. Further, the behaviors exhibited at constituent system level also impacts the SoS MOEs.

D. MOE Relationship Matrix

As discussed earlier, one of the characteristics of SoSs is that the stringing together of the constituent systems results in unique behavior and functionality that gets exhibited at the boundary of the

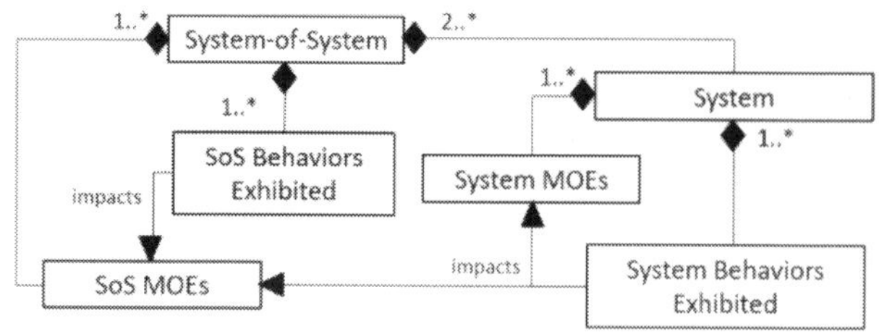

Figure 2. SoS-System Behaviors

Relative importance of each SoS MOE

System Of System - MoEs	SoS MoE Weight	SysA-MoE-1	SysA-MoE-2	SysA-MoE-3	SysB-MoE-1	SysB-MoE-2	SysC-MoE-1	SysC-MoE-2
		MOEs of constituent Systems						
SoS-MoE-1	9	9	9	7				
SoS-MoE-2	7			5	7	7	7	
SoS-MoE-3	5	7	9	5				
SoS-MoE-4	1	9	9	7				7
	Raw score	125	135	130	49	49	49	7
	Relative Weight	21%	22%	21%	8%	8%	8%	1%
	Rank	3	1	2	5	5	5	8

Relative impact of each System MOE on each SoS MOE

System A is a key player in the SoS

Figure 3. MOE Relationship Matrix

SoS, i.e., the behavior may not be attributed to any of the constituent systems functioning independently. With this being the case, the relationships between the MOEs of the SoS vis-à-vis the MOEs of the constituent systems might turn out to be complex and dynamic. There are different means to analyze the MOE relationships between the constituent systems and SoS. SoS-System MOE relationship matrix [6][12] is one of the means to analyze the relationships, as indicated in Figure 3. The impact of different system MOEs on the SoS MOEs could vary. There might be scenarios where a specific constituent system might be meeting all its MOEs, but the SoS MOEs might not be met. Similar scenarios will be discussed later in this paper.

E. SoS MOE Evolution

Evolution is often considered as a major challenge in system-of-systems, given the heterogeneity of constituent systems, hyper-connectivity of systems involved, the emergent behavior and the evolutionary development processes [13]. Architecture evolution deals with changes to the static SoS architecture - for instance, changes to how the constituent systems are networked to each other. On the other hand, behavior evolution pertains to evolution in emergent behavior, based on dynamic SoS architecture - for instance, in terms of changes in set of resources and environment parameters. As the SoS evolves, there might be changes in the impact of an existing constituent systems' MOEs on the MOEs of the SoS, or on the MOEs of other constituent systems. Further, there might also be changes in the relationships of an existing constituent system's MOEs on the MOEs of the SoS, or on the MOEs of other constituent systems. Many other such inherent dynamics would play a role in the SoS evolution. While the MOE relationship matrix (Figure 3) would provide a good sense of the intertwining relationships from the functional and behavioral properties of the SoS, factoring in these additional constraints would be a challenge for complex SoS.

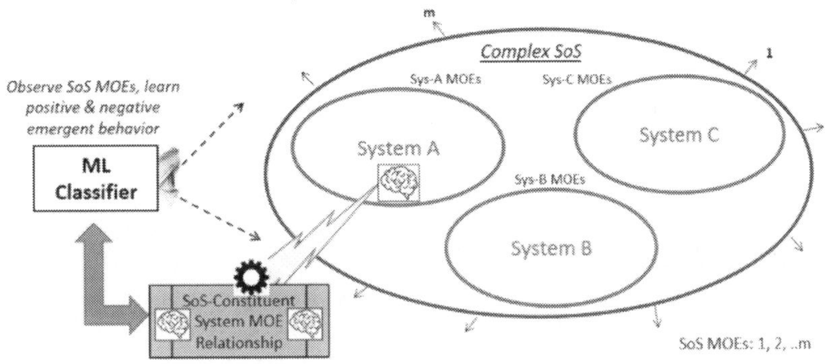

Figure 4. Overview of Proposed Approach

F. Reinforcement Learning

Reinforcement learning is a type of machine learning approach that allows *agents* to automatically learn optimal control strategies through trial-and-error interactions with its environment [14]. As shown in Figure 5, a RL agent iteratively performs *actions* on the environment and in response, it receives the description of the environment (called *state*) and feedback (called *reward*) that indicates the impact of the action on the environment. While positive rewards indicate desired behaviour, negative rewards are penalties of bad actions. Based on the reward, the agent learns an optimal strategy or *policy* for choosing its next action that would receive higher reward. The training typically involves *exploration* in which random actions are selected, and *exploitation* which uses prior learned knowledge to select the best action. Striking a balance between exploration and exploitation is essential for maximizing rewards at minimal cost.

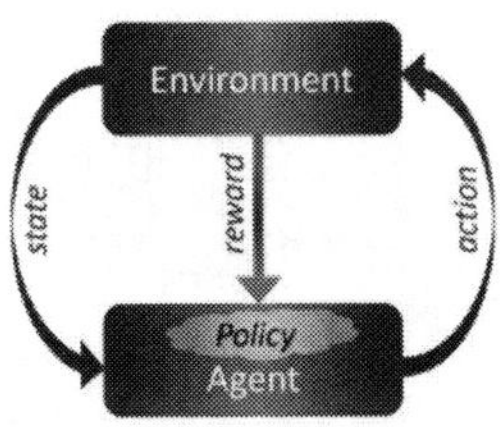

Figure 5. Reinforcement Learning

In the last decade, RL has become increasingly successful in solving complex systems in various fields such as robotics [15], gaming [16], and safety critical systems [17]-[19]. Typically, most of the existing RL literature concerns training single, or multiple agents that cooperate/compete [20][21] within the same environment, in which the agent observes a single scalar reward function and the goal is to find a policy that maximises the expected rewards [22]. However, since SoS is characterized by multiple constituent systems that have independent objectives and varying priorities, single agent or single objective training approaches are generally unsuitable in SoS context. Although there are theoretical discussions about multi-agent and multi-objective optimization approaches [23][24], to the best of our knowledge, the application of these techniques in a SoS context has not been previously explored. On the contrary, in this paper, we focus on training agents independently to achieve their own-goals, as well as the SoS-level goals by leveraging the relationships between SoS and constituent system MOEs for designing the rewards.

III. Proposed Framework

This section discusses the proposed framework towards application of reinforcement learning for constituent systems to learn the implications of its behaviors on the MOEs of the SoS and the emergent behavior witnessed at the SoS level.

A. Overview

Figure 4 provides an overview of the proposed approach. The complex SoS has a set of defined MOEs. The SoS comprises independent constituent systems, with each having their own corresponding system MOEs. A Machine Learning (ML) Classifier [25][26], that observes the various MOEs at SoS level and constituent system level and learns the positive and negative emergent behavior, is leveraged. In the proposed approach, the ML Classifier is used to advise the SoS-Constituent System MOE Relationship (SSMR) on positive and negative emergent behaviors. SSMR is built with the required intelligence to serve as the Environment (per Figure 5) for the constituent system, and provide the required feedback based on the positive and negative emergent behaviors witnessed at the SoS level. The constituent system is embedded with a reinforcement learning Agent (per Figure 5) to learn and evolve its behavior. Figure 6 provides details of the proposed approach.

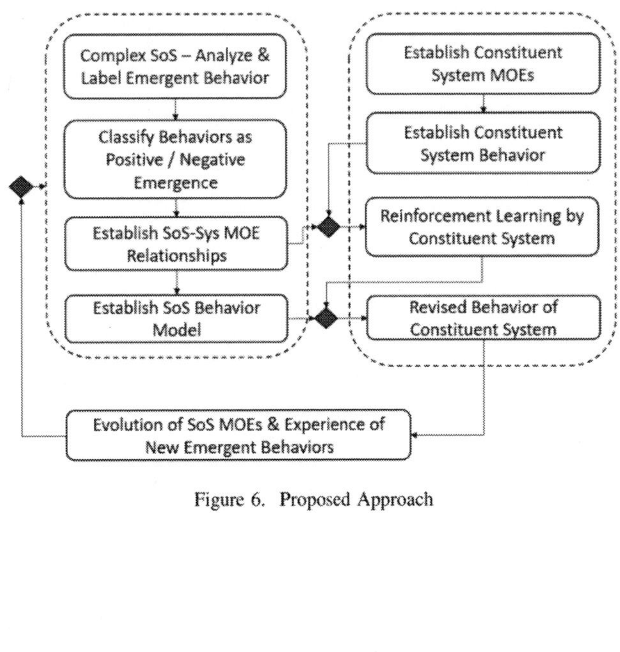

Figure 6. Proposed Approach

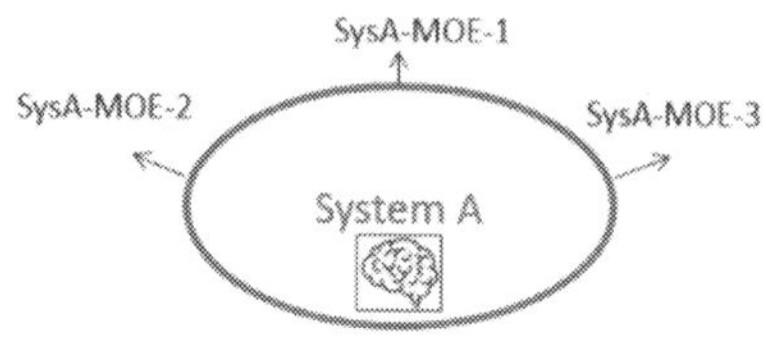

Levels of Performance of System-A in terms of MOEs

SysA-MOE-1	SysA-MOE-2	SysA-MOE-3
V1-1	V2-1	V3-1
V1-2	V2-2	V3-2
V1-3		V3-3

States as mapped to various performance levels of MOEs

STATES	SysA-MOE-1	SysA-MOE-2	SysA-MOE-3
S1	V1-1	V2-2	V3-1
S2	V1-2	V2-1	V3-3
S3	V1-3	V2-1	V3-2
...	...	...	...
S18	V1-3	V2-2	V3-3

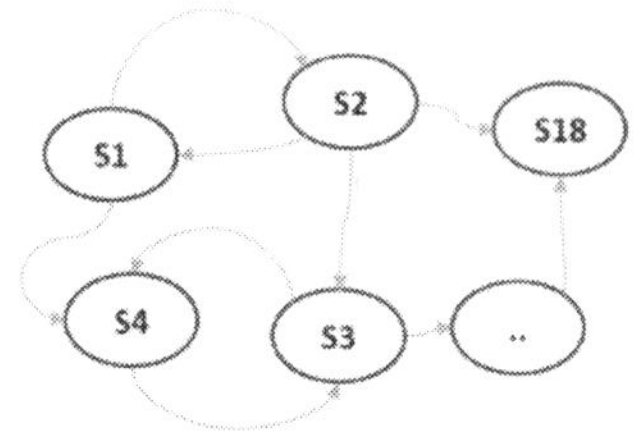

State Transitions

Figure 7. System-A: MOEs and State Transitions

B. Framework Illustration

Towards illustrating the adoption of proposed approach, the generic case of a constituent system, System-A, having a set of three MOEs: SysA-MOE-1, SysA-MOE-2 and SysA-MOE-3 is considered. The behavior exhibited by System-A is considered in terms of the specific levels of performance being exhibited in terms of its MOEs. The states of System-A, as mapped to the various performance levels of the MOEs are illustrated in Figure 7. For instance, System-A meets SysA-MOE-2 at two possible performance levels: V2-1 and V2-2. The figure also illustrates the various transitions permissible between the different states, as in state transition diagram. For instance, from state S2, the possible transitions are S1, S3 and S18. The System-A is a constituent system in SoSx. Let S^U denote the set of all systems. The definitions below illustrate the elements discussed (Z^+ is the set of positive integers) .

$$S^U = \{S_1, \ldots S_n\}, \text{ where } n \in Z^+ \tag{1}$$

$$SoSx \subset S^U; |SoSx| > 1 \tag{2}$$

$$MOE^{SoSx} = \{m_1^{SoSx}, \ldots m_x^{SoSx}\} \tag{3}$$

$$MOE^{S_A} = \{m_1^{S_A}, \ldots m_w^{S_A}\}, \; S_A \in S^U \tag{4}$$

A subset of MOEs of S_A contribute towards a subset of the MOEs of SoSx, represented by $RMOE_{S_A}^{SoSx}$. It is to be noted that this relation has at least one element. Note that $RMOE_{S_A}^{SoSx}$ is defined iff $\exists\, m_w^{S_A} \in MOE^{S_A}$ contributing to $m_x^{SoSx} \in MOE^{SoSx}$.

$$Relation\; RMOE_{S_A}^{SoSx} = \{(m_w^{S_A}, m_x^{SoSx})\} \tag{5}$$

$$m_w^{S_A} \in MOE^{S_A} \text{ contributes to } m_x^{SoSx} \in MOE^{SoSx} \tag{6}$$

With various MOE performance levels being mapped to different states, the constituent system essentially has multiple means to transition from one state to another state. If given the narrow focus of achieving its own MOEs only, the system would perform at a level that maximizes its MOEs performance. In the proposed framework, the SSMR provides the required feedback to the constituent system on the impact of its MOE performance levels on the positive/ negative emergent behavior at the SoS level. This enables the constituent system to learn on the required MOE performance levels that balances its own mission along with the SoS objectives.

IV. Simulation & Experimental Results

In this section, we illustrate our approach using the Grid World example, in which the goal is to allow the agent learn the optimal set of transitions from an initial state to a terminal state. The Grid World serves as an abstract representation of a real world agent's state transition, where each state has implications both at system-level and SoS-level MOEs as described in the previous section. The goal for the agent is to navigate through states such that the SoS MOEs are met in addition to not unduly compromising the MOEs of the system.

A. Experiment Details & Results

We implemented our approach using MathWorks® MATLAB R2020b Reinforcement Learning toolbox [27]. For training, we used a Windows 10 OS with an Intel I-5 Core processor and 8 GB RAM.

Figure 8. Grid World

We programmed a 2-dimensional 5 x 5 Grid World matrix [28], as shown in Figure 8. Each cell in the grid, that corresponds to each state, has an assigned reward value per the SSMR. The agent (visualized as a red circle in the Figure 8) begins from a programmed initial state and learns to traverse to the terminal state (colored blue). The agent has four possible actions in each grid state: west, north, south, and east. Further, certain states are defined as obstacles (black cells) to represent the infeasible states and transitions. The goal of the agent is to learn an optimal state transition through the grid, given the obstacles, such that the total rewards received is maximized. The parameters used for this training are shown in Table I.

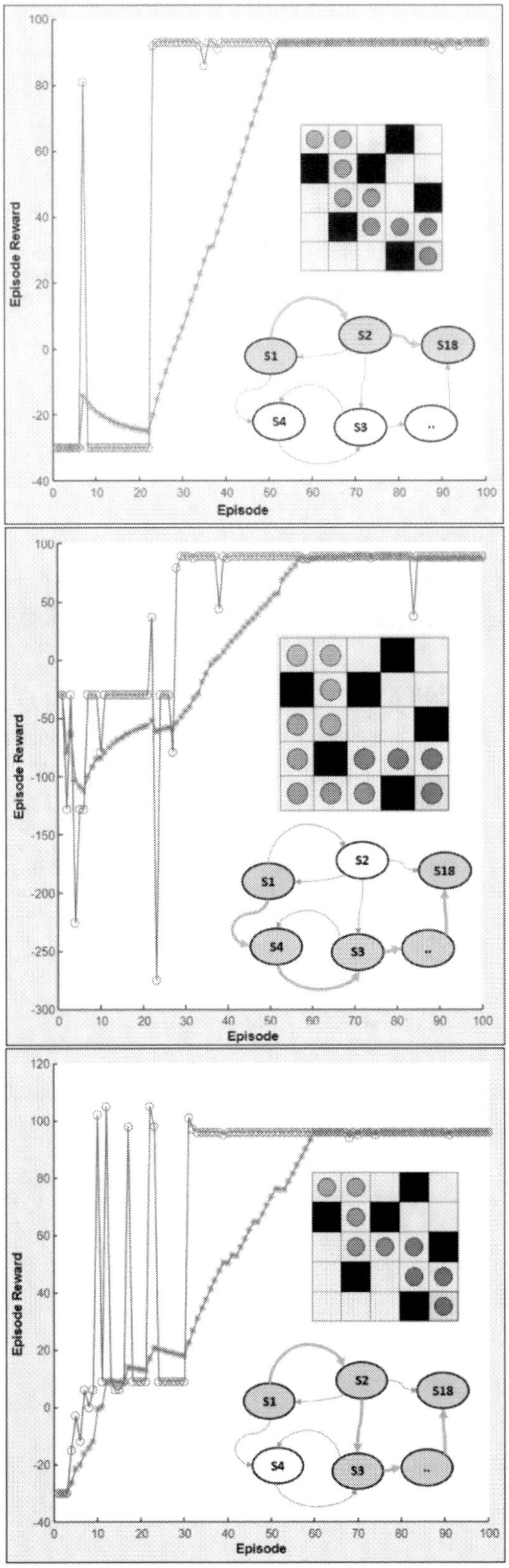

(a) (b) (c)

Figure 9. Training Visualization Plots and Learned Path

TABLE I. TRAINING PARAMETERS

Parameter Name	Description	Value
Epsilon	Probability threshold to select a random action or an existing action that maximizes the state-action value.	0.25 (Fig 9 a,b) 0.45 (Fig 9 c)
MaxEpisodes	Maximum number of episodes to train the agent.	100
MaxStepsPerEpisode	Maximum number of steps to run per episode	30
StopTrainingCriteria	Training termination condition	AverageReward
StopTrainingValue	Critical value of the training termination condition	100

First, to observe the learning in a non-SoS context, we trained the agent by assigning only system-level MOEs as rewards to each cell of the grid. We considered high MOE for the terminal state, a low positive reward for all intermediate states and a negative reward for the obstacles states. Figure 9(a) shows a plot of (i) rewards obtained by agent in each episode during the training (shown in blue line with circles),(ii) average rewards obtained after each training episode (shown in orange line with asterisks), (iii) the learned policy visualised in the grid environment, and (iv) the learned policy visualized in the state transition diagram (traversed states and transitions colored in beige and green respectively).

Next, to understand the emergent behaviours in a SoS context, we altered the reward for each state based on a predefined SSMR. We programmed the agent in a such a way that, at run-time if the learning context is set to SoS, it will adapt to learn a policy to traverse the grid to maximize the reward per the SSMR. For example, in one of the experiments, when an intermediate state ([3,3] in the grid) has low SoS-level MOE (i.e., negative SoS-level reward), the agent learnt to traverse avoiding that cell, as shown in Figure 9(b). Further, when we re-defined a higher SoS-level MOE for another intermediate state ([3,4] in the grid) in the SSMR arrangement and trained the agent again, it learnt another path that favors traversing that state, as shown in Figure 9(c).

The various paths learnt by the agent depending upon the SSMR, demostrates how the agent adapts to maximize SoS-level MOE. As one can observe, while the path taken by the agent could be sub-optimal at the system-level in some cases, it is optimal at the SoS-level, which is ultimately the desired behavior.

B. Limitations: Reward Hacking

While RL with appropriately designed rewards can help effectively train agents without expert supervision, it is not completely fool-proof. One of its well known failure modes is *reward hacking*, which happens when the agent attempts to learn to obtain high rewards in unexpected, rather undesired, ways. For example, when training the agent in the Grid World with higher SoS-level reward for a specific state transition (to [3,4] in Figure 9(c)), we found that the agent did not learn to reach the terminal state even after numerous training episodes. On examining the root cause, we found that the agent tried to accumulate rewards by just moving back and forth to accumulate more rewards, rather than moving past it to reach the terminal state with highest reward. While we addressed this problem in the case example by suitably adjusting the exploration factor as well as the SSMR values, we believe that RL designers of SoS should carefully evaluate the domain and design appropriate rewards to overcome this problem.

V. Conclusion

In this paper, we presented a novel approach towards using RL models and techniques for evolving MOEs of the constituent systems and SoS towards addressing emergent behavior. The proposed approach, through SoS-Constituent System MOE Relationship, enables constituent systems to learn and adapt their behaviors in tandem with the evolution of emergent behavior at SoS level. While the implementation and results described are specific to the case example considered, we believe that this serves as a promising proof of concept for a general, scalable and practical approach to train machine learning based systems in SoS context. In order to further realize the promise of this approach, we are currently working to make the approach applicable for dynamic MOE evolution scenarios in large complex systems and SoS. We are also exploring the use of deep RL approaches that incorporate deep neural networks for superior decision making capabilities and scalability.

References

[1] INCOSE, *Systems Engineering Handbook, 4th Edition*. INCOSE, 2015.

[2] M. Jamshidi, *Systems of Systems Engineering: Principles and Applications*. CRC Press, 2008.

[3] INCOSE, "International Council on Systems Engineering INSIGHT : Feature on System of Systems," vol. 19, pp. 3–78, Oct 2016.

[4] J. A. Lane and D. Epstein, "What is a system of systems and why should I care?," *University of Southern California*, 2013.

[5] C. B. Nielsen, P. G. Larsen, J. Fitzgerald, J. Woodcock, and J. Peleska, "Systems of systems engineering: Basic concepts, model-based techniques, and research directions," *ACM Computing Surveys*, vol. 48, pp. 18:1–18:41, Sept. 2015.

[6] R. Raman and M. D'Souza, "Decision learning framework for architecture design decisions of complex systems and system-of-systems," *Systems Engineering*, vol. 22, no. 6, pp. 538–560, 2019.

[7] W. Kinsner, "Complexity and its measures in cognitive and other complex systems," in *7th IEEE International Conference on Cognitive Informatics*, pp. 13–29, Aug 2008.

[8] J. Ladyman, J. Lambert, and K. Wiesner, "What is a complex system?," *European Journal for Philosophy of Science*, vol. 3, no. 1, pp. 33–67, 2013.

[9] M. Aiguier, P. L. Gall, and M. Mabrouki, "A formal definition of complex software," in *Proceedings of the 2008 3rd International Conference on Software Engineering Advances*, ICSEA '08, pp. 415–420, IEEE Computer Society, 2008.

[10] K. Giammarco, "Practical modeling concepts for engineering emergence in systems of systems," in *2017 12th System of Systems Engineering Conference (SoSE)*, pp. 1–6, June 2017.

[11] N. Smith and T. Clark, "A framework to model and measure system effectiveness," *11th ICCRTS Coalition Command and Control in the Network Era*, 2006.

[12] R. Raman and M. D'Souza, "Knowledge based decision model for architecting and evolving complex system-of-systems," in *Incose International Symposium*, vol. 27, pp. 30–44, Wiley Online Library, 2017.

[13] M. H. Fendali, D. Meslati, and I. Borne, "Understanding evolution in systems of systems," in *2017 IEEE International Systems Engineering Symposium (ISSE)*, pp. 1–6, IEEE, 2017.

[14] R. S. Sutton and A. G. Barto, *Reinforcement learning: An introduction*. MIT press, 2018.

[15] J. Kober and J. Peters, *Reinforcement Learning in Robotics: A Survey*, pp. 9–67. Cham: Springer International Publishing, 2014.

[16] I. Szita, "Reinforcement learning in games," in *Reinforcement learning*, pp. 539–577, Springer, 2012.

[17] K.-L. A. Yau, J. Qadir, H. L. Khoo, M. H. Ling, and P. Komisarczuk, "A survey on reinforcement learning models and algorithms for traffic signal control," *ACM Comput. Surv.*, vol. 50, pp. 1–38, June 2017.

[18] A. Coronato, M. Naeem, G. De Pietro, and G. Paragliola, "Reinforcement learning for intelligent healthcare applications: A survey," *Artificial Intelligence in Medicine*, vol. 109, p. 101964, 2020.

[19] B. R. Kiran et al., "Deep reinforcement learning for autonomous driving: A survey," *arXiv preprint arXiv:2002.00444*, 2020.

[20] R. Lowe et al., "Multi-agent actor-critic for mixed cooperative-competitive environments," *arXiv preprint arXiv:1706.02275*, 2017.

[21] I. Mordatch and P. Abbeel, "Emergence of grounded compositional language in multi-agent populations," *Proceedings of the AAAI Conference on Artificial Intelligence*, vol. 32, Apr. 2018.

[22] D. M. Roijers, P. Vamplew, S. Whiteson, and R. Dazeley, "A survey of multi-objective sequential decision-making," *Journal of Artificial Intelligence Research*, vol. 48, pp. 67–113, 2013.

[23] R. Rădulescu, P. Mannion, D. M. Roijers, and A. Nowé, "Multi-objective multi-agent decision making: a utility-based analysis and survey," *Autonomous Agents and Multi-Agent Systems*, vol. 34, pp. 1–52, 2020.

[24] P. Stone and M. Veloso, "Multiagent systems: A survey from a machine learning perspective," *Autonomous Robots*, vol. 8, pp. 345–383, 2000.

[25] R. Raman and Y. Jeppu, "Formal validation of emergent behavior in a machine learning based collision avoidance system," in *IEEE International Systems Conference (SysCon)*, pp. 1–6, IEEE, 2020.

[26] R. Raman and Y. Jeppu, "An approach for formal verification of machine learning based complex systems," in *INCOSE International Symposium*, vol. 29, pp. 544–559, Wiley Online Library, 2019.

[27] "Reinforcement learning toolbox." https://www.mathworks.com/help/reinforcement-learning/index.html. [Accessed 1-Apr-2021].

[28] "Grid world." https://www.mathworks.com/help/reinforcement-learning/ref/creategridworld.html. [Accessed 1-Apr-2021].

A Capability Based Approach for Warship Design

Paola Gualeni
DITEN - UNIGE
Genoa, Italy
email: paola.gualeni@unige.it

Lucio Tirone
Fincantieri S.p.A.
Genoa, Italy
email: lucio.tirone@fincantieri.it

Paola Bonofiglio
Fincantieri S.p.A.
Genoa, Italy
email: paola.bonofiglio@fincantieri.it

Maria Giovanna Scognamiglio
Fincantieri S.p.A.
Genoa, Italy
email: maria.scognamiglio@fincantieri.it

Abstract— **Traditional Naval Warship design is based on a rather sharp separation between two domains: the Platform and the Combat System. Naval engineers are primarily concerned with the Platform, with tight interaction with other disciplines such as mechanical and electrical engineers. On the other hand, Combat Systems engineers are more concerned with the technological component of the Warship, working in tight coordination with electronic, software or telecommunications engineers. The resulting system (the Warship) is often closer to a *Federation of Systems*, with more or less controlled interactions among each other, rather than to a truly *integrated system*. The focus of this paper is to present a novel approach to the design of a Warship that avoids the a-priori distinction between Platform and Combat System, but considers the Warship as a single, coherent whole. Thus, the approach shifts the focus on the level of the whole warship's capabilities, and its related measures of effectiveness and performance, rather than on its components and subsystems. The aim of such effort is to increase the mutual awareness of the problems specific of each of its components among the entire range of teams called to design, develop, produce, integrate, test and maintain a system as complex as a modern Warship.**

Keywords-capabilities; systems engineering; naval; ship design.

I. Introduction

Naval ships are increasingly large, complex and technologically advanced systems, suggesting a review of the traditional ship design procedure to better tackle with the interdependent ship aspects and to rationally identify the ship final configuration, able to meet operational requirements within technical an programmatic constraints.

Along the decades, interesting discussions and proposals about new ship design philosophy have been launched [1][2], mainly exemplified with applications in the naval ships' fields [3]. In particular, the Systems Engineering approach is recognized as a powerful guide to rationally and successfully develop complex systems [4][5][6].

In the perspective to capture and manage the interactions between the vessel (the ship meant as a platform) and the different installed systems on board (the so called "payload"), from multiple points of view and in a concurrent accomplishment, Systems Engineering appears to offer an effective support, based on a system thinking paradigm rather than on a reductionist and mechanistic view. In fact, it enables to overcome the traditional approach limitations and to focus, since the early design phase, on the naval ship functions rather than on the several singular components the ship is made of.

This radical change of mindset implies that ship performance is to be pursued and observed as an emergent property i.e., as arising from the collaborative functioning of different parts of a system, but not expressed by any of the individual items alone. Typical examples are ant colonies, a flock of birds, the bees hive and, of course, our brain. In other words, emergent properties manifest themselves as the result of various system components working together, not as a property of any individual component.

The term "emergent" is used within systems theory, biology, chemistry, ecology, science, philosophy. Since emergent properties are accessible and evident at higher levels of analysis, only examining individual parts of the system will prevent one from seeing them.

The necessity of a comprehensive ship performance prediction regarding the ship system as a whole, characterized by significant complexity, motivates the exploitation of "tools" like the "measurements of performance" and the "measurement of effectiveness", suggested by Systems Engineering.

As a starting point, ship capabilities need to be identified and discussed. In the perspective of what stated above, they may represent, in fact, the Warship emergent properties to pursue as design goals, and required to comply in turn with the customer expectations.

The paper is structured as follows:

- Section I: the present Introduction
- Section II: a description of the Capability approach
- Section III: a detailed description of the taxonomy of Capabilities
- Section IV: a preliminary analysis of Capability interdependencies
- Section V: the Conclusions

II. THE CAPABILITY BASED APPROACH

The INCOSE Systems Engineering Handbook [7] defines a Capability as "an expression of a system [...] ability to achieve a specific objective under stated conditions". It is rather common in Warship specifications to find descriptions of the abilities of the "Combat System" to achieve specific objectives, such as "Command and Control", "Combat" or "Surveillance" [8][9]. Very few references can be found [10][11] to the basic abilities of the Warship itself, in its quality of "ship" before anything else, such as the ability to float on the surface of the sea, or the ability to remain stable in an upright position in order to allow any activities to be carried onboard.

Section III of this paper describes an innovative effort, to further deepen the topic and contribute to the relevant naval literature, aimed at the definition of the Warship Capabilities in order to provide a coherent framework for the categorization of the key performance requirements of the Warship. This is achieved by reducing the complexity of the Warship through a decomposition of the *problem* (the Capabilities that the Warship has to exhibit), rather than of the *solution* (the systems and subsystems that will be part of the Warship). Nevertheless in the following the Warship Capabilities are discussed in their details in order to start paving the link with the solution domain.

III. DEFINITION OF THE WARSHIP CAPABILITIES

A possible categorization of the capabilities related to a Warship should start with the obvious recognition that the Warship itself is a ship in its own right, and even before, that it is a platform floating on the sea, used by and interacting with human operators.

The basic Capabilities for any sea faring "platform" are shown in Figure 1 and can be recognized as:

- **Buoyancy**: the platform has to float on the waters, carrying its load
- **Stability**: it has to avoid capsizing
- **Structural Strength**: it has to avoid falling apart

Following the analysis, any such platform needs to be operated by humans, and will interact with them, with man made infrastructures, and with the environment, and so needs the following Capabilities:

- **Safety**: no humans, or their properties, or the environment, should be harmed
- **Security**: it should not be tampered with malicious intent

The next step is to consider the Capabilities that are necessary to make use of such platform as a "ship":

- **Power Generation**: either by oars, sails, or engine and propeller, the platform needs to sail
- **Controllability**: the operators need to control its heading and speed
- **Navigation**: the operators need to know where it is located on the earth surface, and where they intend it to sail

The type of ship we are interested in is a modern platform, with automated functions, and technology aiding the human operators in all their tasks, and this brings to the next required Capabilities:

- **Command and Control**: the computer based automation of all operations performed through the ship's equipment
- **Communications**: the means to exchange voice, data, and other types of information, among the on board persons, and with the outside world

Finally, we have to consider the ultimate Capabilities that make our ship a Warship, able to carry out its intended missions:

- **Surveillance**: the Capability to discover and monitor any potential threats
- **Combat**: the Capability to neutralize those threats

The following Figure 1 shows a representation of all the identified Warship Capabilities, which are described one by one in the next sections:

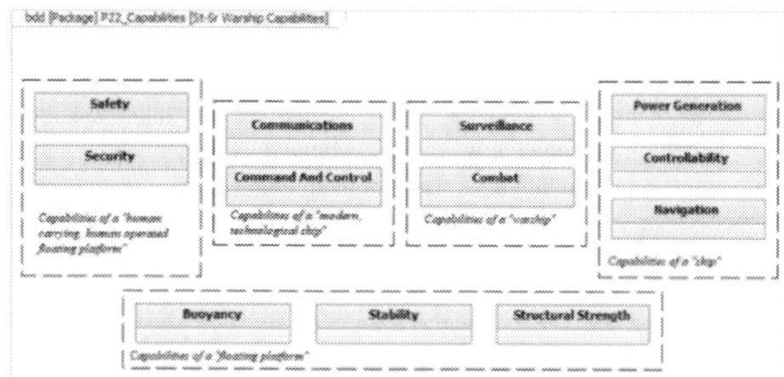

Figure 1. Warship Capabilities.

A. Buoyancy

Buoyancy is the Warship's Capability to float above the sea surface.

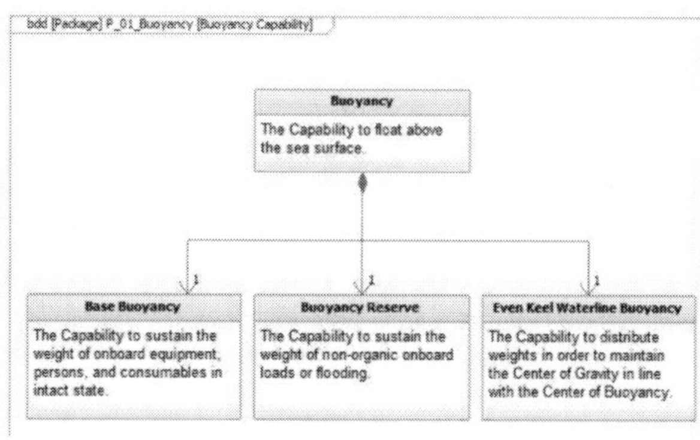

Figure 2. The Buoyancy Capability.

As evidenced in Figure 2, the Buoyancy can be further divided in "base buoyancy" and "reserve of buoyancy" as discussed in the following. A comprehensive watertight hull volume is to be guaranteed, normally able to provide "base buoyancy", exceptionally able to provide "reserve of buoyancy" in case it is needed.

Moreover the waterline that is identified by the ship floating position should be suitable for operations i.e., the ship shall be upright and even keel (a small trim by stern can be accepted).

1) Base buoyancy

The ship capability to float is enabled by the buoyancy force (Archimedes's law) experienced by the ship in relation with the weight of the water that the immersed hull volume displaces. The hull geometry is to be selected is such a way that the buoyancy force (directed upward) balances the total amount of weights force (directed downward) identified by the total amount of weights the ship is made up of.

2) Buoyancy reserve

It might happen however that during the ship operational life, some further accidental situations require an additional buoyancy as a reserve (i.e., the above mentioned hull water-tightness is to be guaranteed also in case of a possible draft increment).

3) Even keel waterline buoyancy

The floating position of the ship cannot be whatever. The operational profile of the ship requires suitable condition. This state can be achieved paying particular attention to the position of the centre of gravity of the ship (application point of the total weight force) and of the centre of the immersed volume (application point of the buoyancy force). Their relative position in terms of longitudinal coordinate x and transverse coordinate y generate the equilibrium waterline features.

B. Stability

Stability is the Warship's capability to resist to inclining actions, and a further characterization is given in Figure 3.

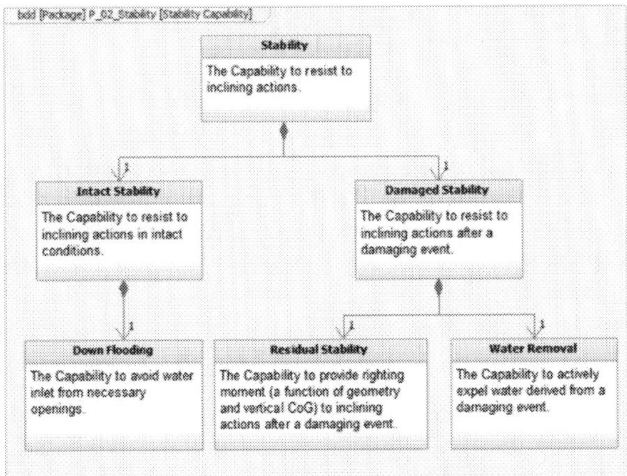

Figure 3. The Stability Capability.

The capability of the ship to resist and respond to inclining actions (e.g., wind and waves action, shift of weights, turning at speed, ...) is to be guaranteed both in the intact and in the damaged condition. In the latter case often it is referred to as residual stability.

In case large heel angles are reached, some (necessary) ship openings might be immersed; this is going to further jeopardize the ship stability performance due to the possible ingress of water and due attention is to be given to the issue. (Actually, the accidental ingress of water can also jeopardize the buoyancy performance).

In the specific case of damage, the capability to pump out the flooding water might be requested as a recovery measure, to improve both residual buoyancy and residual stability.

1) Intact Stability

The capability of the ship to react to inclining actions and to return to the upright position is given by the righting moment. A satisfactory performance of ship stability is defined acting on the ship geometry and on the vertical position of the center of gravity.

2) Damaged stability

Also in case of a damaged ship, some inclining moments can act on the ship and further worsen the emergency situation. In this case, the capability of the ship to react to the inclining actions, i.e., the righting moment, is influenced by the ship flooded condition.

3) Down flooding

For the operational activity of the ships, some openings are necessary. They represent a critical point both for the intact stability and the damage stability.

An opening can be

- Unprotected
- Protected by weathertight closure
- Protected by watertight closure

In case of the intact ship, an opening can be submerged by the waterline due to a large heel angle. In this case, to eliminate the critical situation, it is enough to provide a weathertight closure (if possible).

In case of ship in damaged condition, the final waterline after a damage can reach an opening. In this case to eliminate the critical situation, it is necessary to provide a watertight closure (if possible).

4) Residual Stability

Notwithstanding a damage, a ship is requested to guarantee a residual buoyancy and a residual stability also in degraded conditions.

A specific attention is to be paid to the internal subdivision in order to manage the flooding extent and to provide the sufficient residual stability.

Different levels of residual capability can be requested, in order to resist a sufficient amount of time to wait for emergency support or to sail back home toward protected water or to maintain an operational capability.

5) Water removal management

The water ingress due to the damage compromises the residual buoyancy capability and can be a serious threat for the residual stability, especially in case of large free surfaces.

To recover from this situation, specific systems (e.g., high capacity bilge pumps) and operational measures can be applied, to guarantee the water amount removal in reasonably short time.

Equalization systems can be also provided in order to reduce and balance the list angle after damage.

C. Structural Strength

Structural Strength is the capability to ensure the vessels structural integrity in normal and damaged conditions, as evidenced in Figure 4.

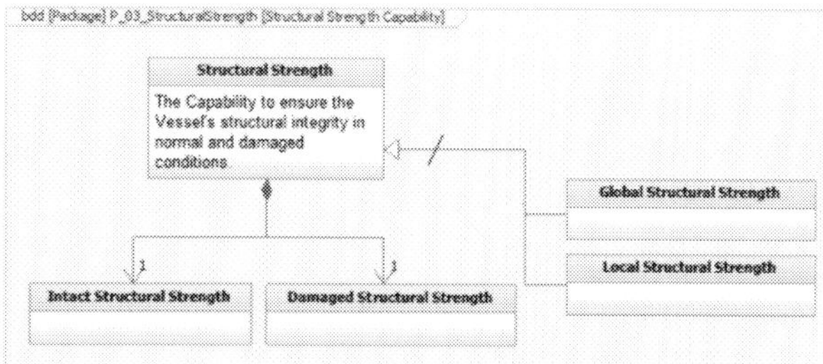

Figure 4. The Structural Strength Capability.

The ship hull and superstructures are usually built in steel and/or aluminum alloy and/or composite materials. Structure scantlings and details are to be designed in such a way that enough strength is guaranteed against local and global loads. For ships with significant length, in fact, the hull girder is characterized by global stresses that are to be properly addressed in such a way that the ship shall not suffer structural damage during her operational life in waves. At the same time, local stresses (e.g., due the presence of a crane in deck or a fluid head action on a bulkhead) are to be considered.

As already mentioned, the ship is supposed not to suffer a structural damage in operating condition, even in extremely rough seas; nevertheless an accidental damage (e.g., collision, grounding) might happen and the ship can be requested to guarantee a residual structural strength in the damaged conditions.

1) Intact Structural Strength

The ship structure (basically made of shell plates, girders and stiffeners) in operational condition is under the effect of local and global loads. The structure scantling are defined in relation with regulation requirements, which are defined with refence to safety margins, in order to avoid structural collapse and permanent deformation. Possible corrosion and fatigue effects on structures are also taken into account.

2) Damaged Structural Strength

Even though the ship is designed in order not to suffer structural damage, it may happen that for accidental events like collisions, grounding, fire, hits, the structure is damaged. A residual capability can be requested, especially as far as residual longitudinal strength is concerned, in order to resist a sufficient amount of time for emergency support or to sail in protected water or to maintain an operational capability.

3) Global Structural Strength

The ship girder is under the stress created by the weight distribution along the ship length, the buoyancy given by the submerged watertight hull, in calm water and in waves.

This is going to create, along the ship, shear forces and bending moment that are to be tackled with by the whole ship seen as a girder. In the evaluation of the ship structures able to guarantee the longitudinal strength, only longitudinal elements are to be considered.

4) Local Structural Strength

Beside the scantlings of ship structures in charge of sustaining the longitudinal strength, also assessment at local level are to be carried out (e.g., the scantling of transverse bulkheads), with specific reference to local loads.

D. Controllability

Controllability is the capability to control the vessels speed and heading in order to accomplish a defined objective, as described in Figure 5.

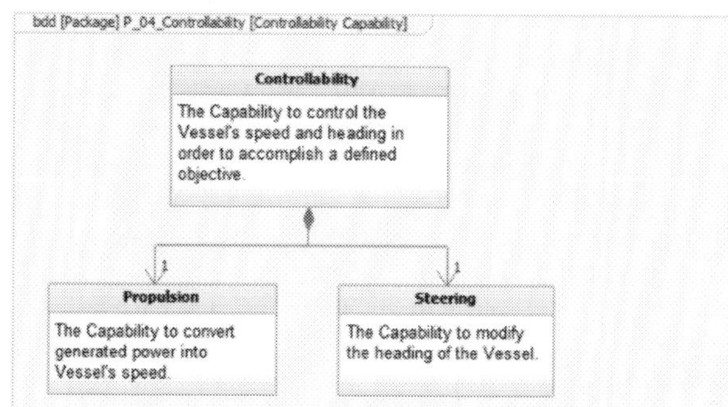

Figure 5. The Controllability Capability.

The ship is assumed able to sail at the desired speed, with the capability to arrange the suitable route, even in heavy adverse environmental conditions.

1) Propulsion

The capability to use the generated power to produce thrust and therefore ship speed is usually obtained by means of a propulsion system like shaft lines with propellers. Other possible propulsion devices, not very much common for naval ships applications actually, are pump-jets, Voith-Schneider systems, azipods.

2) Steering

In the traditional solution where shaft lines and propellers are used, the ship maneuvering is guaranteed by rudders controlled by steering systems, in the stern part of the ship.

The other above mentioned propulsion systems are intrinsically provided with a steering devices.

The proper maneuvering of ships in restricted water can be supplemented also by bow and stern thrusters placed in the symmetry plan of the ship.

E. Power Generation

Power Generation is capability to generate power for the entire vessel including all organic equipment, and it can be further discussed as represented in Figure 6.

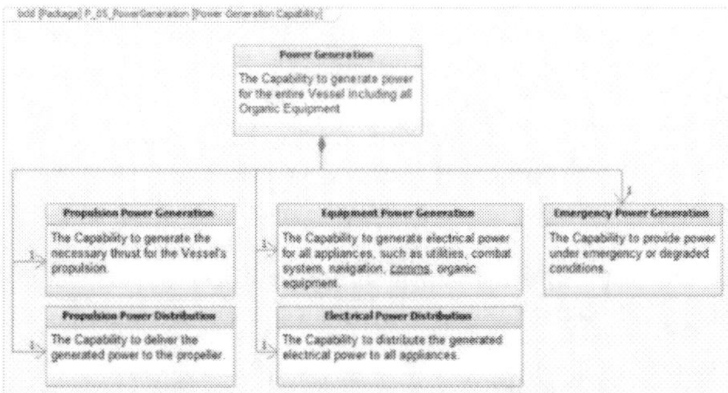

Figure 6. The Power Generation Capability.

A sufficient amount of power generation on board is to be guaranteed in order to provide the ship propulsion and to provide support for all the other possible electrical load requests onboard.

In naval ships the distribution of power generation systems onboard is requested to be adequate to provide energy to the ship also in a residual mode in degraded condition after a damage. Also in this case (see residual buoyancy, stability, structural strength) different levels of residual power generation can be requested after the damage, in relation with the capability to resist waiting for emergency support, to sail in protected waters, to express a residual operational capability.

1) Propulsion Power Generation

The typical power generation system on board navy ships in made of diesel engines and gas turbines with several possible combinations. These are properly able to provide power for propulsion in relation with the power distribution systems described later. In some cases also electrical engines are used for the propulsion and the power supply is guaranteed by the electrical power distribution system, properly powered.

2) Propulsion Power Distribution

In general, the propulsion power distribution is guaranteed by a gear box/boxes (more or less complex in relation with the number and the typology of the power generator units) and shaft lines, provided with appropriate joints and bearings.

3) Equipment Power Generation

Shipboard power is generated using prime movers and an alternators working together. Typically diesel generators are used on board in the sufficient number to provide the necessary power, enough flexibly and redundancy.

In some cases the alternators are able to derive power from the main propulsion shaft lines of the ship.

4) Electrical Power Distribution

The electrical power distribution is to be guaranteed with the proper technical characteristic (e.g., voltage and frequency) in relation with the final electrical users.

Beside the power generation units, the propulsion power distribution systems is made of main switch board, bus bars , circuit breakers, transformers, wires and cables. The distribution systems is designed in such a way to provide redundancy and reliability.

5) Emergency power Generations

It can be requested to provide an emergency power generation for supply in case of ship total black out. The size is selected making reference to the selected electrical load requests that are to be guaranteed in emergency situation.

F. Safety

Safety is the capability to achieve and maintain a state in which all embarked persons, tangible properties interacting with the vessel and the environment surrounding the vessel are free from risk. This definition is also shown in Figure 7.

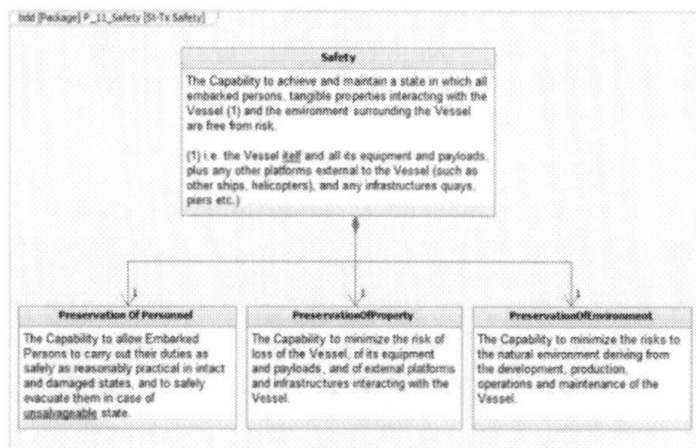

Figure 7. The Safety Capability.

Safety is generally meant as a freedom from risk. In the case this is impracticable, it can be accepted to focus on the reduction of risk at a level as low as reasonably possible. In this perspective, attention is paid on both the probability of occurrence of an hazardous event and on the severity of its consequences. It is important to point out that the loss (total or partial loss) is the result of an hazardous situation that in a specific scenario has evolved in a loss. Since it may be difficult to foresee an unexpected scenario, it is difficult to have control on it. Therefore during the design process, the attention is more focused on the hazard identification and relevant avoidance or countermeasures.

1) Preservation of Personnel

The safety of life at sea has not been the same along the history and still now it is not practically the same all around the world. Nevertheless at present this is a very well addressed issue by means of application of the most demanding international safety rules. In the merchant ships context, the SOLAS convention is the most important IMO international safety rule and it prescribes, among others, requirements for residual buoyancy and stability, fire fighting, evacuation and life saving appliances, dangerous goods transportation, safe management of ships.

It is important to point out that the ship safety is meant as the safety of the system and not as professional safety that is ruled by other international conventions (STCW, MCL2006)

2) Preservation of Environment

Attention on the effect of ship navigation on the environment is rooted in the seventies of the twentieth century. The most important international regulation is the MARPOL convention, developed by IMO, often used as a reference for the navy fleets, where appropriate.

At first, the attention was only on the sea pollution (e.g., due to oil leakage, sludge water, garbage) but recently the attention is very much on the air pollution relevant to the engines exhaust gases (MARPOL annex VI)

3) Preservation of Property

This aspect is not explicit in the safety regulation, but it is implied in the concept of safety of life at sea that in any case has the priority.

The attention to the preservation of property is reasonable due to the huge economical value of a ship (e.g., several hundreds of millions of dollars), but it is even more sensible in case of naval ships that usually have an even higher value and financially supported by public money.

G. Navigation

As evidenced in Figure 8, **Navigation** is the capability to perform Warship positioning and route planning, and to monitor and control the Warship's adherence to the planned route.

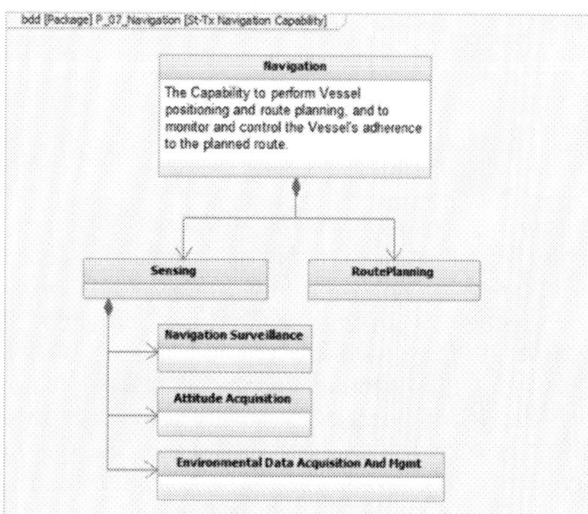

Figure 8. The Navigation Capability.

Two main elements compose the Navigation capability: Sensing and Route planning:

1) Sensing

Sensing is the capability to acquire information about the Warship position, heading, motion and attitude, and the operational environment (both natural and tactical) surrounding it. In detail, the Sensing capability is composed by other specific capabilities:

- **Navigation Surveillance** refers to the detection, localization, recognition/classification and tracking of external sea surface contacts
- **Attitude Acquisition** refers to the precise determination of the tilts of the Warship's frame with respect to "local" coordinate axes. This capability is tightly connected to the Warship performance, for example, successful missiles launch, or successful detection and tracking of missile threats are deeply influenced by precise attitude data acquisition.
- **Environmental Data Acquisition and Management** refers to the capability to perform data acquisition about meteorological and marine/oceanographic environment surrounding the Warship and about its global position and reference time.

2) Route Planning

Route Planning refers to the capability to plan and establish the Warship route. Wind, waves and currents and sea ice cover are crucial factors in choosing a route at sea. Advanced routing systems support the crucial decisions about the route. Avoiding hostile entities or rough weather and having the best possible advance route planning can minimize damage and allow more precise control of the Warship. Choosing the optimum route also lays the foundation for reducing fuel consumption. All these aspects highlight the importance of the Route Planning Capability.

H. Command and Control

Command and Control is the Capability to allow the operators to perform full control of the Warship's equipment, in order to optimize the tactical use of the Warship within its naval task force. Further details to this regard are given in Figure 9.

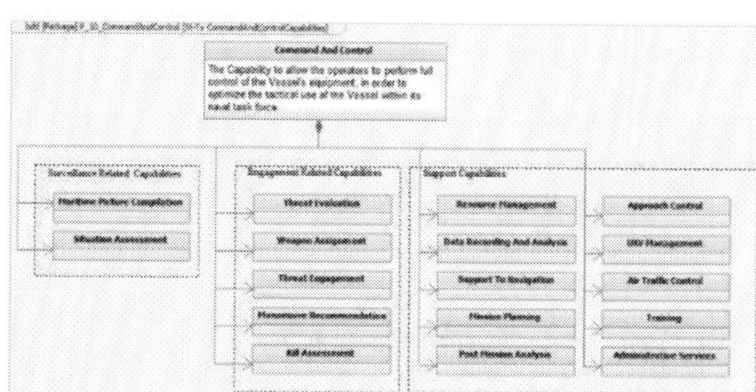

Figure 9. The Command and Control Capability.

Command and Control (C2) includes a wide range of specific capabilities, which can be grouped in the following broad categories: "Surveillance", "Engagement" and "Support", as described below.

1) C2 Surveillance Related Capabilities

Maritime Picture Compilation is the Capability to process the data received from passive and active sensors, from Data Links and from manual insertion by Operators. The scope is to display to the Operator a unique representation of the Real World Objects (RWOs) around the Warship.

Situation Assessment is the Capability to identify and to classify any tracks in the maritime picture as friends or possible threats. Many track functionalities for identification are necessary: initialization, association, coupling, splitting, merging etc.

2) C2 Engagement Related Capabilities

Capabilities dedicated to the management of potential threats around the unit and the coordination of any reactions.

Threat Evaluation is the Capability to evaluate threats and set priority levels in their engagement.

Weapon Assignment is the Capability to identify the suitable weapon system to use against given threats. The reaction must be coherent with kinematics features, doctrine elements, threat category, weapon system limitations.

Threat Engagement is the Capability to perform engagements against given threats through the identified weapon systems. Typically an Engagement Plan is defined with a detailed schedule of reactions, and adaptation margins to handle unpredicted situations.

Manoeuvre Recommendation is the Capability to recommend the motions and attitude the Warship should assume during an engagement in order to minimize the vulnerability against a specific threat.

Kill Assessment is the Capability to evaluate the result of the neutralization action on an engaged threat, based on data acquired from sensors, telemetries in downlink from the used weapon when available, or operator manual inputs.

3) C2 Support Capabilities

Resource Management is the Capability to monitor and control the status of organic equipment, including the management of alarms and the control of electromagnetic emissions.

Data Recording and Analysis is the Capability to store, extract and process data exchanged among all Warship equipment.

Support to Navigation is the Capability to support safe navigation of the Warship through navigation aids management.

Mission Planning is the capability to define mission parameters and relevant data for the Warship.

Post Mission Analysis is the Capability to analyze mission recorded data for the purpose of validating actions taken during the tactical phase, potentially generating new contact data based on discovered missed detection/ classification opportunities.

Approach Control is the Capability to support aircraft operations, including approach, deck landing and take off.

UXV Management is the Capability to manage Unmanned Aerial, Surface or Underwater Vehicles operations.

Air Traffic Control is the capability to direct air traffic in coordination with ATC centers.

Training is the Capability to simulate possible scenarios in which the Warship could be involved in order to support Operator training.

Administrative Services is the Capability to provide administrative services such as mail, intranet, data processing, printing facilities etc.

I. Communications

As better detailed is Figure 10, **Communications** is the Capability to manage the exchanges of information both internally among the Warship components, and with other units or land centers to receive data and orders and participate as a force asset.

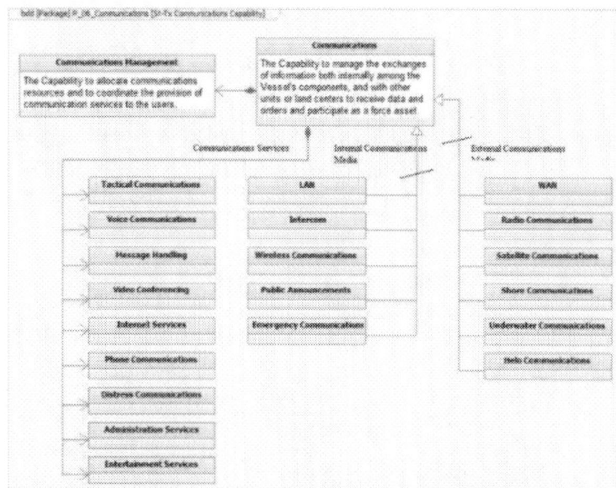

Figure 10. The Communications Capability.

The first relevant component of this Capability is **Communications Management**, the Capability to allocate communications resources and to coordinate the provision of communication services to the users.

Following, Communications can be categorized according to the type of Service that is conveyed (voice, data, entertainment, etc.), and the media through which the services are delivered, both internally on the Warship, and externally.

1) Communications Services

The following Services are typically delivered by the internal and external communications networks:

- **Tactical Communications**
- **Voice Communications**
- **Message Handling**
- **Video Conferencing**
- **Internet Services**

- **Phone Communications**
- **Distress Communications**
- **Administration Services**
- **Entertainment Services**

2) Internal Communications Media

The following list reports the typical Internal Media through which the communication services are delivered:

- **Local Area Networn (LAN)**
- **Intercom**
- **Wireless Communications**
- **Public Announcements**
- **Emergency Communications**

3) Internal Communications Media

The following list reports the typical External Media through which the communication services are delivered:

- **Wide Area Networn (WAN)**
- **Radio Communications**
- **Satellite Communications**
- **Shore Communications**
- **Underwater Communications**
- **Helo Communications**

J. Surveillance

Surveillance is the Capability to detect, localize, recognize and classify and track contacts in all domains related to the Warship's Area of Operations, as shown in Figure 11.

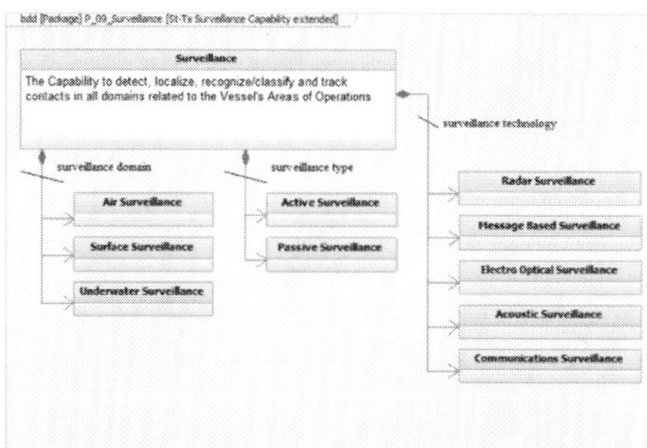

Figure 11. The Surveillance Capability.

Based on the Surveillance domains, types and employed technology, three different categorizations can be made:

1) Surveillance domain

The Surveillance Capabilities are related to the Aerial, Sea Surface or Underwater domains:

Air Surveillance allows detecting air based objects such as aircrafts, or missiles.

Surface Surveillance allows detecting objects on the surface of sea, lakes, oceans or located near the coast.

Underwater Surveillance allows detecting underwater objects, such as submarines or mines.

2) Surveillance Type

Active Surveillance is performed involves the emission of signals, typically in the form of electromagnetic or acoustic waves. Exploiting this capability, the Warship can cover a wide range of kilometers in the domain where detecting occurs. The drawback of the active surveillance consists in being more visible and easily discovered by other entities.

Passive Surveillance on the other hand is performed by receiving signals emitted by other systems but not issuing any interrogation. Lesser performance in sensitivity and range of the detection is traded off by the ability to remain more effectively hidden from enemy detection.

3) Surveillance Technology

This categorization is related to the technology employed to perform the Surveillance activities.

Radar Based Surveillance allows the Warship to detect both fast and slowly moving non-cooperating objects, through the acquisition of their radar echo. Their position and velocity are determined using distance and azimuth information for 2D radar surveillance, and also with elevation for 3D radar surveillance.

Message Based Surveillance is performed through the exchange of coded messages for the mutual exchange of identity and voyage related information, and is implemented using base stations and transponders. Typical examples of message based surveillance are Interrogation Friend or Foe (IFF), used for determining the identity of an unknown contact on the basis of the response to a direct interrogation message, and the AIS, a relay network connecting all commercial and military vessels on the VHF Maritime Mobile Band, carrying information such as departure and destination ports, transported cargo or precise positioning.

Electro Optical Based Surveillance consists in the optical and infrared spectrum scanning through high performance cameras, able to operate both during day and night and in all possible weather conditions.

Acoustic Based Surveillance allows the Warship to detect underwater objects, through the acquisition of their acoustic echo. Acoustic surveillance makes use of several types of sonar sensors, either active or passive, and which can be installed directly attached to the hull, or as arrays of multiple elements towed by cable.

Communication Based Surveillance consists in performing analysis on emissions from radio channels in order to achieve information related to the source, such as the relative direction of emission, the type of equipment used for transmission, or even the gathering of intelligence based on the content of the communications.

K. Combat

Combat is the Warship Capability of denying the enemy the effective use of threats against the Warship itself, its protected assets, or tactical/operational/strategic interests.

More details are schematically provided in Figure 12.

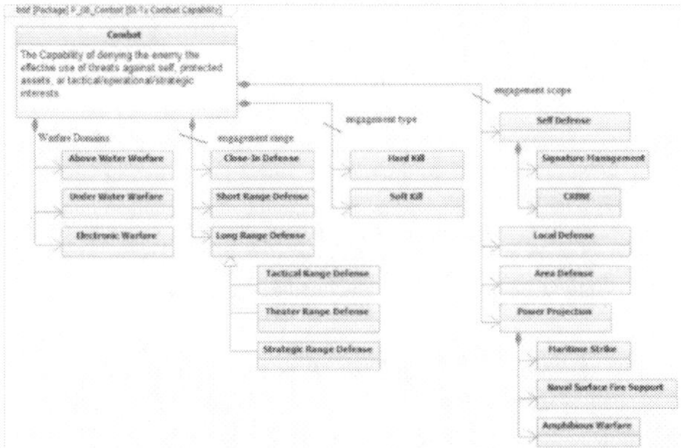

Figure 12. The Combat Capability.

There are four main categorizations of the Combat Capability, starting from the warfare domain to which a given threat belongs, to the type, scope and range of the engagement that is required to neutralize such threat.

1) Warfare Domain/Area

The warfare Domain is related to the environment to which the threat to be faced belongs:

- **Above Water Warfare** concerns threats that originate above the water surface, and is divided in two Warfare Areas: Anti Air Warfare (AAW), including threats such as airplanes, missiles, or helicopters; and Anti Surface Warfare (ASuW), including threats such as ships or land based platforms
- **Below Water Warfare** concerns threats that originate below the water surface, and is divided in two main Areas: Anti Submarine Warfare (ASW) and Mine Warfare (MW)
- **Electronic Warfare** (EW) concerns threats that affect the electromagnetic spectrum, independently from the physical domain of their bearer. EW is further characterized by Electronic Attack Measures, and Electronic Protection Measures

2) Engagement type

Two types of Engagement can be performed by the weapons carried on board the Warship:

- **Hard Kill**, when the weapons physically engage threats by destroying/altering their payload/ warhead in such a way that the intended effect on the target is severely impeded
- **Soft Kill**, when the weapons alter the electromagnetic, acoustic or other signature(s) of a target thereby altering the tracking and sensing behavior of an incoming threat

3) Engagement range

Entirely different weapons are devoted to the facing of threats according to their range:

- **Close In Defense** relates to the neutralization of threats within a few Nautical Miles (NM) from the Warship, and is typically performed with small caliber artillery
- **Short Range Defense** relates to the neutralization of threats within tens of NM, and is typically performed with large caliber artillery, missile systems, torpedoes and so on
- **Long Range Defense** relates to the neutralization of threats within several thousands of NM from the protected asset; Long Range is further divided in Tactical Range (12-50 NM), Theater Range (up to several hundred NM), Strategic Range (up to national or regional range)

4) Engagement scope

Engagement Scope regards the definition of the asset(s) that the Warship is assigned, by a specific mission, to protect:

- **Self Defense** is concerned with avoiding/neutralizing threats against the Warship itself, and includes other capabilities, such as Signature Management and CBRNE (the Capability to resist to Chemical, Bacteriological, Radioactive, Nuclear or Explosive threats)
- **Local Defense** is concerned with the neutralization of threats against a protected asset (High Value Unit, HVU), such as another ship within the same convoy, or a port
- **Area Defense** is concerned with the neutralization of threats against a specific protected geographical area, such as a Sea Line Of Communications (SLOC)
- Finally, **Power Projection** is devoted to the protection of strategic level interests, by actively employing force against enemy assets, and is further divided in Maritime Strike when the target is naval, Naval Surface Fire Support (NSFS) when the target is land based, and Amphibious Warfare when the contribute of the Warship is essentially logistic

IV. Capabilities Interdependencies

The thorough description of all Whole Warship related Capabilities can be followed by a discussion on mutual interactions and interdependency. For example the Surveillance Capability can be enhanced by increasing the Radar's height, however this will have a direct impact on the Warship's Stability; or at the same time, optimizing Surveillance will have an impact on the Warship's Controllability in terms of required Power Generation. This in turn will affect the Buoyancy due to the different weight of the power generators.

These considerations become really effective when all Capabilities are taken into account comprehensively at the same time, allowing an holistic view of the entire Warship as a whole in its operational environment. This type of effort will be the objective of future works based on the findings presented in this paper.

V. Conclusions

In the paper it is postulated that, during the design process of complex Warships, a shift of attention is necessary to an initial activity of thorough analysis focused on the problem domain. Thus, the approach shifts the focus on the level of the whole warship's capabilities, rather than on its components and subsystems that belongs to the solution domain.

A set of twelve Capabilities characterizing the naval vessel has been proposed, further detailed and commented. Their identification enables and instructs the investigation and development of the solution domain. They are assumed to be effective to comprehensively represent all the necessary Capabilities for the Warship to fulfill a superior mission by means of proper implementation of the operational requirements.

All the identified Capabilities are meant as Warship emergent properties deriving from the successful and concurrent interaction among the different parts and systems. In this perspective, an overcoming of the typical separation between the Warship platform and the Warship combat systems is pursued.

As a further step it will be possible to discuss how the different Capabilities are related to each other and with the Warships technical characteristics as well. In this perspective the relation of the contents of this paper and the traditional naval ship design process is elucidated: the traditional design spiral provides an effective model for the assessment and the relevant discussion.

The Capability formulation enables also:

- the systematic identification of the necessary technology to be installed onboard with specific reference to their interfaces and interference characteristics with the ship platform.
- the identification of workable Measures of Effectiveness and derived Measures of Performance, to afterwards give evidence of the Warship compliance with design goals.

In conclusion the content of this paper represents a proposal to better set out the naval ship design process since the very beginning for a comprehensive and robust final fulfilling of the customer needs following a documented and informed process.

REFERENCES

[1] F. Mistree, W. F. Smith, B. A. Bras, J. K. Allen and D. Muster, "Decision-Based Design: a Contemporary Paradigm for Ship Design", SNAME Annual Meeting, san Francisco, California, 1990.

[2] D. J. Andrews, "A Comprehensive Methodology for the Design of Ships (and Other Complex Systems)", Proc. R. Soc. Lond. A 454, pp. 187-211, 1998.

[3] S. Esbati "Design for Support in the Initial Design of Naval Combatants", PhD Thesis in Naval Architecture and Marine Engineering, Department of Mechanical Engineering, University College London, 2018.

[4] C. N. Calvano, O. Jons and R. G. Keane, "Systems Engineering in Naval Ship Design", Naval Engineers Journal July 2000.

[5] W. J. Tudor and N. Harrison, "Virtual integration: managing complex warship design through model based engineering", Engine As A Weapon International Symposium, 2019.

[6] H. Wang, D. Pei, L. Gan, R. Chen and Z. Li "A Short Review of U. S. Naval Ship Concept Design Technology Development Features", International Journal of Maritime Science & Technology, Vol. 64, Issue 2, ISSN: 0469-6255, EISSN: 1848-6320, 2017.

[7] INCOSE, "Systems Engineering Handbook – a guide for System lifecycle processes and activities", published by John Wiley & Sons, 2015.

[8] M. Manfredi and L. Tirone "Application of the Model Based Systems Engineering Approach for Modern Warship Design", 28th Annual INCOSE International Symposium, Washington DC, 2018

[9] L. Tirone, C. Agostinelli, P. Petrinca, E. Guidolotti, L. Fornaro, M. Nardini, S. Solazzi, "Application of the Unified Architecture Framework for the Definition of a Generic System Architecture of a Combat System", Conferenza INCOSE Italia su Systems Engineering, CIISE'17, Naples, November 2017

[10] J. P. Olivier, S. Balestrini-Robinson and S. Briceño, "Approach to capability-based system-of-systems framework in support of naval ship design", IEEE International Systems Conference Proceedings, pp. 388–395, 2014.

[11] J. P. Olivier and S. Balestrini -Robinson "Capability -Based System-of-Systems Approach in Support of Complex Naval Ship Design" , Complex Systems Design & Management (CSD&M) conference, 2014.

Chaotic-based Security for Near Field Communication in Internet of Things Devices

Colin Sokol Kuka
Department of Electronic Engineering
University of York
Heslington
York YO10 5EZ
United Kingdom
sk1759@york.ac.uk

James Chandler
The City of Liverpool College
Liverpool L3 6BN
United Kingdom
James.Chandler@liv-coll.ac.uk

Mohammed Alkahtani
University of Liverpool
Liverpool L69 3BX
United Kingdom
m.alkahtani@liverpool.ac.uk

Abstract—**The security of wireless systems has become a growing challenge resulting from the expansion of the Internet of Things (IoT) into everyday life. Despite the many advantages driving the adoption of IoT devices, their proliferation increases the surface susceptible to advanced attacks that aim to misuse their resources and cause interruptions, delays, losses and degradation of the offered services in IoT. This paper introduces a chaotic transmission for Near Field Communication (NFC) Topology, based on the Wireless Power Transfer (WPT) systems. Traditional WPT circuits are based on inverters to create an oscillation for the transmitter coil. This results in systems relying only on software security. Therefore, we have introduced this topology which adopts chaotic encryption for NFC security. Furthermore, the proposed system is immune to Man-in-the-Middle (MitM) attacks. The simulation results and tests prove the functionality of the chaotic WPT based on the Chua's diode and their synchronisation between transmitter and receiver. The chaos generated is sampled by an electronic board and can be used for cryptography coding based on Python. The application for this system is a new NFC digital code for accessing the IoT services.**

Keywords–Cryptography, Chaotic transmission, Digital key, High Security, Chua diode, Man-in-the-Middle (MitM) attack immune, Near Field Communication (NFC), Wireless Power Transfer (WPT), Internet of Things (IoT).

I. INTRODUCTION

The Internet of Things (IoT) is the product of recent developments in energy and cost-efficient computing and cloud/wireless infrastructure. The IoT has been a major driver of scientific, technological, economic, and social change 1. IoT also comes with a set of requirements [1]: ultra-low power consumption for long-term autonomous operation without the ability to recharge the battery; the need to communicate with other devices; the need to operate efficiently in harsh environments; and the ability to withstand malicious cyber-attacks (including both: remote attacks mounted through network connections and physical attacks by adversaries) [2]. Our everyday lives are intertwined with modern cryptographic schemes. The majority of available cyber-defenses are based on securing electronic systems' software or their communication interfaces [3].

Most everyday IoT devices use the Near-Field Communication (NFC), which is a recent short-range communication system that can be used for anything from physical access control to contactless payments [4]. The NFC transponder is the most important part of the device because it enables data to be read and written. There are several different types of NFC tags, each with its own form, scale, and construction material, but they all fall into two categories [5], [6]. One group is the active NFC, in which the system uses its own power source, which is normally a long-lasting battery. The other type is passive, which means they don't have their own energy source and instead rely on the electromagnetic field produced by the transponder [7], [8]. To relay information over a short distance, NFC uses electromagnetic induction between two loop antennas at a particular frequency. The data is stored in tiny microchips (or tags) and sent to readers within a certain physical range [9].

NFC devices using the WPT operating principle rely on the resonance by magnetic means of an alternating current in coupled LC circuits. In near-field, the mutual inductance at high frequency of both antenna coils acts as a loosely (roughly) magnetically coupled transformer, where energy is magnetically induced and propagated from the primary to the secondary coil. For short-range tasks such as a gap of few centimetres, the working frequency of the resonant circuit is generally in the range from 10 kHz to a few MHz [10], [11].

In this work, we present a WPT topology with advanced security capabilities based on the Chua's diode. The circuit exhibits a typical two attractor chaotic behaviour. Thanks to this unique non-linearity, it is possible to adopt a mutual authentication key based on the last state and its subsequent encryption and decryption. Furthermore the WPT system is immune to man-in-the-middle (MitM) attacks.

The memristor or Chua's diode is a circuit element based on the electrical charge q and the magnetic flux φ. Its constitutive relationship is theorised by Prof. Leon Chua [12]. This device can create chaos from the well known Chua's circuit shown in Fig. 2. Memristors with their non-linearities are properly integrated into existing electronic circuits to create several new chaotic behaviour circuits [13], [14] as depicted in Fig. 3. Dynamic behaviours, such as chaos and hyper-chaos [15], [16], coexisting multiple attractors [17], [18], hyper-chaotic multi-wing [19], [20] and hidden attractors [21], [22] have been studied and analysed by numerical simulations and hardware experiments.

Figure 1. Example of IoT devices used in everyday life which rely on the NFC and the WPT techniques.

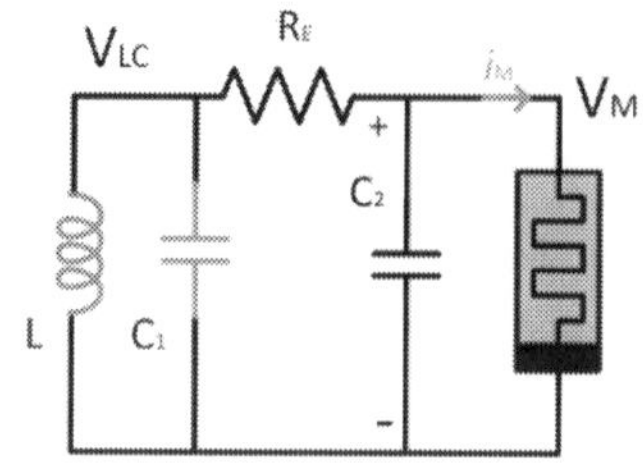

Figure 2. Traditional Chua's circuit

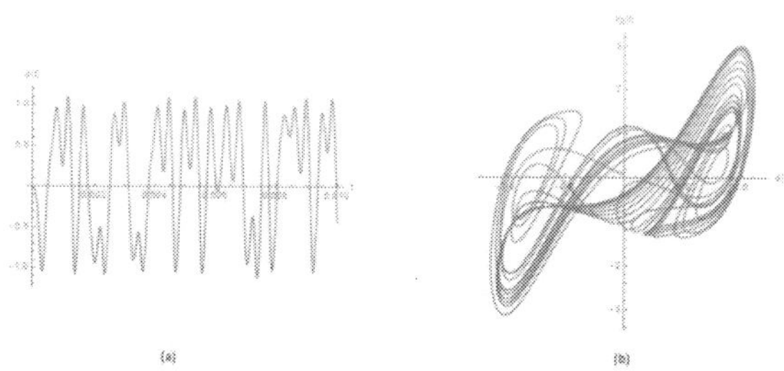

Figure 3. Typical chaotic behaviour waveform of the voltages in the inductor (**a**) and capacitor in a XY mode representation (**b**).

In this work, we therefore propose a low power Chua's diode circuit architecture for WPT systems. The system has the quality of transmitting power and data wirelessly. In addition, the system has the ability to achieve the highest level of encryption due to the chaotic behaviour. One of the biggest advantage for this system is the low power consumption. The rest of the document is organized as follows. The wireless power transmission circuit and encryption and decryption capabilities are shown in the next section. In Section III, there is an analysis of the WPT based on memristor. System functionality and simulation results are presented in Section IV. Finally, Section V concludes the document.

II. Wireless Power Transfer and Chua's Diode

Near Field Communication (NFC), which is commonly used in smartphones as presented in Figure 1. The NFC are also used contactless credit cards and digital keys, is a special form of WPT device that is very sensitive to the problem of cryptography [23], [24]. NFC is a low-bandwidth, two-way wireless communication technology that uses electromagnetic induction to transfer data between devices separated by up to ten centimeters. Internal user data on access cards and digital keys is encrypted by software and stored in a computer. The Hash function has historically been used to encrypt data. This form of algorithm is well-known and subject to a number of attacks easily accessible through the Internet [25]–[27]. This confidential information must be secured by an internal electronic system in high-security applications. We present an NFC device based on a chaotic communication between two circuits in this paper. By adopting this technology, there are three major advantages:

- Ability to develop chaotic behaviour.
- Avoid man-in-the-middle (MitM) attack.
- Provides less power consumption than transistors or switches.

In this way, the WPT device with Chua diode can create highly encrypted security without the use of external circuits to drive their synchronisation. It is not based on a tamper-proof algorithm. The developed waveform is chaotic and is based on the state variables' most recent state. Every time the device reads from the memristor, the internal state of the memristor changes to a new point of stability that is completely random and unrelated to the previous one.

There is no such method in the literature [28]. The cryptography suggested in the reference [29] is based on a shift in transmission frequency that knocks out other receivers. The frequency and correspondence with the receiver are generated by causal variation of the capacitor array according to the algorithm for maximum power output. The transmitted power can then be packed with various frequencies and delivered to the receiver in a predetermined time interval. Nonetheless, discrete algorithm adjustments, finite choices, and simple cloning affect these types of switched capacitor cryptography. In contrast, the memristor has been successfully used in imaging and communication encryption, achieving the highest degree of encryption. Circuit instability is crucial in deciding on chaotic encryption and decryption in a chaotic model of memristor-based cryptography. A user key, for example, has a chaotic generation of sequences because its initial values triggered the chaos of the memristor circuit. Encryption and decryption was built from this series. As a result, WPT technology and a chaotic memristor-based circuit can be used together.

A. *Wireless Communication*

Figure 4 depicts a WPT device made of memristors. Since the inductor is a reciprocal inductance the memristive Chua's

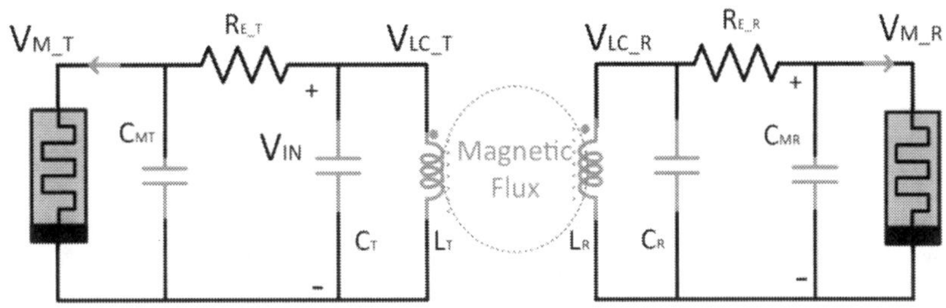

Figure 4. Symmetric Chua circuit proposed in the article.

TABLE I. PARAMETERS OF THE SYSTEM PROPOSED.

Parameter	Transmitter	Receiver	Value
C_1	C_{MT}	C_{MR}	6.8 nF
C_2	C_T	C_R	68 nF
R_E	R_T	R_R	2.18 kΩ
L	L_T	L_R	8 mH
M			4 mH

circuit introduced has been strengthened. The system is totally symmetric with two copies of the Chua circuit, as shown in Fig. 4. The above circuit produces an oscillation that may result in equilibrium, disorder, or instability. The parameter values shown in Table I have been considered in reference to a memristive Chua's circuit. As can be shown, the inductors have a value of 8 mH, which is lower than the typical value of 12 mH in Chua memristive circuits due to the use of the mutual inductance of the coupled circuits. The current flowing through L_T, the transmitter coil, generates a magnetic field around it, with some of these magnetic field lines going through the receiver coil, resulting in reciprocal inductance. Since the square root of two equal values is the same as one single value, when the inductances of the two coils are the same and equal, L_T and L_R are equal to L, the reciprocal inductance between the two coils would equal the value of one single coil, as shown:

$$M = k\sqrt{L_T L_R} = kL \tag{1}$$

where k denotes the coupling coefficient as a fractional number between 0 and 1, with 0 denoting no inductive coupling and 1 denoting complete or maximum inductive coupling. Since one coil induces a voltage in the next, the transmitter L induces a voltage V in the receiver, and vice versa. The oscillation of the circuit is not possible with more than one receiver at the same time because it will create an over mutual inductive M load as shown in the equation below.

$$\begin{cases} v_R^{in} = L_R \frac{dL_R}{dt} + M \frac{dL_T}{dt} \\ v_T^{in} = L_T \frac{dL_T}{dt} + M \frac{dL_R}{dt} \end{cases} \tag{2}$$

Using these relationships, lower inductances can be used than in Chua's circuit, and the circuitry's symmetry allows the chaotic behaviour to be transmitted. The transmitter and receiver would have the same resonant frequency:

$$f_0 = \frac{1}{2\pi\sqrt{LC_T}} = \frac{1}{2\pi\sqrt{LC_R}} \tag{3}$$

When the values in Table I are used, the result is 6.8 kHz. It is important to note that high efficiency is not needed for this application. The receiver only requires a small amount of power to begin its own oscillation and the chaotic actions needed for encryption.

B. Memristor state variables

Moreover, it is crucial to demonstrate that the device has no difference when compared to the typical Chua's diode circuit equations. When both sides of the system are in close proximity to each other, they must be capable of engaging in disorderly actions. The circuit's behaviour is derived from the classic third order Chua circuit by adopting the ideal voltage regulated active memristor shown in Fig. 5. Since the two circuits are symmetric, we will only look at the transmitter in this study. For the study, we call $C_{MT} = C_1$, $C_T = C_2$ and $L_T = L$ in series with a resistor (resistance of the coil) R_0. Let us consider that the state equations are obtained by computing the currents through the two voltage at the capacitors and the voltage across the inductor and remembering that $i_1 = C_1 \frac{dv_1}{dt}$, $i_2 = C_2 \frac{dv_2}{dt}$ and $V_3 = L\frac{di_3}{dt}$. We obtain:

$$\begin{cases} \frac{dv_1}{dt} = \frac{1}{C_1}[(v_2 - v_1)G - f(v_d)] \\ \frac{dv_2}{dt} = \frac{1}{C_2}[(v_2 - v_1)G - i_L] \\ \frac{di_3}{dt} = -\frac{1}{L_T}[v_2 - R_0 i_3] \end{cases} \tag{4}$$

where the $f(v_d)$ is the diode function:

$$f(v_d) = G_b v_1 + 0.5(G_a - G_b)[|v_1 + B_p| - |v_1 - B_p|] \tag{5}$$

To plot these equations,, usually we are sizing the time, voltages, and currents by RC_2, B_p, and B_pG, respectively. Assuming the variables $\tau = \frac{t}{RC_2}$, $x = \frac{v_1}{B_p}$, $y = \frac{v_2}{B_p}$ and $z = \frac{i_3}{GB_p}$, we obtain the following dimensionless state equations:

$$\begin{cases} \frac{dx}{d\tau} = \alpha(-x + y - f(x)) \\ \frac{dy}{dt} = x - y + z \\ \frac{dz}{dt} = -\beta y - \gamma z \end{cases} \tag{6}$$

where $\alpha = \frac{C_2}{C_1}$, $\beta = \frac{R^2 C_2}{L}$ and $\gamma = RR_0\frac{C_2}{C_1}$. These are the typical equations for the Chua circuit computed in almost all computer simulators analysing the chaotic behaviours.

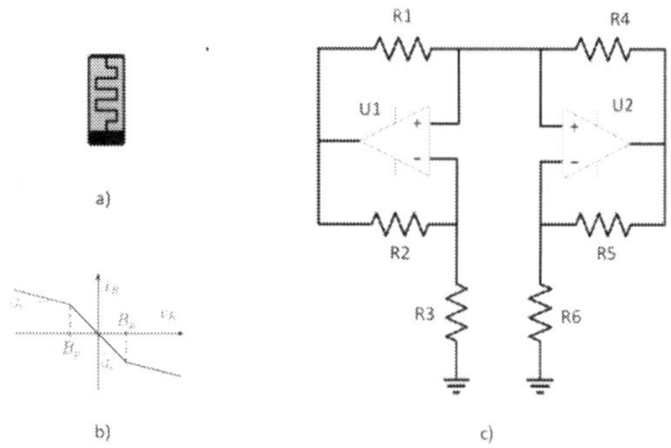

Figure 5. Chua's diode (**a**) typical I-V characteristic (**b**) and the equivalent circuit used in this article.

TABLE II. Circuit Parameters in reference to the Chua's diode equivalent circuit.

Circuit Parameters			
Resistor	Value	Resistor	Value
R_1	220 Ω	R_4	22 kΩ
R_1	220 Ω	R_4	22 kΩ
R_1	2.2 kΩ	R_4	3.3 kΩ

III. Communication Sequence

In this Section, we list all the steps and a flowchart of the new chaotic NFC procedure. The system is described as a door opening mechanism but can be adopted in all the IoT applications mentioned above such as payment.

A. NFC procedure proposed

Memristor-based chaotic cryptography system model consists of two parts shown in Fig. 4, which are two symmetrical Chua's circuits, Transmitter and Receiver respectively. In a typical Chua circuit, the initial condition is applied on the Capacitor C_T from external digital source. Therefore, in the $L_T C_T$ and $L_R C_R$ there is a connection to A/D or D/A converters. According to the cryptosystem model shown in Fig. 6, the process of chaotic encryption key data generation for opening an access door is described as follows:

1) The high security lock has a database of customers and each lock has in internal memory the ID of the customer.
2) The digital key or Access Card has an internal ID encrypted by the last Memristor chaotic status.
3) At the attempt to open the door, the lock and digital key (Receiver) are connected to each other. Both Memristors will develop a chaotic behaviour.
4) The chaotic behaviour generated in the transmitter circuit depends on the receiver status because it induces a voltage in the transmitter coil and consequently giving a new initial condition V_{IN}. In this way, the security lock's digital logic can immediately recognise the authenticity of the user decrypting the data received.
5) If the Memristor status of the digital key is the same as the last status check, the digital logic can convert data. Otherwise, the receiver will bring the transmitter Memristor into a state with unknown variables, and hence the lock will be prevented from opening.

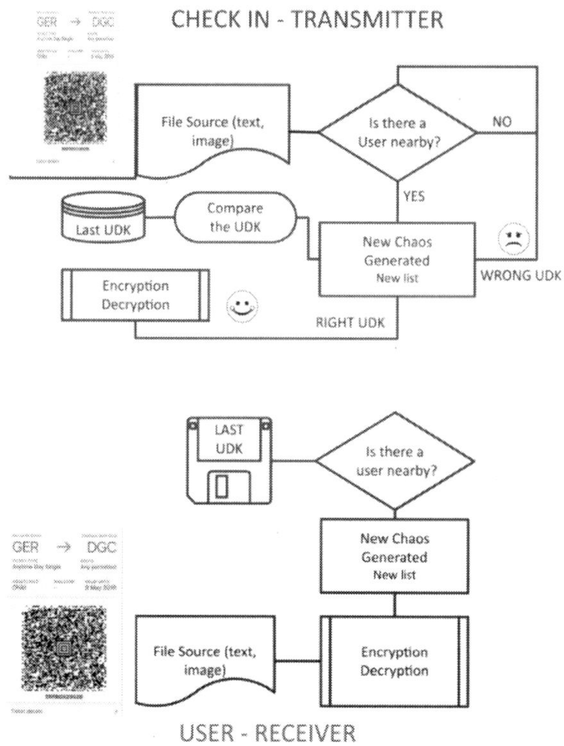

Figure 6. Flowchart of the entry system described in steps.

6) When the WPT system has reached an End Of File, both digital logic stages will disconnect the Memristor storing their last status.

Furthermore, any attempt to forge the digital key or smartphone would leave an indelible mark, as it will cause the memristor internal status for the authentication key to change irreversibly to an unexpected value from which their is no way to derive the previous value. True, the electronic system can be duplicated, but the internal value of the memristor can never be estimated, and there is no algorithm that can do so.

IV. System Performance Results

The system has been simulated with the advanced software NI multisim 14.2 with commercial devices and Labview functionality. The coils are designed as coupled inductors with a variable coupling factor. In order to start the chaotic behaviour memristors develop the chaotic waveform following the Chua's memristive circuit. The key design specifications and parameters are listed in Tables I and II. The whole system has been verified showing a chaotic behaviour. The time plot can only partially give an understanding of the chaotic behaviour, therefore the system has been plotted with an oscilloscope in X-Y mode. We have shown the waveforms in the receiver as XY plot in 0.2 V/div and 1 V/div in Fig. 7 for V_{M_R} vs V_{LC_R} , respectively. In Fig. 8 is shown V_{M_R} vs i_{LC_R} in XY mode in 1 V/div and 1 V/div, respectively. In Fig. 9 is shown the v_{LC_R} vs i_{LC_R} in 0.2 V/div and 1 V/div, respectively.

The synchronisation of the phase portraits of the chaotic

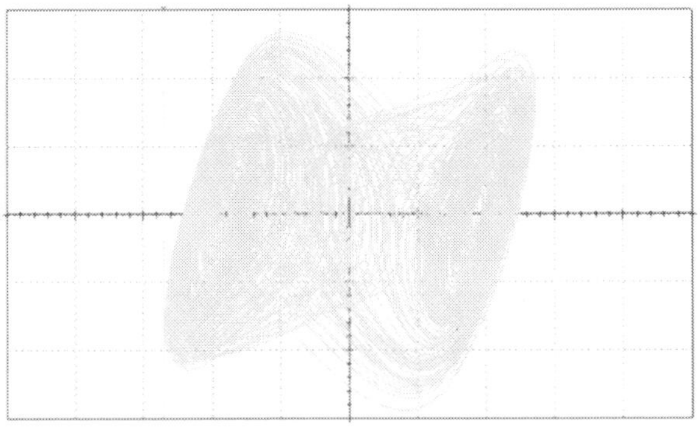

Figure 7. Receiver V_{M_R} vs V_{LC_R} shown in XY mode in 0.2 V/div and 1 V/div, respectively.

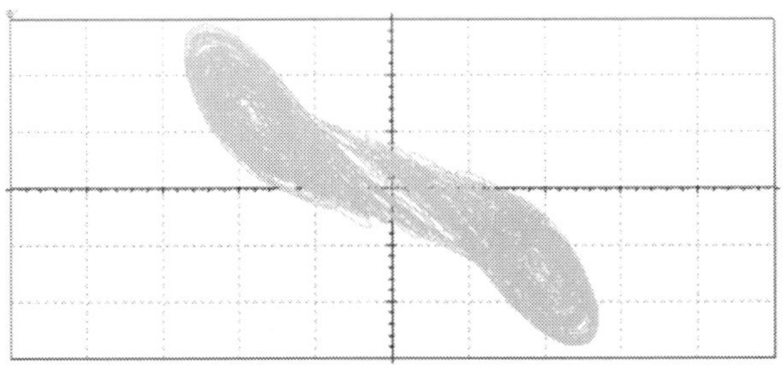

Figure 8. Receiver V_{M_R} vs i_{LC_R} shown in XY mode in 1 V/div and 1 V/div, respectively.

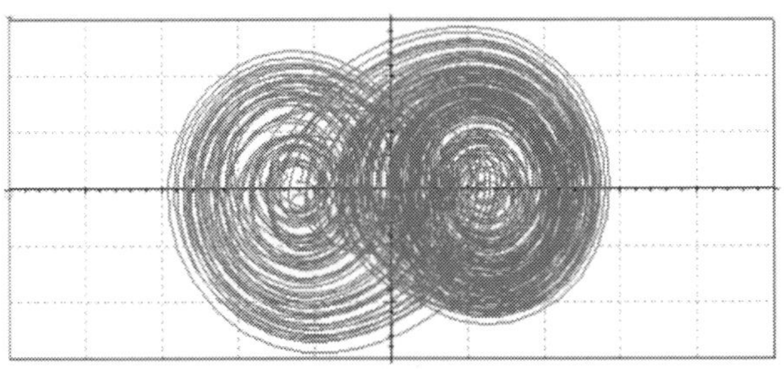

Figure 9. Receiver v_{LC_R} vs i_{LC_R} shown in XY mode in 0.2 V/div and 1 V/div, respectively.

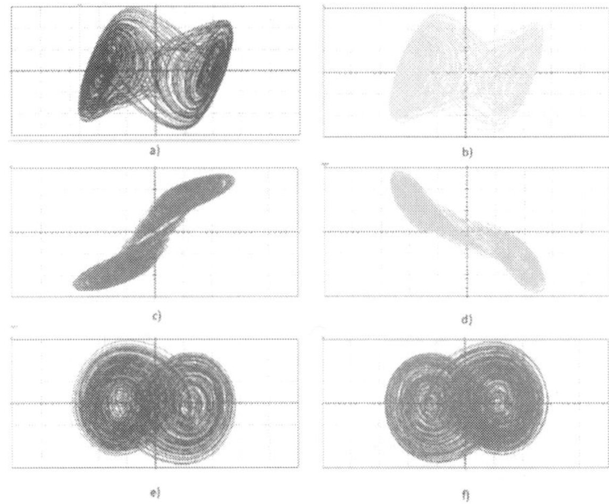

Figure 10. Synchronisation of the phase portraits of a chaotic attractor: voltage in the inductor V_{LC} referred to the memristor voltage V_M in the transmitter (a) and receiver(b) coil; current in the inductor i_L referred to the memristor voltage V_M in the transmitter (c) and receiver (d) coil; the memristor voltage V_M referred to its internal voltage status V_0 in the transmitter (e) and receiver (f).

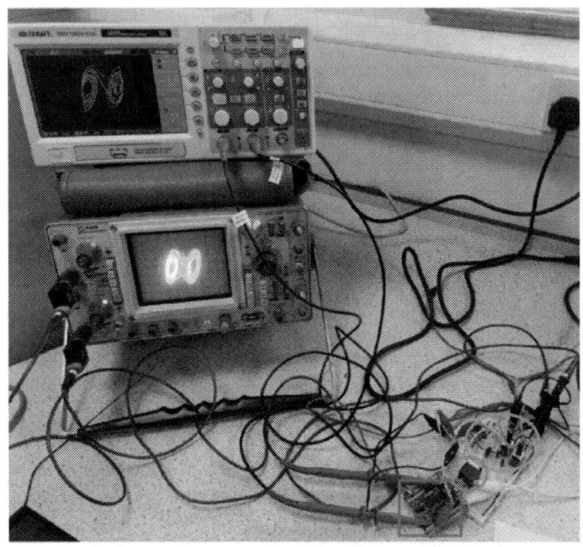

Figure 11. The prototype transmitter highlighted in orange, the receiver in red and the coupling transformer in blue.

attractors are fully synchronised as shown in all the plots of the transmitter (left) and the receiver (right) in Fig. 10.

A. *Experiment*

A prototype of the system has been built, as shown in Figure 11, on two different electronic breadboards which are jointed by a transformer representing the two coils. The memristor model has been built using the the ideal voltage regulated active Chua's diode introduced in Figure 5. The physical design of the memristors and the coils require advanced manufacturing technology which is outside of the scope of this article. In place of the coils a 6 mH 1:1 transformer has been used (resulting in a total inductance of 12 mH). The chaotic behaviour developed by the system is visualised on the transmitting side using a Tektronix 465 analogue oscilloscope and at the receiver with a Voltcraft digital storage oscilloscope and is in accordance with our simulations.

For the IoT application, we have sampled the waveforms and used the Arduino Firmata library and Python to record the data on a host PC and an online service, as shown in Figure 12. In this way the chaotic behaviour is available online. The chaotic data is used in a Python code by using Flask libraries and HTML Python. We have created a database and webpage by using Python and sampling data by arduino.

V. CONCLUSIONS

The security of the new electronic and Internet of Things devices has become a great challenge. The data protection of these devices are only based on the web or on well-known algorithms and software. Therefore, the unique behaviour of the

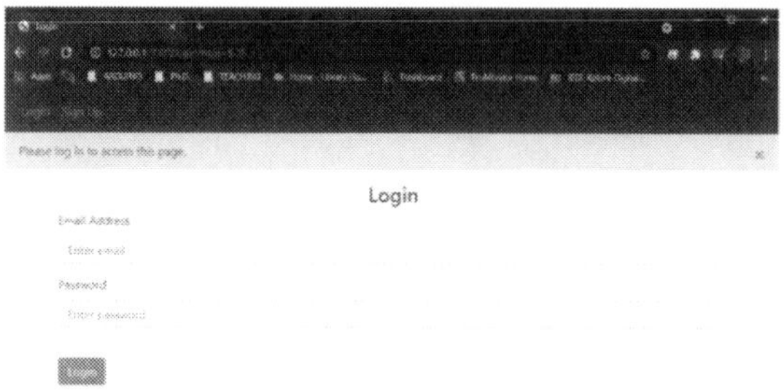

Figure 12. Use of Python and use chaotic encryption for web resources.

Chua's diode has attracted a lot of research studies and interest in developing new encryption characteristics. Furthermore, the memristor in a modified Chua's circuit is able to facilitate power and data transmission, provided that the inductors are mutually coupled. For this reason, we created two symmetrical Chua circuits able to transmit chaos. This new technique is an interesting solution, due to the fact it can be used to implement near-field wireless communication and encryption using a true random number generator. We are introducing an innovative implementation of the Chua circuit, which is applied in the NFC. In the article we have not mentioned the algorithm used in Python.

Future work will be focused on improving the data encryption and the realisation of multi-coil synchronisation, because they show a great and interesting advantage in comparison with the traditional Chua's circuit.

REFERENCES

[1] D. Minoli, K. Sohraby, and B. Occhiogrosso, "Iot considerations, requirements, and architectures for smart buildings—energy optimization and next-generation building management systems," IEEE Internet of Things Journal, vol. 4, no. 1, 2017, pp. 269–283.

[2] I. Stellios, P. Kotzanikolaou, M. Psarakis, C. Alcaraz, and J. Lopez, "A survey of iot-enabled cyberattacks: Assessing attack paths to critical infrastructures and services," IEEE Communications Surveys & Tutorials, vol. 20, no. 4, 2018, pp. 3453–3495.

[3] F. Restuccia, S. D'Oro, and T. Melodia, "Securing the internet of things in the age of machine learning and software-defined networking," IEEE Internet of Things Journal, vol. 5, no. 6, 2018, pp. 4829–4842.

[4] A. Dohr, R. Modre-Opsrian, M. Drobics, D. Hayn, and G. Schreier, "The internet of things for ambient assisted living," in 2010 seventh international conference on information technology: new generations. Ieee, 2010, pp. 804–809.

[5] V. Coskun, B. Ozdenizci, and K. Ok, "A survey on near field communication (nfc) technology," Wireless personal communications, vol. 71, no. 3, 2013, pp. 2259–2294.

[6] G. Jain and S. Dahiya, "Nfc?: Advantages, limits and future scope," vol, vol. 4, 2015, pp. 1–12.

[7] F. Di Rienzo, A. Virdis, C. Vallati, N. Carbonaro, and A. Tognetti, "Evaluation of nfc-enabled devices for heterogeneous wearable biomedical application," IEEE Journal of Radio Frequency Identification, vol. 4, no. 4, 2020, pp. 373–383.

[8] I. Yoon and H. Ling, "Investigation of near-field wireless power transfer under multiple transmitters," IEEE Antennas and Wireless Propagation Letters, vol. 10, 2011, pp. 662–665.

[9] Y. Sun, S. Kumar, S. He, J. Chen, and Z. Shi, "You foot the bill! attacking nfc with passive relays," IEEE Internet of Things Journal, 2020.

[10] J. I. Cairó, J. Bonache, F. Paredes, and F. Martín, "Reconfigurable system for wireless power transfer (wpt) and near field communications (nfc)," IEEE Journal of Radio Frequency Identification, vol. 1, no. 4, 2017, pp. 253–259.

[11] S. Kuka, K. Ni, and M. Alkahtani, "A review of methods and challenges for improvement in efficiency and distance for wireless power transfer applications," Power Electronics and Drives, 2019.

[12] R. Barboza and L. O. Chua, "The four-element chua's circuit," International Journal of Bifurcation and Chaos, vol. 18, no. 04, 2008, pp. 943–955.

[13] T. Matsumoto, "A chaotic attractor from chua's circuit," IEEE Transactions on Circuits and Systems, vol. 31, no. 12, 1984, pp. 1055–1058.

[14] Q. Xu, Q. Zhang, B. Bao, and Y. Hu, "Non-autonomous second-order memristive chaotic circuit," IEEE Access, vol. 5, 2017, pp. 21 039–21 045.

[15] B. Bao, T. Jiang, Q. Xu, M. Chen, H. Wu, and Y. Hu, "Coexisting infinitely many attractors in active band-pass filter-based memristive circuit," Nonlinear Dynamics, vol. 86, no. 3, 2016, pp. 1711–1723.

[16] A. L. Fitch, D. Yu, H. H. Iu, and V. Sreeram, "Hyperchaos in a memristor-based modified canonical chua's circuit," International Journal of Bifurcation and Chaos, vol. 22, no. 06, 2012, p. 1250133.

[17] Q. Xu, Y. Lin, B. Bao, and M. Chen, "Multiple attractors in a non-ideal active voltage-controlled memristor based chua's circuit," Chaos, Solitons & Fractals, vol. 83, 2016, pp. 186–200.

[18] J. Kengne, Z. Njitacke Tabekoueng, V. Kamdoum Tamba, and A. Nguomkam Negou, "Periodicity, chaos, and multiple attractors in a memristor-based shinriki's circuit," Chaos: An Interdisciplinary Journal of Nonlinear Science, vol. 25, no. 10, 2015, p. 103126.

[19] P. Zaiping, W. Chunhua, L. Yuan, and L. Xiaowen, "A novel four-dimensional multi-wing hyper-chaotic attractor and its application in image encryption," Acta Physica Sinica, vol. 63, no. 24, 2014, p. 240506.

[20] H. Wu, Y. Ye, B. Bao, M. Chen, and Q. Xu, "Memristor initial boosting behaviors in a two-memristor-based hyperchaotic system," Chaos, Solitons & Fractals, vol. 121, 2019, pp. 178–185.

[21] B. Bao, H. Bao, N. Wang, M. Chen, and Q. Xu, "Hidden extreme multistability in memristive hyperchaotic system," Chaos, Solitons & Fractals, vol. 94, 2017, pp. 102–111.

[22] M. Chen, M. Li, Q. Yu, B. Bao, Q. Xu, and J. Wang, "Dynamics of self-excited attractors and hidden attractors in generalized memristor-based chua's circuit," Nonlinear Dynamics, vol. 81, no. 1, 2015, pp. 215–226.

[23] P. Pourghomi and G. Ghinea, "A proposed nfc payment application," arXiv preprint arXiv:1312.2828, 2013.

[24] M. Q. Saeed and C. D. Walter, "Off-line nfc tag authentication," in 2012 International Conference for Internet Technology and Secured Transactions. IEEE, 2012, pp. 730–735.

[25] D. Schürmann, S. Dechand, and L. Wolf, "Openkeychain: an architecture for cryptography with smart cards and nfc rings on android," Proceedings of the ACM on Interactive, Mobile, Wearable and Ubiquitous Technologies, vol. 1, no. 3, 2017, pp. 1–24.

[26] V. Coskun, K. Ok, and B. Ozdenizci, Near field communication (NFC): From theory to practice. John Wiley & Sons, 2011.

[27] N. Ramya, U. Sandhya, and L. Gayathri, "Biometric authentication to ensure security in epassports," in 2018 International Conference on Communication, Computing and Internet of Things (IC3IoT), Feb 2018, pp. 342–346.

[28] C. S. Kuka, Y. Hu, Q. Xu, and M. Alkahtani, "An innovative near-field communication security based on the chaos generated by memristive circuits adopted as symmetrical key," IEEE Access, vol. 8, 2020, pp. 167 975–167 984.

[29] Z. Zhang, K. T. Chau, C. Qiu, and C. Liu, "Energy encryption for wireless power transfer," IEEE Transactions on Power Electronics, vol. 30, no. 9, Sep. 2015, pp. 5237–5246.

New Approach to Efficiently Assess the Power Consumption of Field Programmable Gate Array Devices

Esteve Hassan
Electrical and Computer Engineering Technology
Mohawk College of Applied Arts and Technology
Hamilton (ON), Canada
e-mail: esteve.hassan@mohawkcollege.ca

Bilal Al Momani
Electrical and Computer Engineering Technology
Mohawk College of Applied Arts and Technology
Hamilton (ON), Canada
e-mail: bilal.al-momani@mohawkcollege.ca

Abstract— In this paper, the design application is a telemetry system intended for health monitoring applications. The Field Programmable Gate Array (FPGA) is used as the brain control unit at both transmitter and receiver sides. The transmitter side is recording data packets through external interfaced sensors. Verilog Hardware Description Language (Verilog-HDL) has been used to implement the various functionalities required by the FPGA device. The power performance of the FPGA-based design will be assessed using the XILINX Xpower tool. A Model sim Code coverage feature has been incorporated to make sure that the test bench will cover all the nets branch statements of the design and create the most accurate Value Change Dump (VCD) file for the power consumption assessment process.

Keywords- FPGA; Telemetry system; power assessment.

I. INTRODUCTION

Electronic systems development is becoming more and more complex, fast, powerful, and power-consuming. Indeed, the transistor miniaturization dramatically increases the power consumed by a whole chip [1]. The main consequences of this trend are the addition of elaborated cooling circuits and the reduction of battery life for the embedded systems. As for timing and die area, power consumption becomes a critical constraint for electronic system design. A previous study [2] has demonstrated the beneficial effect of power optimization at high-level; it is then necessary to develop high-level estimation tools which use power models for all kind of components (Application-Specific Application Circuit (ASIC), FPGA) in a system. Playing many important roles in recent applications, FPGAs devices are used in a wide scale of designs ranging from small glue logic replacement to System-on-Chip. The main advantage of FPGA compared to ASIC chips is the flexibility: a design can be reprogrammed partially or totally in-situ. This functionality is realized by a configuration plan and requires a large number of transistors for Static Random Access Memory (SRAM) FPGA; therefore, the drawback is important static power consumption. Moreover, FPGA builders are currently improving this circuit characteristic to facilitate their integration in System on Chip (SoC). The health care field became one of the most recent applications of the FPGA designers [3].

The challenge is to raise or at least maintain the present level of health care provision without ending up in an uncontrolled cost explosion. The increasing number of researchers and manufacturers who are working on a new generation of wireless technology applications for the medical field has led to improved quality and reduced cost of patient care. One of the areas in healthcare that best lend itself to wireless technology is patient monitoring, also known as wireless telemetry.
FPGA vendors are facing the difficult task to accurately specify the energy consumption information of their products on the device data sheets because the energy consumption of FPGAs is strongly dependent on the target circuit including resource utilization, logic partitioning, mapping, placement, and route. While major Computer Aided Design (CAD) tools have started to report average power consumption under given transition activities, energy optimal FPGA design demands more detailed energy estimation. This work aims to present a useful methodology for estimating the power consumption of an FPGA-based system designed for medical applications. Modelsim code coverage capability will be used to investigate the different styles of test bench coding on the overall power consumption estimation of the FPGA device.

In Section 2, a system overview is presented. Section 3 is outlining the power estimation methodology for FPGA devices. Modelsim code coverage is explained in Section 4. Section 5 is giving the merits of the new method to perform an accurate power consumption assessment. Finally, conclusions are drawn in Section 6

II. SYSTEM OVERVIEW

The main blocks of the transmitter side FPGA are shown in Figure 1. The different units of the system were coded with Verilog HDL simulated with ModelSim SE V6.0a and implemented with ISE14.7. The final implementation was targeting the Spartan-3 device since it provides the various features that solve the designer's challenge throughout the entire system. The transmitter FPGA consists mainly of an SPI (Serial Peripheral Interface), RLE (Run Length Encoding) compressor, and framer units. The operation of the system units and the flow of data through the system are controlled by the main FSM (Finite State Machine) controller.

At the receiver side, a data recovery unit is needed to extract the clock from the received bitstream. The de-framer and the RLE decompresser blocks are designed to reconstruct the original data bytes sent by the transmitter.

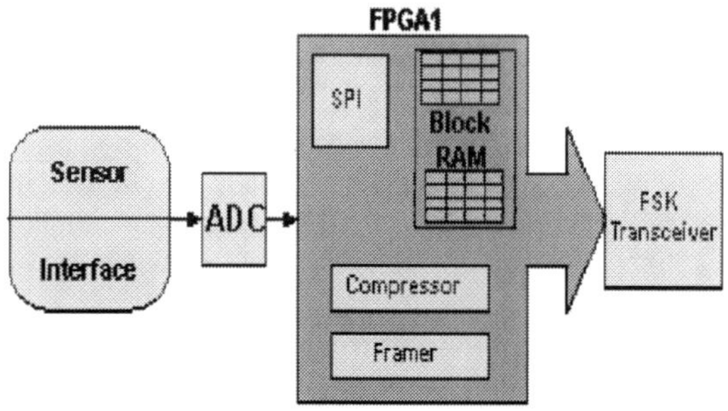

Figure 1. Building blocks of the transmitter FPGA

A. *SPI main units*

An efficient SPI unit has been modeled, as shown in Figure 2. The Master out Slave in (MOSI) signal has been omitted from the design based on the hardware requirements where data only needed to be transferred from the ADC to the FPGA system. The main units of the SPI are functioning as follows:

1. Clock Divider Unit: Divides the system clock by a certain factor to generate the required SPI clock frequency.
2. Data out clock synchronizer: used to generate both the rising edge (dout7) and the falling edge (dout16) of the ADC clock.
3. ADC Enable unit: triggered on when the start_conv signal is asserted to generates the following signals:
    a. Capture signal to capture data transfer from the ADC to the SPI register after each byte transfer.
    b. Increment signal used to change the address inside the Block RAM unit.
4. Slave Chip Select (CS).
5. SPI Register Unit: contains the SPI serial in/parallel out register, which is enabled when the capture signal is asserted and receives input serial data through ADC_Din signal. Spiout (output) signal carries the information data bytes to the Block RAM unit.
6. Distributed Block RAM: stores the data bytes in locations determined by the increment signal.

Typically, test benches have become the standard method to verify HDL designs. Test benches invoke the functional design, and then simulate it. Accordingly, an efficient test bench has been written to mimic the behaviour of the ADC and verify the operation of the SPI system units.

III. FPGA POWER ESTIMATION

Power consumption is mandatory information in modern digital system design.

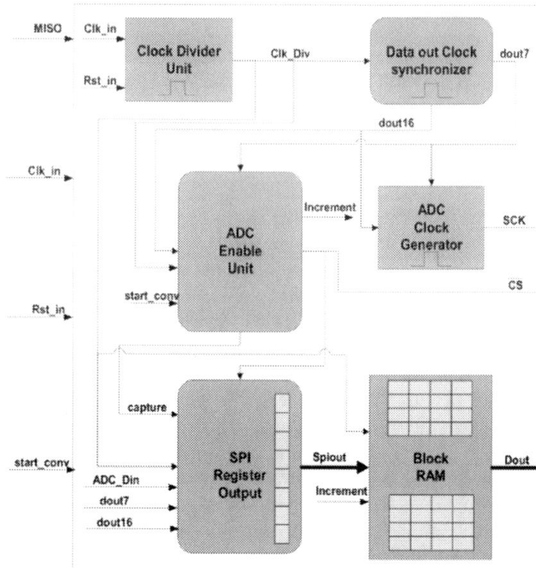

Figure 2. Block units of the developed SPI inside the FPGA

Chip vendors are naturally in charge of supplying energy consumption information of their products on the device data sheets. However, it is not possible for vendors to specify power consumption information of SRAM-based FPGAs because it is not only dependent on the target device and operating frequency, but is highly dependent on the design and operating conditions. Power consumption is strongly dependent on the target circuit including resource utilization, low-level features such as logic partition, mapping, placement and route.

A. *Related Work*

For FPGA, some methodologies and models have already been developed to estimate the power consumed specifically by the logic elements. For example, a probabilistic model is proposed by [4]; developed for a CAD tool, this model estimates, at the transistor level, the 0.18 μm Complementary Metal Oxide Semiconductor (CMOS) FPGA power consumption based on place and route. The switching activity used to calculate the dynamic power is determined by the transition density of the signal. The static power is evaluated by a sub-threshold current estimation. The resulting absolute error of this model is 23% compared to measurements. Some techniques are proposed in [5] to reduce both static and dynamic power consumption like drowsy mode, clock gating, guarded evaluation, counter and state machine encoding, but no estimation model is proposed. For a design in Virtex-II, [6] proposes an estimate of the dynamic power consumed by logical elements after routing. Lastly, [7] has presented a Register Transfer level power estimator based on determination of wire length and switching activity with an average error of 16.2%. The first parameter is calculated by applying Rent's rule during high-level synthesis. The second parameter is evaluated by a fast switching activity calculation algorithm. The model developed by [8] allows estimating the power consumption of distributed memory (using logic elements) in past FPGA families with technical parameters. Another model proposed in [9] uses technical parameters such as effective capacitance of each resource which is hardly obtained. All these methodologies and models use low-level parameters and technical characteristics which are not available before place and route. More precise approaches to estimate FPGA power consumption were described in [11] and [12].

B. XPower XILINX Tool

XPower is a commercial-off-the-shelf tool to estimate power consumption of Xilinx SRAM-based FPGAs. The design flow of the XPower is shown in Figure 3. In this paper the implementation of the Xilinx XPower will be investigated. XPower reads in either pre-routed or post-routed design data, and then makes a power model either for a unit or for the overall design based on the power equation: $P=CVf$ where P is average power consumption, C is equivalent switching capacitance, V is supply voltage and f is operating clock frequency or toggle rate. It considers resource usage, toggle rates, input/output power, and many other factors in estimation. Because XPower is an estimation tool, results may not precisely match actual power consumption. The frequency, f, is determined by users or provided by simulation data from the ModelSim family of HDL simulators.

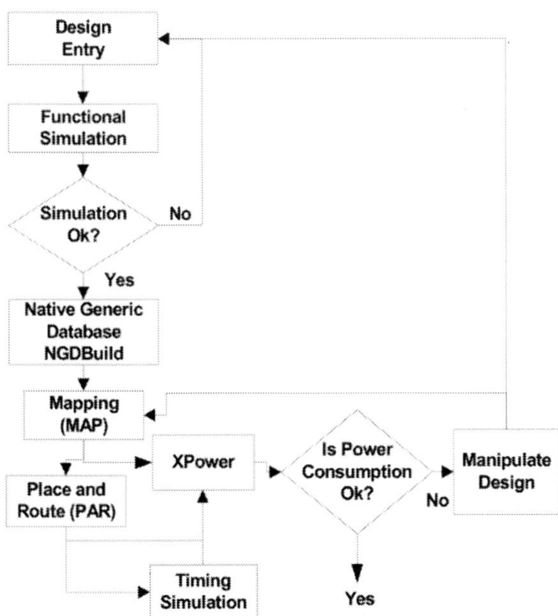

Figure 3. XPower tool design flow

XPower provides two types of information called data view and report view. The data view shows the power consumption of individual parts of a design such as signals, clocks, logic and outputs. The report viewer represents the total power consumed by a given design, which is again classified into power consumption of clocks, logic and outputs, and static (leakage) power. The power consumption of clocks, logic and outputs are calculated by equivalent switching capacitance models. The static power is based on constant value quoted in a data book or calculated by an equation associated with temperature, device utilization and supply voltage.

IV. ModelSim Code Coverage

ModelSim code coverage can display a graph and report file feedback on which statements, branches, conditions, and expressions in the source code have been executed. It also measure bits of logic that have been toggled during the execution. Therefore, it can be considered as trace tool and probe at the same time that provides history of the software execution.

As code execution is almost invisible without an accurate trace tool, it is common for the entire blocks or modules of code to go unexecuted during test routines or redundant user-case suites. Coverage metrics showing which functions are not executed are useful for writing new, additional tests or identifying unused "dead" code. In applications where code size is critical, removing dead code reduces both waste as well as risk in the targeted design. In many cases, code coverage can also be used to analyze errant behavior and the unexpected execution of specific branches or paths. The FSM can be extracted with code coverage as in Figure 4 for the compressor unit.

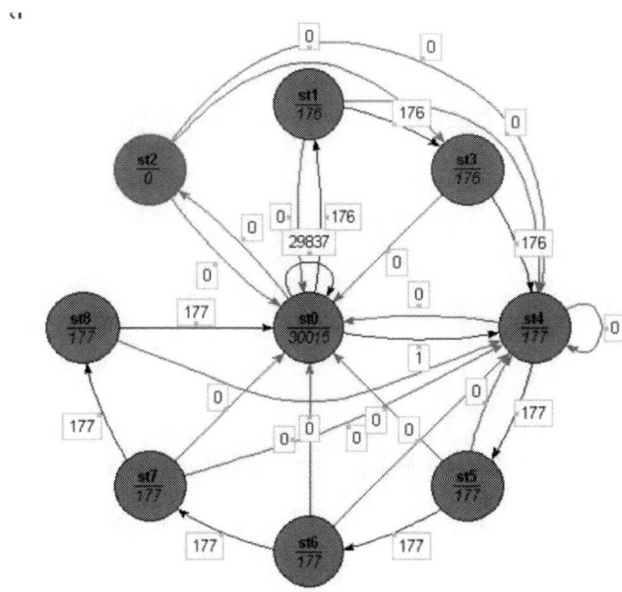

Figure 4. Transmitter FPGA-Compressor unit FSM

The FSM figure clarifies the number of the states involved in the design and the interaction between these states. A test bench has been written to examine the behavior of the HDL design. The code coverage is enabled to check the covered and uncovered parts of the design code by the test function which can lead to alter the design and consequently change the power consumption.

Figure 5 shows some uncovered statements indicated by red X mark. In addition, an example of missed branches is shown in Figure 6 where the X_T mark indicates that the true branch of the conditional statement was not covered.

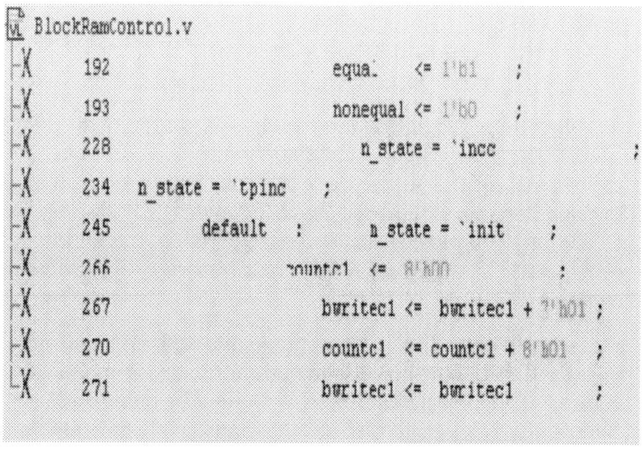

Figure 5. Not covered design statements

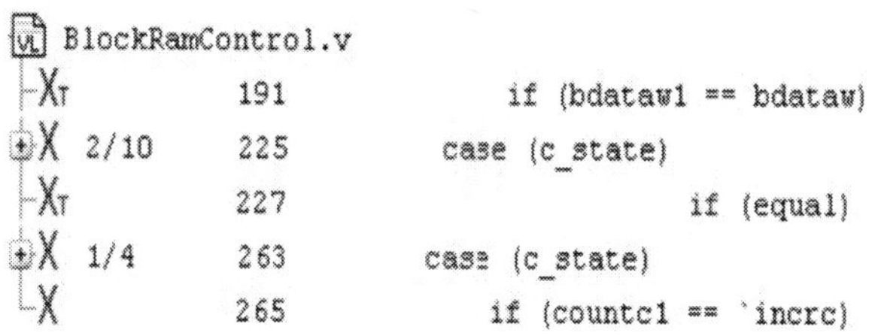

Figure 6. Not covered design branches

V. ACCURATE FPGA POWER ESTIMATION

The power characterization using XPower tool is done and based on the mapped/placed/routed design. In general, the total power consumption of a CMOS component is given by Equation.1. The dynamic power is due to the component activity while static power represents the power consumed by the leakage current.

$$P_{total}=P_{dynamic}+P_{static} \quad (1)$$

The static power given by the XPower is constant, and calculated by the multiplication of maximum leakage current absorbed by the FPGA core and its supply voltage. On the other hand, dynamic power is varying according to the switching activity of the design. Therefore, two factors determine the accuracy of the XPower analyzer estimation: the accuracy of the data within Xpower analyzer and the stimulus provided by the user. It is necessary to mention that XPower relies upon stimulus data to estimate the power consumption for internal components. Valid input frequencies and toggle rates are necessary parameters to generate a proper power estimate. The main four important files that need to be invoked by the tool is the design (*.ncd), simulation (*.vcd), physical constraints (*.pcf) and setting (*.xml) files.

There are few strategies that can be implemented to reduce the power consumption of the FPGA device; these are:

1. Turn off clocks when they are not in use.
2. Make Block RAMs to operate in "no read on write" mode. This reduces toggling of the output of the BRAM.
3. Use clock enables to reduce switching activity on the output of Flip Flops (FFs).
4. Partition logic driven by global clocks into clock regions and reduce their number to which each global clock is routed.
5. Reduce the total number of columns to which a clock is routed.
6. Reduce the total length of heavy loaded signals.

Mainly, we followed the recommendations in 3 &4 to reduce the power consumption of our design. Therefore, the global design has been partitioned into a lot of small blocks.

In order to investigate the impact of test bench writing style on the accuracy of the power estimate, two methods have been exercised. In the first one, the ADC_Din (line carrying input data coming from the ADC) has been stimulated by variable 8-bits data samples, as expected in the practical case. In the second method, only 0 data value is stimulating the ADC_Din. As an example, the control logic of the compressor BRAM has been considered to see the difference in the code coverage represented by the summary reports given in Figures 7 and 8.

File: BlockRamControl.v

Enabled Coverage	Active	Hits	% Covered
Stmts	86	80	93.0
Branches	52	47	90.4
Conditions	6	6	100.0
States	9	8	88.9
Transitions	26	10	38.5

Figure 7. BRAM control coverage report without adc_in

File: BlockRamControl.v

Enabled Coverage	Active	Hits	% Covered
Stmts	86	83	96.5
Branches	52	50	96.2
Conditions	6	6	100.0
States	9	9	100.0
Transitions	26	12	46.2

Figure 8. BRAM control coverage report with adc_in

The hits count shows the number of times the indicated code part has been reached or executed. It is obvious that this count has been increased for all the design parts except the conditions. The states of the design have been fully covered in Figure 8 because the system is dealing with all the possible design options that are required in the verification stage. Sample ModelSim waveforms for the two adc_in condition are shown in Figures 9 and 10.

To investigate the effect of adc_in on the power consumption of the FPGA device, XPower tool has been used for this purpose. Table.1 summarizes the total power and current estimates for both configurations.

TABLE 1. TOTAL CURRENT AND POWER ESTIMATES

Total Power and Current estimates	I(mA) With adc_in	P(mW) With adc_in	I(mA) Without adc_in	P(mW) Without adc_in
Device		59		51
Vccint 1.20V	12	16	11	13
Vccaux 2.50V	16	41	15	38
Vcco25 2.50V	1	2	0	0
Quiescent Vccint 1.20V	10	12	10	12
Quiescent Vccaux 2.50V	15	38	15	38

As given above, more power is needed for the design when ADC_Din is clocking with different serial data. This leads to the conclusion that the FPGA device will consume higher power if the analog input signal to the ADC is rapidly changing. IN this case, the compressor unit of the design will be fully functioning with all the possible transition state.

The second case is assuming that the analog input has steady value which is rare in practical, but useful to have a power estimates for different working conditions. Thus total dynamic power is more depending on the states of the input signals. In comparison, the power values in the two cases are different due to the code coverage analysis that has been discussed earlier. As more code has been covered with ADC_Din is varying, then we can consider that the obtained power estimate with such case has more credibility.

Quiescent power is the same for both configurations since it depends on the device itself using default conditions in moderate environments. To reduce the power consumption of the FPGA without loosing the accuracy, more work need to be done outside than inside the device. For examples, reduce the ADC resolution or the analog input can be good options. The test bench should be written in a very optimum way to provide stimulus for all the inputs and read efficiently all the outputs. This is an important issue in the XPower tool since it provides one of the main files for the tool to estimate the power. The code coverage sometimes can help to extract the unnecessary parts from the design which has a great benefit for the power consumption. As a final comment, obtaining the high code coverage can lead to higher but more accurate power estimate using XPower.

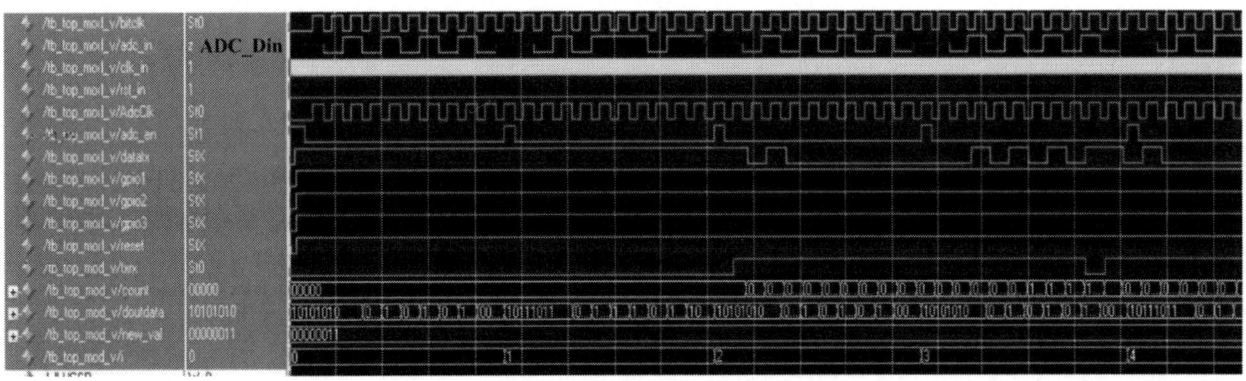

Figure 9. Simulation output waveform of the design with for variable adc_in

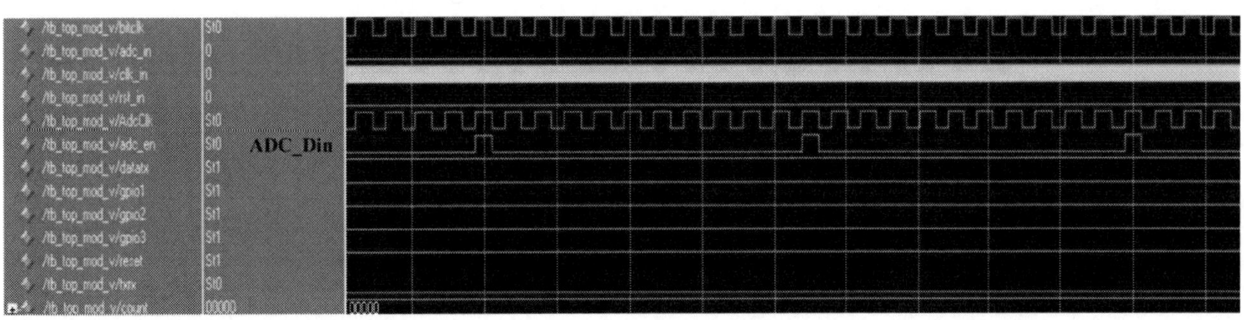

Figure 10. Simulation output waveform of the design with 0 data on adc_in

VI. CONCLUSIONS

In this paper, the power consumption of an FPGA-based system designed for medical applications has been investigated. The use of XPower from XILINX was the main focus of this work as an efficient tool to get good power estimates for the target FPGA device. The relation between the test bench coverage and power estimate accuracy was studied under different design conditions. It has been found that a good test bench with higher design code coverage capability can achieve more accurate power estimates. The presented results reflected clearly the efficiency of this method which can be applied with similar performance on any other Xilinx FPGA devices.

REFERENCES

[1] N. S. Sung et al., "Leakage Current: Moore's Law Meets Static Power", IEEE Computer Magazine, December 2003, pp 68 – 75.

[2] J. M. Rabaey,M. Pedram, Low Power Design Methodologies, Kluwer Academic Publisher, 1996, ISBN 0-7923-9630-8.

[3] P. Dillinger, J. F.Vogelbruch, J. Leinen, S. Suslov, R. Patzak, H. Winkler, and K .Schwan, "FPGA based real-time image segmentation for medical systems and data processing", IEEE 14th NPSS Real Time Conf Proc., June 4-10 Sweden, 2005.

[4] K. W. Poon, Power Estimation For Field Programmable Gate Arrays, Ph.D Thesis, department of Electrical and Computer Engineering, University of British Colombia, Vancouver BC, Canada 1999.

[5] X. Guo-Lin, "Power-sensitive design techniques on FPGA devices," Electronics Quality Journal, 2002.

[6] L. Shang, A. S. Kaviani, K. Bathala, " Dynamic Power Consumption in VIRTEX-II FPGA Family", in FPGA'02, February 24-26,Feb 2002, Monterey, California, USA.

[7] D. Chen, J. Cong, Y. Fan, "Low-Power High-Level Synthesis for FPGA Architecture", ISPLED'03, August 25-27 Seoul Korea, 2003.

[8] A. D. Garcia, Estimation et optimisation de la consommation de puissance des circuits logiques programmables du type FPGA [Estimation and Optimization of the Power Consumptionlogic circuits of the FPGA type], Ph.D Thesis, Ecole nationale suprieure des télécommunications de Paris, 2000.

[9] D. Elleouet, N. Julien, D. Houzet, J. Cousin, and M. Martin, "Power consumption characterization and modeling of embedded memories in XILINX", IEEE Digital System Design Conf Proc., 2004, pp.394-401.

[10] H. Gyu Lee, S. Nam, and N. Chang, "Cycle-accurate Energy Measurement and High-Level Energy Characterization of FPGAs", IEEE Quality Electronic Design Symp Proc. 2003, pp.267-272.

[11] T. Fryza and M. Waldecker, "Precise Measurement of Power Consumption and Execution Time for Embedded Platforms," 25th International Conference on Systems, Signals and Image Processing (IWSSIP), Maribor, Slovenia, 2018, pp. 1-4.

[12] N. Lawal, F. Lateef and M. Usman, "Power consumption measurement & configuration time of FPGA," Power Generation System and Renewable Energy Technologies (PGSRET), Islamabad, Pakistan, 2015, pp. 1-5.

Metamorphic Thinking in Cartesian Systemic Emergence

Marta Franova, Yves Kodratoff
LISN, UMR9015 du CNRS & INRIA Saclay
Bât. 660, Orsay, France
e-mail: marta.franova@lri.fr, yvekod@gmail.com

Abstract— **Cartesian Systemic Emergence (CSE) is a theory developed in order to formalize the process of a human *creation* relative to particular problem-solving systems. Its final aim is to enable to design (semi-) automated tools that favor this creation. The creation process considered here concerns the context of informally specified systems and working with underspecified notions in incomplete environments. The aim of this paper is to show that this non-standard research approach is epistemically justified. In particular, the paper focuses on justifying inspiration-conduciveness of the CSE-experiments-generation-and-handling process relative to the invention of primitive notions needed in order to create the intended problem-solving system.**

Keywords*— *Cartesian Systemic Emergence; Symbiotic Recursive Pulsative Systems; Metamorphic Thinking; deductive-like problem-solving systems; systems design methodologies.

I. Introduction

The design of a problem-solving system S is usually based on the well-known 'divide-and-conquer' strategy. Such a particular design can thus be expressed as a paradigm (called here P1-paradigm) represented by the paradigmatic formula

$$\forall \text{ pb } \exists \text{ st solves(st,pb)} \qquad \text{(P1)}$$

in the following sense: Some already existing different tools T_i are recognized (maybe after a relevant adaptation) as suitable for solving a subset Pb_i of the set {pb}. An adequate modular composition of these different tools T_i (or, rather the systems st_i obtained from each of these tools) then constitutes (a subset of) the system st.

Instead of this usual modular approach, in this paper, we consider a system design paradigm represented by the paradigmatic formula

$$\exists \text{ S } \forall \text{ pb solves(S,pb)}. \qquad \text{(P2)}$$

Relying on this paradigm (called here P2-paradigm), the intention is to build a system S that *solves all problems in the same way*. This means that such a system S is not built as a modular composition of independent sub-systems. An obvious question is:

How to design S? (1)

Cartesian Systemic Emergence (CSE) introduced in [15] attempts to answer this question for particular systems (specified in Section II.D). CSE is a generalization of

c1. the experience acquired in an exploration of the genesis of ancient deductive systems [11],
c2. the experience acquired in the design of a P2-system (i.e., a system that is built relying on P2-paradigm) for Program Synthesis of Recursive Programs Specified by Formal Specification in Incomplete Domains – PS for short [14],
c3. the experience acquired from an original construction of ack [17] and a study of its computation process [16],
c4. the experience coming from the use of Descartes' method [10] for PS mentioned in c2.

These experiences confirm that the experiments-generation-and-handling process belongs to the important topics to be considered *before* a P2-design (i.e., before the design of a P2-system).

The primary goal of CSE experiments is the invention of primitive notions needed in order to create the intended P2-problem-solving system. In particular, we are concerned with the creation of Symbiotic Recursive Pulsative Systems (SRPS) intended as P2-problem-solving systems (see Section III.F of [18]). One of the suitable P2-design strategies for the experiments-generation-and-handling is called Resonance Thinking (RT) [18]. RT is based on a particular 'oscillation' between P2-paradigm and a simultaneous consideration of the formulas (P1) and (P2). We call RT-oscillation this process. This paper will justify that RT-oscillation is an inspiration-conducive one, i.e., it provides useful ideas concerning the parts of an intended P2-system S. The justification presented is 'epistemic' in the sense that it follows mainly from the active knowledge of c1. This paper, therefore, presents a minimal knowledge description necessary for building such an active knowledge. We say that knowledge is active when it is acquired through its active (re-) construction requiring the same effort as its first construction. We call 'Metamorphic Thinking' the particular 'epistemic justification' constructed here. It is on-purpose created for and in the framework of CSE. As a by-product, the epistemic justification presented in this paper provides also an epistemic justification for CSE as a non-standard, but justified, scientific way to do research in the context of informally specified systems, while working with underspecified notions in incomplete environments. Such a justification is necessary as many modern computer scientists and experts usually lack epistemic knowledge related to *creating 'from scratch'* new scientific pluridisciplinary theories.

The paper is structured as follows. Section II contains the fundamental notions used in this paper. Section III presents Metamorphic Thinking. Section IV briefly discusses related work, some applications and challenges. We conclude the paper in Section V.

II. FUNDAMENTAL NOTIONS

Roughly speaking, the goal of CSE is to formalize strategic aspects of human creation of *informally* specified *symbiotic deductive-like problem-solving systems*. In this section, we recall three terms by which this goal is expressed, namely

- informal specification,
- symbiosis, and
- deductive (deductive-like problem-solving) systems.

Since, in the CSE-context, the rigorous definitions of these terms are highly interdependent (more precisely, they are symbiotic), let us give first a rough description of their meaning. Such imprecise descriptions might then also be exploited in modular contexts.

An informal specification of a system is a description of this system that is somewhat vague, i.e., what it means or what the words in this description exactly mean may be unclear or even it may seem absurd or impossible to achieve. The symbiotic nature of a system parts means that, if even only one of these parts is eliminated, not only the system collapses but also all the other symbiotic parts collapse as well. Deductive-like problem-solving systems are systems that are defined exactly by their corresponding axiomatic system. We now will provide more precise descriptions of these notions.

A. *Informal Specification*

Let us consider the sentence: "Knife without a blade, for which the handle is missing." In a usual context, we may agree with the claim that this sentence is absurd [9]. However, we can consider another context in which this sentence represents an informal specification of an object to be constructed. Indeed, a surgeon may express a desire for a perfect cutting tool exactly by this sentence. The absence of a blade expresses his desire to cut with an unbelievable (for a knife) precision. The absence of a handle expresses his desire for a guarantee that this perfect 'knife' is out of reach for an incompetent person. Considering thus the words 'knife', 'blade' and 'handle' not as words with their usual 'material' meaning, but as underspecified words with the desired relevant 'characteristics' meaning, we obtain that a laser is a convenient solution for the surgeon's wish. An informal specification thus expresses a goal that may seem unachievable though, in fact, it implicitly contains a strong intention to reach this goal as much as possible. Of course, it is accepted *in advance* that some reasonable trade-offs may arise in order to reach this goal.

In the framework of CSE, an ***informal specification*** of a system is thus a description of this system by a *sentence* in which occur terms that are not yet exactly defined; they are *underspecified*. When considered out of a particular context, such a description, i.e., informal specification, may even seem absurd (as we have seen above for the 'knife-without-blade-...' specification) or the goal specified by it may seem impossible to reach (as might be argued, for instance, for a goal expressed by P2-paradigm). The meaning of these terms, in which a particular given informal specification is expressed, will evolve during the system construction. In other words, depending on some constraints and opportunities that will arise during the construction of the system, the meaning of the terms used in the starting specification will evolve and will make a part of the solution. The initial ambiguity of terms occurring in a given informal specification is eliminated by the provided solution. The evolution of these terms will also bring an exact specification of the context to be considered. Thus, in order to work with an informal specification, we must agree (and be aware) that the definitions and the exact context (or interpretation) are not given from the start, as it is usual for contemporary exact sciences. Therefore, in order to consider research working with informal specifications as a justified part even of contemporary exact sciences, this paper presents some arguments that have to be taken into account. The notion of 'epistemic justification' described in the next sub-section helps us in this task.

B. *Epistemic Justification*

As [23], p. 22, states, "justification is at issue only where something is untoward; there is *prima facie* violation of a norm or expectation that constrains action."

There are two facets of such a violation when working with informal specifications and underspecified contexts (frameworks, interpretations) in contemporary exact sciences.

The first facet concerns the necessity to consider 'fruitful' as well as 'luminous' experiments. As Bacon states in [2], fruitful experiences are concerned with the research starting from already rigorously defined 'building blocks' (definitions, tools, strategies, frameworks). However, luminous experiences express the fact that, in order to reach a goal, all the building blocks have to be created, usually from scratch. From a technological point of view, it means that fruitful experiences aim at improving on an existing technology (this is called 'innovation' in modern vocabulary), while luminous experiences aim at inventing a new technology (Bacon calls this 'progress' – a term that modern science tries to forget, as can be illustrated by the contemporary mutilated perception of creativity denying the possibility of creation from scratch [8]).

The second facet concerns the necessity to understand and accept a somewhat unusual kind of verbal expression (communication) when working with informal specifications and underspecified contexts. In other words, if we want to persuade an audience about a reasonable and realizable character of a goal that seems absurd or impossible to achieve (as it may seem for a system creation via P2-paradigm), we need to better specify a particular interpretation context (or, referential context) in which this goal has to be understood. In other words, we need to dissolve the rigidity of usual expectations (relying exclusively on a limiting 'logical exact reasoning') of the audience that constrains and impedes upon action oriented towards 'rigorous creativity'. In other words, as we have done for the above 'knife-without-blade-...' specification, we need to be convincingly 'talkative' in order to dissolve such rigidity. This 'talkative' character is typical of the argumentation in which one relies on 'recusation' instead of 'refutation'. To our best knowledge, such a kind of argumentation took place already in Francis Bacon's work [3] [1]. As stated on the fourth cover page of [3], refutation supposes a common ground on which the discussion starts. In contrast to this, recusation starts from scratch by building a new unusual ground in which the discussion will start and take place. In other words, in refutation, we are concerned with the same 'measure' (roughly speaking, a measure is here a system of measurement, i.e., an exact specification of the context and the tools to be used) and we are refuting a usual 'order' (roughly speaking, an order is here a way how we use these tools) by specifying some weaknesses or incoherencies of this order. We then introduce small improvements of (or in) this order or we suggest a completely new order in the same measure. Inversely, in recusation, we do not rely on an already known and agreed upon existing measure, but we introduce a new measure with a relevant order. In a standard 'logical' measure, there is no possible order which would allow us to consider some absurd goals as realistic goals. Therefore, the recusation here consists in specifying a new 'rigorous creation' measure in which these goals become realistic. Of course, we need to be concerned with the reliability of this new measure (see [23], p. 33-36). A method (or a measure) is reliable provided it is used in 'normal conditions'. 'Normal conditions' are those for which the method (or measure) was designed for. This means that the condition of intentionality is heavily present [23], p. 33. It is known (see [20], for instance) that intentionality cannot be present in formal logical reasoning in other way than as the 'intention of a formal manipulation'. This is the first point where our 'recusation' of the 'impossibility' of P2-goal (i.e., of creating a system built via the P2-paradigm) starts. Namely, our *intention* is to *create* a measure (i.e., a referential rigorous context) in which creating P2-systems is realistic. (Our intention is not a formal manipulation.) It is known that when people do not share the same intention there is little or no possibility to reach a common agreement (see the first paragraph of [10]). Since we are in a scientific context, we have a slight advantage that lies in dissimulating the notion of intention by employing the notion of hypothesis instead. In other words, we may ask our audience to 'study' with us our hypothesis of a possibility to consider our P2-goal as a realistic goal. Nevertheless, there exists a serious problem. Namely, in this particular case, the 'study' of our hypothesis is nothing but a construction of a referential rigorous context (i.e., a measure) in which creating a P2-system can be considered as a realistic goal. This 'study' requires from each one of the audience to employ the same effort, the same 'tools' and to have a strong 'intention' to create a solution for this goal. As we know, scientists do not usually share this vision of 'study of a hypothesis'. This is why, in agreement with [23] and [27], we call our justification 'epistemic' in order to express explicitly the requirement to rely on the same intention, the same tools and the same effort.

Epistemic justification is usually concerned with truth-conduciveness [23]. In other words, in the traditional sense, epistemic justification is concerned with the *verdict* 'true'. Note that, here, we are not concerned with 'verdicts'. We are concerned with the question:

How we can create a reasonable system that solves all the problems in the same way. (2)

We are not questioning whether this is possible. We simply have a strong intention to create such a system. In other words, we expect to have to make a few reasonable trade-offs in our process and we are decided to provide all the effort and ingeniosity necessary to create a system that solves all the problems in the same way. Since we are preoccupied here with 'How?' (see (2)), the verdict 'true' is of no interest during the creation process. However, in order to find an answer to (2), we are concerned with the 'inspiration-conduciveness' of a particular experiments-formation in the process of a particular system that solves all the problems in the same way. The notions of symbiosis and of deductive-like problem-solving systems presented just below will allow us to refer to this topic in Section III.

C. *Symbiosis*

In the process of a search for an answer for (2), we need to be aware of a particular interdependence, called here symbiosis, of the parts of some existing systems developed by humankind. By ***symbiosis***, we understand a composition of several parts that is vitally separation-sensitive and, by *vital separation-sensitivity* of a composition, we mean that eliminating one of its parts has three possible consequences. It may be a complete destruction or a non-recoverable mutilation or uselessness of the remaining parts. This implies that the divide and conquer strategy, as well as analysis and synthesis, are inappropriate tools when creating and observing symbiotic systems. Symbiosis is therefore different from synergy, since synergy is a mutually profitable composition of elements that are not destroyed nor mutilated by separation.

A well-known picture (available on the Internet) may be used for an intuitive understanding of what we mean by 'destruction' in our definition of symbiosis. It is the 'Young Girl-Old Woman Illusion' (YGOWI) as given, for instance, in [29]. The symbiotic parts, however, do not necessarily need to coincide in the final symbiotic object as it is in YGOWI. From a systemic point of view, symbiosis of a system is embodied by the *vitally separation-sensitive interdependence* of all the notions and the parts of this system. This shows up by a 'circular' character of the definitions in the following sense: Consider two notions n_1 and n_2 describing two symbiotic parts of a system S. Then, the definitions of these notions look schematically like

$\mathrm{Def}(n_1) = \mathrm{description\_in\_terms\_of}(\ldots,n_2, \ldots)$ (3)

and

$\mathrm{Def}(n_2) = \mathrm{description\_in\_terms\_of}(\ldots,n_1, \ldots)$. (4)

For instance, if we want to give the instructions to draw the YGOWI to a painter that has never seen such a kind of illusion, we must describe the 'young girl' of this illusion by referring also to the 'old woman' in the picture, and *vice versa*. We shall introduce the symbol ♦ to denote a symbiotic composition. Then, we shall represent symbiotic systems with the help of a particular systemic representation. For instance, for YGOWI we have the symbiotic representation

YGOWI = Young_Girl ♦ Old_Woman, (5)

where

Old_Woman = Old_Woman ♦ Young_Girl (6)

and

Young_Girl = Young_Girl ♦ Old_Woman. (7)

This concrete representation illustrates that symbiotic descriptions are usually considered as fallacious.

Note that mathematical recursion is a particular case of circular definitions that are accepted. However, (5) illustrates that, in general, (3) and (4) are not an instance of recursion. This means, that symbiotic descriptions are not fallacious, they only represent a complexity for which the usual analysis (such as modular thinking) is inappropriate.

A non-trivial example of a symbiotic system the parts of which are programs can be found in Section VI. of [18].

The next section presents Deductive Systems as scientific objects where symbiosis is present. We will show that while a *manipulation* (or use) of a particular deductive system does not require the awareness of the presence of symbiosis, the *creation* of a deductive system does require symbiosis.

D. Deductive-like Problem Solving Systems

Since deductive systems are a natural illustration of systems that 'think of everything' in the same way, or rather that try to capture by a compact finite formulation all true statements of a particular domain (thus 'thinking of everything true' in a particular unified way), explaining what we mean by a deductive system is important. By ***Deductive Systems*** (DS), we understand a particular kind of axiomatic systems in the sense that these systems formalize, in a compact finite way, the knowledge about a Real-World Situation (RWS) with the aim to handle this knowledge in an efficient uniform way. In our work, the notion of DS is always related to a particular RWS (i.e., an intended interpretation). DS are therefore different from the usual formal systems for abstract considerations.

Peano's Axiomatic Definition (PAD) of NAT and Euclid's Geometry (EG) are the best-known examples of DS. As it can be illustrated by the evolution of PAD and EG, a formalization of an RWS leading to a DS consists in a 'selection' of essential primitive notions and axioms representing the essential relationships among these notions.

Primitive notions are the notions that are *not* defined with a help of *previously* defined notions. Before a full formalization of an RWS, the meaning of these notions is informally specified by a *large experience* in RWS which shows that they are useful and essential for considering RWS. For instance, if we consider NAT, a large experience shows that the primitive notions in a formalization of NAT are not only 0 and Suc, but NAT as well. In particular, we cannot (or do not know how to) provide a clear description of what we mean by natural numbers by referring to other already defined notions. Indeed, when defining NAT, we need to refer simultaneously to 0, Suc and NAT themselves. Similarly, we cannot specify what means 0, for instance, without referring to Suc and NAT. In other words, (3) and (4) adapted here for these three primitive notions have to be considered (as will be described by formula (8) just below). This illustrates that the primitive notions of a DS are, *a priori*, symbiotic.

Thus, ***axioms*** of a DS express the statements about the relationships among the primitive notions. The essential particularity of these relationships is that, together, they provide a definition of all primitive notions. In other words, a particular primitive notion is not defined by a particular axiom: all axioms are symbiotically necessary in order to provide a clear description (and thus a definition) of the meaning of a particular primitive notion.

We said above that primitive notions of a DS are not defined with a help of previously defined notions. However, all primitive notions, say p_1, ..., p_n, are defined simultaneously, each depending on all the other primitive notions, by simultaneous considering all axioms of the system. Thus, (3) and (4) can be written in the form

$$\mathrm{Def}(p_i) = \mathrm{AXIOMS}(p_1,\ldots,p_i, \ldots, p_n), \quad (8)$$

where 'AXIOMS' denotes all DS-axioms considered simultaneously. This also means that all primitive notions are of the same, essential, importance. Therefore, no primitive notion plays a secondary (or auxiliary) role.

Note that, to the best of our knowledge, the symbiotic character of the primitive notions and the axioms of a DS has never been mentioned before in the literature.

Since the primitive notions of PAD and EG are symbiotic, their axioms could not be determined via (P1). The axiomatic constructions of both these systems were determined via (P2), since in both cases the aim was to obtain one global system describing the respective RWS. In general, a DS can be represented as a result of an attempt to proceed with a particular P2-paradigm, namely

$$\exists\, \mathrm{DS}\ \forall\, \mathrm{Truth}\ \mathrm{covers}(\mathrm{DS},\mathrm{Truth}). \quad (9)$$

Here, 'covers' means that a 'Truth' is either an axiom of DS or it can be deduced from axioms of DS.

We shall now informally describe what we mean by a deductive-like P2-symbiotic system.

By a ***deductive-like problem-solving system*** we mean a system such that its primitive notions are specified informally and the essential relationships among them, expressed by a finite number of axioms, provide their exact definition.

In our work, we consider deductive-like problem-solving systems S that have the property:

$$S(S) = S. \quad (10)$$

Formula (10) is known as the *Ouroboros equation* [26]. For a human-created system S, (10) can be seen as the final form of a particular evolutive process, that we shall call here Ouroboros process, represented by

$$\lim_{n\to\infty} S_{n+1}(S_n) = S, \quad (11)$$

where S_0 is an initially given informal specification for S. In this process, S creates itself (from its own informal specification). This is why, we characterize a problem-solving system that verifies the Ouroboros equation as a *Generator of assets* (usually, a solution to a problem is an asset) *that is an asset* (since S is a solution to a problem as well) *that self-generates* (i.e., it provides a solution to its own creation). Another way to express this is by saying that such a generator of assets is a symbiotic part of its own creation.

Therefore, it is important to understand that, from a practical point of view, to go from S_0 to S_1 is the most complex task, since this step already must

- anticipate (and thus allow) the whole evolution (11),
- have a solid and efficient strategy for specifying the primitive notions of S_1 and their symbiosis expressed by the resulting axioms,
- incarnate all methodological fundamentals related to the creation of P2-deductive-like problem-solving systems.

In our future work, we will show that the Ouroboros process is a particular form of pulsation (presented in [18]).

Metamorphic Thinking guarantees that these three conditions are satisfied in CSE. More precisely, CSE is created so that these conditions do hold. Note that (11) can be also seen as a process of reaching a consensus in multi-agent systems [35]. This thus relates to the process of *creating* a pluridisciplinary fundamentals theory enabling *symbiotic* collaborations (see Section VI. of [18]) that are able to reach such a consensus for their aimed project. CSE aims exactly to become such a pluridisciplinary fundamentals theory.

III. METAMORPHIC THINKING

The role (and the name) of MT is best understood in the context of the three remaining CSE parts, namely Symbiotic Thinking (ST), Resonance Thinking (RT) and Pulsative Thinking (PT). With respect to the symbiosis of primitive notions and axioms of deductive systems, ST means that we focus on the creation of primitive notions and axioms that are symbiotic procedures. Resonance Thinking means that during such a creation we focus on experientially induced inspirations that are oriented towards the P2-paradigm. PT means that we handle incompleteness of our real-world perception relying on the evolving creation pulsation model of deductive systems. In other words, these parts express the three essential characteristics of building a deductive system. In contrast to this, MT expresses the fact that the formulation of CSE is heavily determined by the explicit emergence of CSE in the process of the creation of a particular Program Synthesis system [12]. In other words, the experiences in creating this PS-system and the 'crystallizing' process of the CSE final structure have been symbiotically intertwined.

The information presented in this paper completes a first tour of an informal presentation of ST (presented in [19]), RT (presented in [18]) and PT (presented in [17]). The symbiotic structure of CSE requires such an unusual presentation (according to modern scientific standards).

This paper focuses on the epistemic justification of relevant inspiration conduciveness of CSE experiments. This justification consists in taking into account, simultaneously

- the specifically oriented presentation of fundamental notions presented above in Section II,
- our previous descriptions of ST, RT and PT mentioned just above.

This means that a self-containing exhaustive presentation of MT is out of reach of a short paper, since it requires a global exhaustive description of CSE. More exactly, a global exhaustive description of CSE is a 'definition' of MT. This is illustrated already by the YGOWI example illustrated above, where we have seen that, in order to define Young Girl, we have to consider simultaneously the whole context, i.e., (5), the 'definition' of Old Woman, i.e., (6) and the 'definition' of Young Woman, i.e., (7). More formally this is described above by (8). Therefore, our future work aims at

- providing such a global presentation of CSE,
- illustrating the advantages of CSE parts (i.e., ST, RT, PT and MT) in a PS context, and
- presenting Ouroboros process as a particular form of pulsation.

Note that an Ouroboros process has already been explicitly illustrated in [13] while creating the CSE-like method called Créativité Formelle (Formal Creativity).

IV. RELATED WORK / APPLICATIONS / CHALLENGES

Since the main particularity of CSE is focusing on 'creating from scratch', there seems to be no other approach aiming at the same task. Moreover,

- focus on epistemically justified creation instead of skilfull observation,
- focus on P2 instead of P1,
- autopoiesis, and
- considering symbiosis

are the main differences of CSE in comparison with several approaches such as [4] [5] [6] [7] [21] [22] [24] - [26] [28].

We have previously given more detailed descriptions of differences and sometimes even suggested a possible cross-fertilization of other scientific disciplines and works with our approach as follows. In [18], we show how CSE and Michie's Ultra-Strong Learning [34] further elaborated in the works like [32] [33] might be fruitfully cross-influenced. In [18] [19] we illustrate how some unconscious cognitive processes, as the so-called Conceptual Blending [30], can be compared to a conceptually similar, but a conscious particular creative process as described by CSE. We illustrate also how research on cognitive processes of the human brain might follow the Ouroboros process. In [18] we compare CSE with some works on General Systems Theory and on Multidisciplinary Design. As the need for CSE became evident in PS, in [31] we compare some classical research works in PS with our application of CSE to this field.

However, we may consider CSE (through Ouroboros process) as an inspiration for creating 'perfect security' systems that do not break but evolve with each attack to a stronger version. A similarity of this idea can be seen also with mutations of Covid virus the main intention of which might be seen as 'living eternally'.

The main challenge of CSE is to underline the impossibility of replacing symbiotic collaborations by the usual synergic ones. Moreover, it is necessary to underline the need for accepting a non-standard, but epistemically justified way of doing and evaluating the research in the field of CSE creation. A non-trivial example of consequences of an attempt to replace a symbiotic collaboration by a synergic one can be found in Section VI. of [18]. See also the note at the end of Section II.D above.

V. CONCLUSION

This paper provides the last missing part in a presentation of a whole set of all the symbiotic parts of Cartesian Systemic Emergence constituting the foundation of a particular kind of scientific creativity necessary for developing Symbiotic Recursive Pulsative Systems. Moreover, this paper implicitly provided the basic principles for achieving a project aiming at implementing this particular scientific creativity.

CSE brings a progress to modern science at least on three points:

- ✓ it justifies P2-creation of SRPS,
- ✓ it shows that P2-creation requires its own particular kind of presentation, collaboration and evaluation, and
- ✓ it shows the inadequate character of the present intellectual property law still unable to protect this atypical kind of long-term research [13].

We hope that this first informal global (even though not exhaustive) presentation of CSE will stimulate the scientific community to explore more actively the potential of CSE in several, possibly new and on purpose created domains, namely whenever dealing with security constraints in any kind of innovative thinking.

REFERENCES

[1] F. Bacon, The wisdom of Ancients (La sagesse des anciens), Vrin, 1997.

[2] F. Bacon, Novum Organum, P.U.F, 1986.

[3] F. Bacon, Rrecusation of philosophical doctrines (Récusation des doctrines philosophiques), P.U.F, 1987.

[4] L. von Bertalanffy, General Systems Theory, George Braziller, 1969.

[5] J. L. Blizzard and L. Klotz: A framework for sustainable whole systems design, Design Studies 33(5), 2012, pp. 456–479.

[6] F. Charnley and M. Lemon: Exploring the process of whole system design, Design Studies 32(2), 2011, pp. 156-179.

[7] J. A. Crowder, Multidisciplinary Systems Engineering: Architecting the Design Process, Springer, 2018.

[8] M. Csikszentmihaly, Creativity - Flow and the psychology of Discovery and invention, Harper Perennial, 1996.

[9] O. De Rudder, Aperto libro ou le latin retrouvé, Larousse, 1989.

[10] R. Descartes, Discourse on the Method, in R. Descartes, translated by J. Cottingham, R.Stoothoff and D. Murdoch: Philosophical Writings of Descartes, vol. 1, Cambridge University Press, 2006, pp. 111-151.

[11] M. Franova, Deductive Systems, a work presented at the national competition (SVOC) of research work of Czechoslovakian university students in section: Epistemology, logic and philosophy, Bratislava, 1980.

[12] M. Franova, An Implementation of Program Synthesis from Formal Specifications, in Y. Kodratoff, (ed.), Proceedings of the 8th European Conference on Artificial Intelligence, August 1-5, Pitman, London, United Kingdom, 1988, pp. 559-564.

[13] M. Franova, Créativité Formelle: Méthode et Pratique - Conception des systèmes "informatiques" complexes et Brevet Épistémologique, Publibook, 2008.

[14] M. Franova, Cartesian versus Newtonian Paradigms for Recursive Program Synthesis, International Journal on Advances in Systems and Measurements, vol. 7, no 3&4, 2014, pp. 209-222.

[15] M. Franova and Y. Kodratoff, Cartesian Systemic Emergence - Tackling Underspecified Notions in Incomplete Domains, in O. Chernavskaya and K. Miwa (eds.), Proc. of COGNITIVE 2018: The Tenth International Conference on Advanced Cognitive Technologies and Applications, ISBN: 978-1-61208-609-5, 2018, pp. 1-6.

[16] M. Franova, Trace of computation for ack(3,2), https://sites.google.com/site/martafranovacnrs/trace-of-computation-for-ack-3-2 (Retrieved: 03/2021).

[17] M. Franova and Y. Kodratoff, Cartesian Systemic Pulsation – A Model for Evolutive Improvement of Incomplete Symbiotic Recursive Systems, International Journal On Advances in Intelligent Systems, vol 11, no 1&2, 2018, pp. 35-45.

[18] M. Franova and Y. Kodratoff, Cartesian Systemic Emergence and its Resonance Thinking Facet: Why and How?, International Journal On Advances in Systems and Measurements, IARIA, 2020, International Journal on Advances in Systems and Measurements, issn 1942-261x, Volume 13 (Number 1 & 2), pp.11-25.

[19] M. Franova and Y. Kodratoff, Symbiotic Thinking ... for Cognitive Modeling as Well, in C. Sennersten and O. Dini (eds). : COGNITIVE 2020, The Twelfth International Conference on Advanced Cognitive Technologies and Applications ; ISSN: 2308-4197, ISBN: 978-1-61208-780-1, IARIA, ThinkMind, October 2020, pp. 7-12.

[20] J. Y. Girard, Le champ du signe ou la faillite du réductionnisme, in T. Marchaisse, (dir.): Le théorème de Gödel, Seuil, 1989, pp. 145-171.

[21] H. Kopetz, Simplicity Is Complex: Foundations of Cyber-physical System Design, Springer, 2019.

[22] J. L. Le Moigne, La théorie du système général, théorie de la modélisation, P.U.F, 1984.

[23] J. Leplin, A theory of epistemic justification, Springer, 2009.

[24] M. S. Levin, Modular system design and evaluation, Springer, 2015.

[25] A. Reichel, Snakes all the Way Down: Varela's Calculus for Self-Reference and the Praxis of Paradise, Behavioral Science 28(6), November 2011, pp. 646 - 662.

[26] J. Soto-Andrade, S. Jaramilo, C. Gutiérrez and J.C. Leletier, Ouroboros avatars: A mathematical exploration of Self-reference and Metabolic Closure, in T. Lenaerts, M. Giacobini and al. (eds.), Advances in Artificial Life ECAL 2011: Procs. of the 11th Europ. Conf. on the Synthesis and Simulation of Living Systems, The MIT press, 2011, pp. 763-770.

[27] R. Swinburne, Epistemic justification, Oxford University Press, 2003.

[28] C. S. Wasson, System Engineering Analysis, Design, and Development: Concepts, Principles, and Practices, Wiley-Blackwell, 2015.

[29] E. W. Weisstein, Young Girl-Old Woman Illusion, From MathWorld - A Wolfram Web Resource. (Retrieved: 03/2021) http://mathworld.wolfram.com/YoungGirl-OldWomanIllusion.html.

[30] G. Fauconnier and M. Turner, The Way We Think: Conceptual Blending And The Mind's Hidden Complexities, Basic Books, 2003.

[31] M. Franova, Cartesian versus Newtonian Paradigms for Recursive Program Synthesis, International Journal on Advances in Systems and Measurements, vol. 7, no 3&4, 2014, pp. 209-222.

[32] S. Muggleton, D. Lin, and A. Tamaddoni-Nezhad: Meta-interpretive learning of higher-order dyadic datalog: predicate invention revisited, Machine Learning 100; 2015, pp. 49-73.

[33] S. Muggleton, U. Schmid, C. Zeller, A. Tamaddoni-Nezhad, and T. Besold, Ultra-Strong Machine Learning: comprehensibility of programs learned with ILP, Machine Learning 107, 2018, pp. 1119-1140.

[34] D. Michie, Machine learning in the next five years, Proceedings of the third European working session on learning, Pitman, 1988, pp. 107-122.

[35] Y. Shang, A combinatorial necessary and sufficient condition for cluster consensus, Neurocomputing Volume 216, 5 December 2016, pp. 611-616.

Comparing Kinematics-Based and Learning-Based Approaches to Robotic Arm Tasking – Using Pouring as an Example

Tzu-Chieh Chen
Department of Computer Science
National Tsing Hua University
Hsinchu, Taiwan
Email: jessica990805@gmail.com

Chung-Ta King
Department of Computer Science
National Tsing Hua University
Hsinchu, Taiwan
Email: king@cs.nthu.edu.tw

***Abstract*—The vast advances of machine learning in recent years have encouraged researchers to try learning-based end-to-end neural models for performing robotics operations. On the other hand, traditional approaches that leverage known knowledge as rules also have their merits. In this paper, we focus on robotic arm tasking and compare the learning-based end-to-end approach with a kinematics-based approach in terms of their capabilities in trajectory planning, using pouring as an example. In kinematics-based approach, object detection is obtained from a deep neural network, and arm trajectory is calculated with traditional Inverse Kinematics (IK). In the learning-based end-to-end approach, a single neural network is developed that takes RGBD images as input and outputs joint parameters of the robot arm to move the arm forward. We compare these two approaches with two scenarios, static and dynamic, in terms of their time usage and memory usage. Our experimental results show that the kinematics-based approach is more suitable for static scenarios as it uses less processing time and memory, while the learning-based approach is more suitable for complicated and dynamic scenarios.**

Keywords-machine learning; neural network; Inverse Kinematics; robot tasking; trajectory planning.

I. INTRODUCTION

The vast advances of machine learning in recent years have spurred its widespread adoption across almost all research fields. In robotics, many researchers have tried learning-based end-to-end neural models for performing robot operations. Unlike traditional approaches to robot systems that require extensive programming and human knowledge, learning-based approaches use techniques such as human demonstration and reinforcement learning to train a policy for the robot to follow to accomplish prescribed tasks. Such policies are often realized with end-to-end neural models that take raw sensory inputs and generate control outputs directly.

For complex problems, the end-to-end approach can develop well performed models without deep knowledge of the problems [1]. In addition, it uses a single neural network to replace the many functional modules in traditional robot systems, enhancing the systems by using a single optimization criterion.

On the other hand, the models developed by the end-to-end approach may be difficult to improve or modify. Any structural change, e.g., changing the input dimension, often requires re-training, which may lead to a completely different model [1]. It is also difficult to tell why the model does not work well. This is quite different from the traditional approaches, in which one can check and identify which function modules may cause an error or inefficiency. It is interesting to compare the two approaches for a deeper understanding of their respective merits.

In this paper, we compare these two approaches using trajectory planning of a pouring task as an example. Pouring is a common task used in robotics research. Prior works approach trajectory planning of robot arms from a geometric perspective and kinematics. They normally involve object detection, trajectory planning and object manipulation. Object detection determines where the target object is, including its coordinates and orientation in the space. Recent works mostly detect objects with RGB or RGBD cameras. Object detection then becomes a visual recognition problem, which can be solved very well with deep neural networks [9].

Given the location of the target object, trajectory planning then determines a path for the robot arm to reach the object. Traditionally, the problem is solved by *Inverse Kinematics* (IK), which determines the joint parameters to move the arm to the given location [7]. Once the end effector of the arm reaches the location, it can then manipulate the target object. On the other hand, the learning-based approach trains a neural model to determine the joint parameters [2]. For example, Staffan et al. used Receptive Field Cooccurrence Histograms (RFCH) [3][4] for object recognition and pose estimation. When the human moves the target object, the magnetic trackers placed on the human hand help to recognize the grasp type [2]. They designed and evaluated an automatic grasp generation and planning system, which facilitates grasping of new objects based on the shape similarity with the objects that have already been learned [2].

Sulabh et al. focused on detecting a 'good grasp' from RGBD images. They introduced a robotic grasp detection system for parallel plate grippers to detect good robotic grasps for the robot to grasp [5]. Xinchen et al. focused on parallel jaw gripper's grasping learning in simulation. The system can reconstruct the 3D shape of the target from RGBD inputs by a shape generation network. It then predicts the grasping outcome from an outcome prediction network [6].

The comparison in this paper focuses mainly on robotic arm tasking by comparing the learning-based end-to-end approach with a kinematics-based approach in terms of their capabilities in trajectory planning, using pouring as an example. For the kinematics-based approach, we use a deep neural network (YOLO) [9] for object detection and IK for trajectory planning. For the end-to-end approach, we train a deep neural network using RGBD images as input and joint parameters as output. The training data are collected using the kinematics-based approach to ensure data consistency and fairness in comparison.

We compare these two approaches in performing a pouring task, which is to grab a red cup and pour the contents into a blue cup. The evaluation consists of two scenarios. (1) Static scenario: the cups are at the same locations throughout the task. (2) Dynamic scenario: the red cup will be moved during the task. We evaluate their time usage, memory usage and actions under different scenarios. In the static scenario, both approaches can complete all the tasks. However, in the dynamic scenario, the kinematics-based approach fails to finish some tasks while the end-to-end learning-based approach can complete all of them.

The contributions of our work are as follows: (1) We developed kinematics-based and learning-based end-to-end approaches to pouring task by a robotic arm. (2) To train the end-to-end model, we developed a data collection system based on the kinematics-based method. (3) We evaluate and compare these two approaches, analyzing their performance under static and dynamic scenarios. As far as we know, there is no other work providing such a comparison between these two approaches to robot tasking.

The rest of the paper is organized as follows. Sec. II presents the two approaches for comparison. Sec. III shows the experiments and discusses the results and Sec. IV concludes the paper with possible future extensions.

II. Approaches for Comparison

To compare the kinematics-based approach and learning-based end-to-end approach, we place two cups in the view. The goal is to pour the contents of the red cup into the blue cup. We first introduce our kinematics-based approach, discuss our methodology for training the end-to-end model, and then propose a deep neural network architecture for learning the pouring task.

A. Kinematics-Based Approach

Our kinematics-based model, shown in Figure 1(a), consists of an object detection module and a trajectory planning module determined by IK. The object detection module was based on YOLO [9] and output the 2D coordinates of the center of the cup. The whole pouring task is divided into a number of steps, 64 in our experiments. In each step, the camera takes one image and the model then decides how to move the arm accordingly. The trajectory of the robot in performing the pouring task can be represented as $\tau = (A_0, A_1, .. A_t)$, where $A_0, A_1, .. A_t$ are the joint angles of the robot at each time step.

Let I_0 be the first image taken by the camera. It is used as the input of the object detection module. The object detection module outputs $c = (c_x, c_y)$, which is the 2D coordinates of the target's center in image I_0. With a mapping between the 3D world-space coordinates and the RGB image, output c can be used to get the 3D coordinate of the center of the target cup, $T = (T_x, T_y, T_z)$, from an RGBD camera with the origin of the coordinates being the robot arm.

The trajectory planning module then uses IK to calculate the joint parameters at each time step t to construct a path to reach T. The output of the trajectory planning module $\tau = (A_0, A_1, .. A_t)$ is then sent to the robot arm in order to control the robot to finish the task.

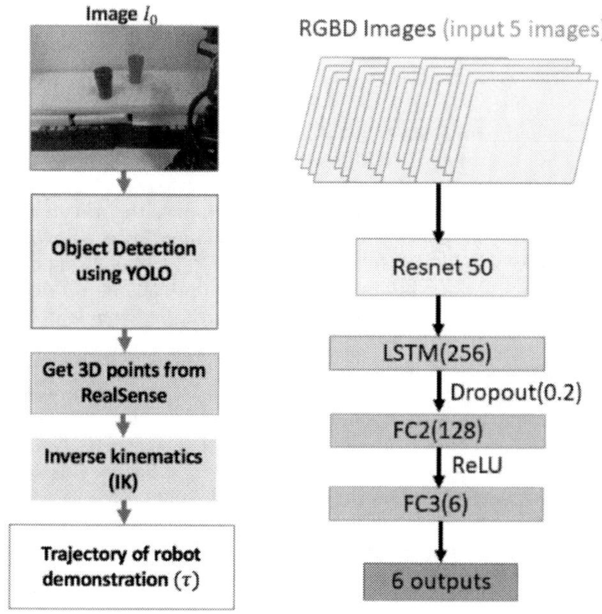

(a) Kinematics-based (b) Learning-based

Figure 1. Appraches for comparison.

B. Learning-Based End-to-End Approach

In the learning-based approach, the pouring task is viewed as consisting of a series of states and actions. The robot arm is controlled by a neural network model with an architecture as shown in Figure 1(b). Let I_t denote the RGBD image seen by the camera at time step t. Our model will take $S_t = [I_{t-4}, I_{t-3}, I_{t-2}, I_{t-1}, I_t]$ as the input state of the neural network, which corresponds to the current image plus four previous images seen by the camera before this time step t.

Our end-to-end model takes the sequence of images at time t as the input and uses a deep residual network (ResNet-50) to extract features from the input images. The last fully connected layers of ResNet-50 is replaced by Long Short-Term Memory (LSTM) [12] with an extra dropout layer and two fully connected layers. The first fully connected layer takes Rectified Linear Unit (ReLU) as the activation function. LSTM is used to deal with the time series data for sequencing the actions, e.g., deciding when to close the gripper. The last fully connected layer is the output layer of the end-to-end model. It predicts the action

$A_t = [a_1, a_2, a_3, a_4, a_5, a_6]$ of the robot arm, where $a_1, ..a_6$ correspond to the settings of the joint motors of the robot arm. We use Adam [13] as an optimizer and mean square error as our loss function.

III. EXPERIMENTS

A. *Environments*

The experiments were conducted on a 6DOF robot arm with an Intel RealSense Depth Camera, D415. The camera was set behind the robot arm to the left with a high angle of around 30 degrees (see Figure 2(a)). The task was to pour the contents of the red cup into the blue cup. Figure 2(b) shows the view of this task from the perspective of the camera.

We used MATLAB R2016B for programming IK and Python deep learning library Keras for training. Our experiments were performed on a NVIDIA GeForce GTX 1070 GPU with AMD Ryzen 5 2600 Six-Core 3.4GHz Processor.

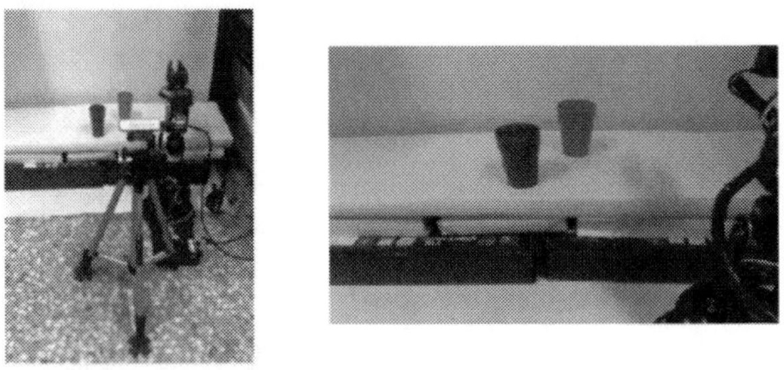

(a) Setup (b) View from robot's camera

Figure 2. Experimental environment.

B. *Data Collection*

The network of the learning-based approach was trained on a dataset that was collected from the data collection system based on the kinematics-based method. The data collection system recorded the states and actions during each demonstration by controlling the robot arm using the kinematics-based approach. In this way, trajectory data were consistent in comparing both approaches. The dataset is composed of 40 pouring demonstrations. Each demonstration contains 64 RGBD images (steps) and 64 corresponding actions. In total, there are 2560 RGBD images and 2560 actions of the six motors of the robot arm. Figure 3 shows a part of our dataset with the states in sequence with the corresponding actions.

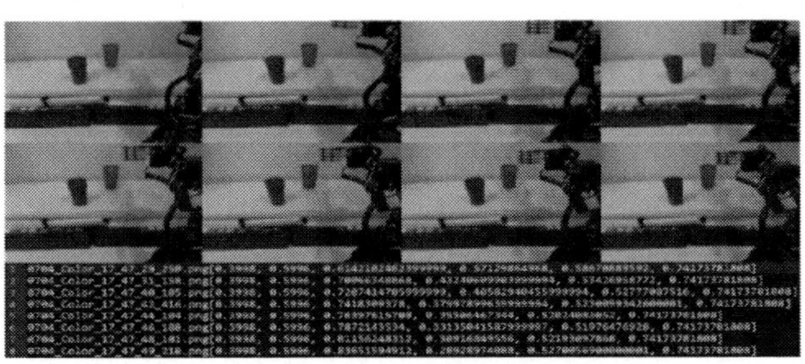

Figure 3. Sample states and actions in our dataset.

C. *Evaluations*

The goal of our experimental evaluation is to compare the kinematics-based approach with the learning-based end-to-end approach. We let both perform the same pouring task. The experiments can be divided into two parts:

- Static scenario: Cups were fixed at the same locations until the task was completed.
- Dynamic scenario: The red cup may be moved dynamically while the task was in progress.

Static Scenario

We placed the red cup in 30 different positions in the area, which the robot arm can reach. The positions spread evenly across the workspace to ensure that the entire area could be tested. Figure 4 shows the 30 positions. Our experiments show that both the learning-based end-to-end approach and the kinematics-based approach can complete all the tasks successfully.

Figure 4. The 30 positions to place the read cup.

We show the computation time and the memory usage of the kinematics-based and the learning-based end-to-end approaches in Table 1. The computation time is the CPU time to execute the model, not counting communication. For the kinematics-based approach, the computation time includes the time spent on object detection and trajectory planning. For the learning-based approach, the computation time is the time to run through the neural model. During the experiments, the number of moving steps of the kinematics-based approach was always 64. On the other hand, although the learning-based approach was trained with the training data that completed the pouring task in a fixed 64 steps, the number of steps taken by the learning-based approach in inference was fewer than 64 steps, with an average of 48. This is because the learning-based approach could identify states similar to those trained and took corresponding actions, thereby skipping steps.

TABLE I. EXPERIMENTAL RESULTS OF STATIC SCENARIO

	Ave. CPU time	*Ave. # steps*	*Ave. time*	*Memory usage*	*Size*
Kinematics	7.83 s	64	119.4 s	2081 MB	236 MB
Learning	10.27 s	48	84.1 s	2574 MB	278 MB

Both approaches used most memory space on model loading. The memory usage of the learning-based approach is higher, because it must process a series of images instead of just one in the kinematics-based approach. For computation time, the learning-based approach spends only 10.27 seconds on model prediction, meaning that our model can output an action in 0.21 seconds. Both approaches spent a lot of time on serial communication. However, since the learning-based approach may skip steps, the computation time can be shortened.

The total computation time of the kinematics-based method remains almost the same, because its step count is fixed and the calculation time of IK does not change a lot. The total time of the learning-based approach depends on the number of steps in moving the robot arm. If the model completes the task with fewer steps, the total time will be less.

We can see from Figure 5 that there is an uptrend of moving steps in the learning-based approach. The red dots show the positions in which more steps are needed to finish the task. The reason is that when the distance between the robot arm and the target is far apart, it may be possible to choose similar states that will finish the task faster by skipping some steps. However, when the robot arm is close to the target, it could only do it step by step.

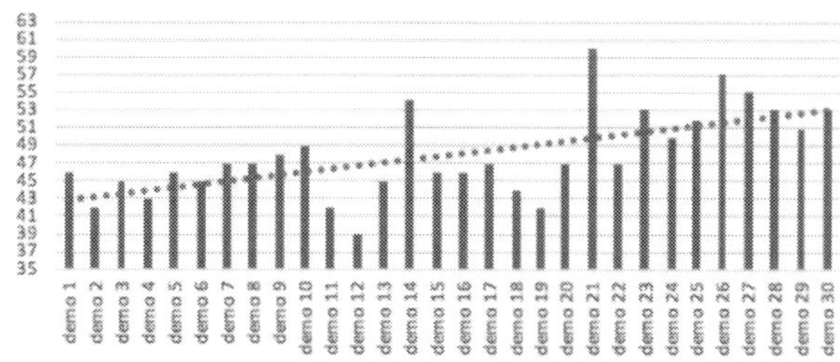

Figure 5. Uptrend of the moving steps of the end-to-end model.

Dynamic Scenario

In the dynamic scenario, the red cup was moved while the robot arm was reaching the cup. To allow the kinematics-based approach to handle moving objects properly, we used the following procedure:

1. **While** the distance between the robot arm and the target object $d >$ a threshold h **do**
2. Detect the target object
3. **If** the target object is moved since last detection and the moving distance $m >$ 1.5mm **then**
4. Re-plan the trajectory
5. Divide the trajectory into n points (n is based on d)
6. Move the robot arm to the next point in the trajectory
7. Grab the target object

We tested both the kinematics-based approach and the learning-based end-to-end approach under 10 different cases. The tests were split into four parts according to the way the target red cup is moved:

- Right-to-left:
  The target red cup was placed at the upper right, middle right and lower right, respectively, in the workspace of the robot arm. We then moved the cup to the left side of the workspace, as shown in Figure 6. It was found that both approaches could complete all the right-to-left tasks. The most important factor for the kinematics-based approach to success was the target cup's final position -- the whole cup could be seen by the camera and not be blocked by the robot arm.
- Left-to-right: The target red cup was placed at the upper left, middle left and lower left, respectively, in the workspace. Then, we moved the cup to the right side of the workspace. Our experiments showed that the kinematics-based approach failed in upper-left and middle-left positions, due to a failure in object detection. This is because the moving robot arm blocked the view of the camera, and, consequently, the target object could not be detected. It follows that the trajectory planning module mistook the blue cup for the target. The lower-left task was successful because the final position of the red cup was in front of others and the view of the cup was not obstructed by the robot arm.
- Top-to-bottom: We placed the red cup at the top of the workspace and then moved the cup to the bottom side of the workspace. Both the kinematics-based approach and the learning-based approach can complete the tasks. It seems that if the object detection module could recognize the target correctly, the kinematics-based approach can complete the task successfully.
- Bottom-to-top: We placed the red cup at the bottom of the workspace and moved the cup to the top side of the workspace. The experimental results were the same as in the top-to-bottom case.

From the experiments, we can see that the learning-based approach succeeded in all the tasks tested, while the kinematics-based approach failed in some cases. For the kinematics-based approach to succeed, it is critical that the target object be visible and identifiable so that its location can be determined. If the location cannot be determined or is detected incorrectly, IK will calculate a wrong path and the robot arm cannot reach the target object.

Furthermore, the kinematics-based method consists of several independent modules, which are optimized separately under different criteria. Even if we add rules to let it handle dynamic scenarios in which objects may be moved, there are always unexpected situations. Figure 7 shows a conflict of the rules. If the distance between the robot arm and the target object is less than the threshold h, the trajectory planning module will not re-plan the path. This may happen when the robot arm is very close to the target object, but it obstructs the view of the camera. The model will mistake the blue cup as the target. Choosing a suitable threshold value is also a difficult problem.

By observing the trajectories generated by the kinematics-based approach, we further find that it could only handle the change of the position of the target cup early in the process. This is perhaps because the joints of the robot arm require sufficient lead time to adapt to new positions. From the above observations and discussions, we find that the kinematics-based approach has limitations in handling complex and dynamic tasks.

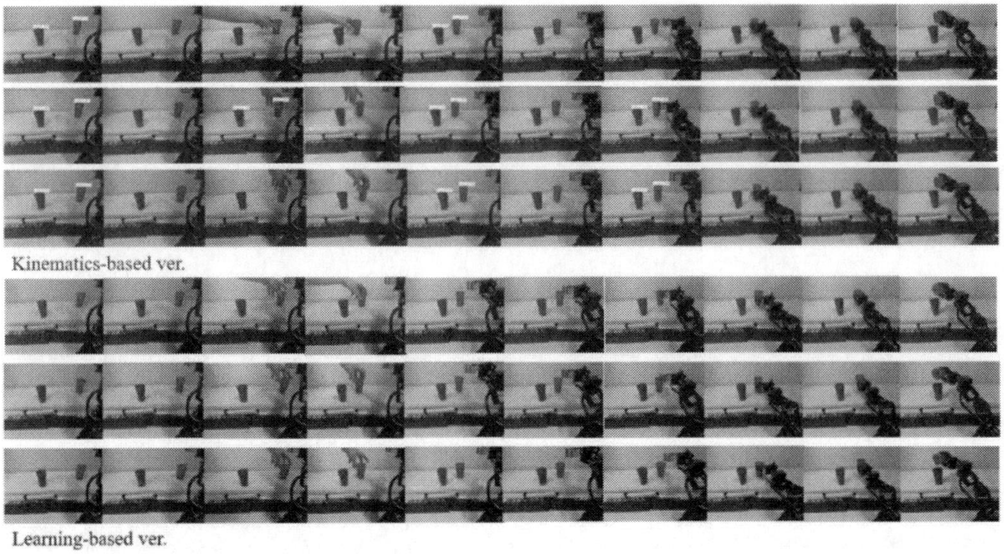

Figure 6. Right-to-left task.

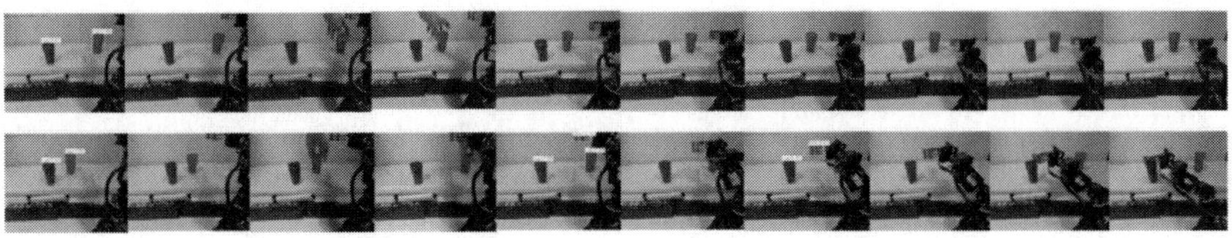

Figure 7. A conflict of the rules in the kinematics-based approach.

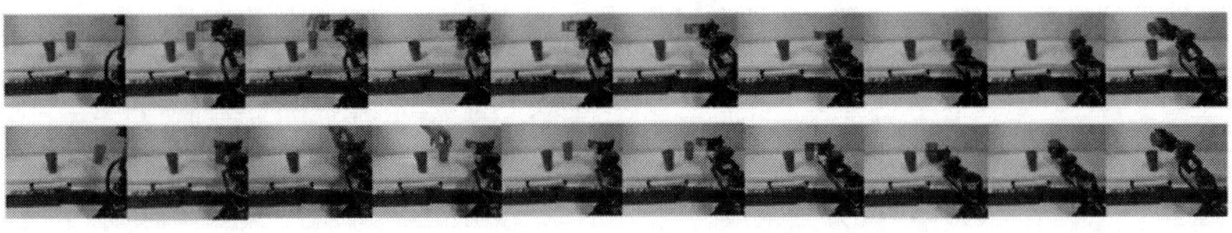

Figure 8. The learning-based approach stilll accomplishes the task.

On the other hand, the learning-based approach succeeds in cases when the target object is obstructed. This is because the learning-based end-to-end approach takes the entire view as the state to decide the action to perform. When it encounters an unseen state, it will try to find a similar known state and act according to that state. Therefore, even when the target is moved and obstructed, the model can still find a proper action to perform.

Furthermore, from Figure 8, we can see that the learning-based approach can still finish the task even if we move the target cup when the robotic arm almost grabs it. The end-to-end model is less affected by the obstructions caused by the moving robotic arm as it knows the end goal of the task. From all our experiments, we conclude that the learning-based end-to-end approach is more suitable for handling complicated and dynamic scenes.

In Table 2, we show the time usage and the memory usage of the kinematics-based and the learning-based end-to-end approaches. The biggest difference between static scenario and dynamic scenario is the computation time. The kinematics-based method spends additional time for object detection and re-planning the trajectory when the target object is moved. On the other hand, the learning-based end-to-end approach can handle the dynamic scenario with the same trained neural model and thus incur similar amount of computation time as in the static scenario. By observing the number of moving steps of both approaches, the learning-based approach completes the task more efficiently in the dynamic scenario too.

TABLE II. EXPERIMENTAL RESULTS OF DYNAMIC SCENARIO

	Avg. CPU time	*Avg. # of steps*	*Avg. total time*	*Memory usage*	*Size*
Kinematics	21.53 s	66	137.2 s	2279 MB	236 MB
Learning	9.33 s	47	81.7 s	2572 MB	278 MB

IV. CONCLUSIONS AND FUTURE WORKS

In this work, we compare the kinematics-based approach and the learning-based end-to-end approach to robot tasking, using pouring as an example. The kinematics-based approach is composed of object detection module and trajectory planning module, in which the trajectory is calculated by IK. The end-to-end learning network was trained by the dataset that was collected by the data collection system based on the kinematics-based approach.

The two approaches are compared in static scenario and dynamic scenario by evaluating their time usage and memory usage, and observing how they complete the tasks. Our experimental results demonstrate that the kinematics-based approach is suitable for static scenario, because it requires less computation time and memory. The learning-based approach is more suitable for complicated and dynamic scenarios, because it can perform properly for unseen and dynamic states.

In the future, we plan to improve the kinematics-based approach by using different object detection methods, e.g., grasp detection model, to handle more dynamic scenarios. Furthermore, we found that it was too troublesome to collect test data, since we need to keep changing the position of the target object manually. It is necessary to develop an automated data collection system for collecting the testing data easier. Additionally, we would like to extend both the kinematics-based approach and the learning-based approach to more complicated scenarios, e.g., blue cup in different positions, complex scenes and background, and obstacles. It is interesting to study how the two approaches handle these complex states.

ACKNOWLEDGMENT

This work was supported in part by the Ministry of Science and Technology, Taiwan, under Grant MOST 109-2218-E-007-023 and by Information and Communications Research Laboratories of Industrial Technology Research Institute, Taiwan.

REFERENCES

[1] "End-to-end learning, the (almost) every purpose ML method" [Online]. Available: https://towardsdatascience.com/e2e-the-every-purpose-ml-method-5d4f20dafee4 [retrieved: March, 2021].

[2] S. Ekvall and D. Kragic, "Learning and evaluation of the approach vector for automatic grasp generation and planning," in *Proceedings IEEE International Conference on Robotics and Automation (ICRA)*, 2007, pp. 4715-4720.

[3] S. Ekvall and D. Kragic, "Receptive field cooccurrence histograms for object detection," in *Proceedings of IEEE/RSJ International Conference on Intelligent Robots and Systems (IROS)*, 2005, pp. 84-89.

[4] S. Ekvall, D.Kragic, and F. Hoffmann, "Object recognition and pose estimation using color cooccurrence histograms and geometric modeling," *Image and Vision Computing*, vol. 23, pp. 943-955, 2005.

[5] S. Kumra and C. Kanan, "Robotic grasp detection using deep convolutional neural networks," in *Proceedings of IEEE/RSJ International Conference on Intelligent Robots and Systems (IROS)*, 2017, pp. 769-776.

[6] X. C. Yan et al., "Learning 6-DOF grasping interaction via deep geometry-aware 3D representations," in *Proceedings IEEE International Conference on Robotics and Automation (ICRA)*, 2018, pp. 3766-3773.

[7] B. Siciliano, L. Sciavicco, L. Villani, and G. Oriolo, *Robotics: Modeling, Planning, and Control*, Springer-Verlag, 2009.

[8] "Program inverse kinematics algorithms with MATLAB" [Online]. Available: https://ww2.mathworks.cn/discovery/inverse-kinematics.html [retrieved: March, 2021].

[9] J. Redmon, S. Divvala, R. Girshick, and A. Farhadi, "You Only Look Once: Unified, real-time object detection," in *Proceedings IEEE Conference on Computer Vision and Pattern Recognition (CVPR)*, 2016, pp. 779-788.

[10] "An overview of ResNet and its variants" [Online]. Available: https://towardsdatascience.com/an-overview-of-resnet-and-its-variants-5281e2f56035 [retrieved: March, 2021].

[11] K. He, X. Zhang, S. Ren, and J. Sun, "Deep residual learning for image recognition," in *Proceedings IEEE Conference on Computer Vision and Pattern Recognition (CVPR)*, 2016, pp. 770-778.

[12] S. Hochreiter and J. Schmidhuber, "Long short-term memory," *Neural Computation*, vol. 9, pp. 1735-1780, 1997.

[13] D. Kingma and J. Ba, "Adam: A method for stochastic optimization," in *Proceedings of 2015 International Conference on Learning Representations*, (ICLR), 2015.

Adversarial Training for Deep Learning-based Intrusion Detection Systems

Islam Debicha

Royal Military Academy
and Université Libre de Bruxelles
Brussels, Belgium
Email: debichasislam@gmail.com

Thibault Debatty

Royal Military Academy
Brussels, Belgium
Email: thibault.debatty@rma.ac.be

Jean-Michel Dricot

Université Libre de Bruxelles
Brussels, Belgium
Email: jdricot@ulb.ac.be

Wim Mees

Royal Military Academy
Brussels, Belgium
Email: wim.mees@rma.ac.be

***Abstract*—Nowadays, Deep Neural Networks (DNNs) report state-of-the-art results in many machine learning areas, including intrusion detection. Nevertheless, recent studies in computer vision have shown that DNNs can be vulnerable to adversarial attacks that are capable of deceiving them into misclassification by injecting specially crafted data. In security-critical areas, such attacks can cause serious damage; therefore, in this paper, we examine the effect of adversarial attacks on deep learning-based intrusion detection. In addition, we investigate the effectiveness of adversarial training as a defense against such attacks. Experimental results show that with sufficient distortion, adversarial examples are able to mislead the detector and that the use of adversarial training can improve the robustness of intrusion detection.**

Keywords–Intrusion detection; deep learning; Adversarial attacks; Adversarial training.

I. INTRODUCTION

With the growth of the computer and telecommunications industry and the expansion of the Internet, there has been a significant escalation of cyberattacks targeting all types of networks, as attackers are increasingly motivated to develop new ways to penetrate systems, given the great reward. As a result, securing these networks has become a crucial area of interest. Intrusion Detection Systems (IDS), which are designed to detect and identify anomalies and attacks, are gaining popularity and are presented as one of the solutions against these cyber-attacks.

There are mainly two types of intrusion detection systems: those based on signatures and those based on anomaly detection. The first one works more or less in the same way as most antivirus systems by maintaining a database with all known attack signatures. An exhaustive comparison of the incoming traffic with the signature database allows the system to determine if it represents an attack. These systems are remarkably effective at detecting known attacks and offer high accuracy but are obviously unable to detect zero-day exploits. This is essentially what drives the use of anomaly-based intrusion detection systems that work by modeling the normal behavior of traffic and network activities and then comparing new traffic to this baseline.

Several research studies have examined the use of different Machine Learning (ML) techniques to improve the accuracy of anomaly-based IDS [1][2]. Nevertheless, the lack of transferability and the dependence of traditional machine learning on domain knowledge (feature engineering) have been among the main reasons for substituting them with DNNs which not only solved these problems but also yielded, in most cases, the highest accuracies, making them the state-of-the-art in the field of anomaly-based intrusion detection [3].

Despite their popularity, DNNs have proven to be vulnerable to adversarial attacks in computer vision where, by introducing imperceptible changes in an image, an adversary can mislead the classifier. When applied to machine learning-based security products, these attacks can lead to a critical security breach. Although a considerable amount of studies has been conducted on adversarial attacks in computer vision, there are very few studies on this issue in intrusion detection. Therefore, the contribution of this paper is double: (1) we study the effect of adversarial attacks on deep learning-based intrusion detection systems. For that, three adversarial attacks are tested: Fast Gradient Sign Method (FGSM) [4], Basic Iterative Method (BIM) [5] and Projected Gradient Descent (PGD) [6] showing that adversarial attacks are able, given enough strength, to mislead the IDS significantly. In addition, (2) this is the first study, to the best of our knowledge, to examine the effectiveness of adversarial training as a defense against adversarial attacks for intrusion detection systems.

In what follows, we briefly recall the concept of DNNs, present an overview of related work and explain the idea of adversarial examples in Section II. The experimental approach is explained in Section III. Results and discussions are presented in Section IV. Concluding remarks and suggestions for possible follow-up work are given in Section V.

II. BACKGROUND

A. Deep Neural Network (DNN)

DNN refers to a machine learning algorithm made up of multiple interconnected layers where each layer is composed of several nodes - called neurons. Within each neuron, an activation function operates as a basic computing unit. The activation function input on a neuron is the parameter-weighted output of the immediately preceding layer, whilst each layer's output is at the same time the next layer's input.

Frequently described as an end-to-end machine learning process, DNN is capable of learning complex patterns based on limited prior knowledge of input data representation. As a result, deep learning models are widely applied to address large-scale data problems that are frequently inadequately handled by traditional machine learning algorithms. DNN layers fall into three categories: the input layer, the output layer, and, in between, the hidden layer. For large-scale input data, it may be necessary to use several hidden layers so as to learn the subjacent correlation.

DNN can be seen as a function $f(\cdot)$, $f \in F$: $\mathbb{R}^n \rightarrow \mathbb{R}^m$. let Θ be the DNN parameters. Training the model involves finding the optimal parameters Θ where the loss function J (e.g., cross-entropy) is minimal.

For the classification task, the outputs of the last layer in DNN are called logits. The softmax function is added after the last layer in order to transform these logits into a probability distribution, i.e., $0 \leq y_i \leq 1$ and $y_1 + . + y_m = 1$ where y_i is interpreted as the probability that input x has class i. The label with the highest probability C(x) = argmax y_i is assigned as the class of the input x.

Let $Z(x) = z$ be the output of all layers excluding Softmax, thus the full DNN is $F(x)$ = softmax$(Z(x)) = y$. At the neuron level, the input is first linearly transformed using weights $\tilde{\theta}$ and baises $\hat{\theta}$, and then subjected to a non-linear activation function σ (e.g., ReLU). The DNN model is a chain function :

$$F = softmax \circ F_n \circ F_{n-1} \circ \cdots \circ F_1 \quad (1)$$

Where:

$$F_i(x) = \sigma(\tilde{\theta}_i.x + \hat{\theta}_i) \quad (2)$$

B. Related work

Several studies have shown the effectiveness of the DNN for intrusion detection systems in different types of networks. [7] has proposed an LSTM neural network for distributed detection of cyber-attacks in fog-to-things communications. [8] used the DNN to develop a framework for the identification of intrusions and attacks at the network and host level. [9] presented a lightweight framework using deep learning for encrypted traffic classification and intrusion detection. Nonetheless, little if any attention was paid to the effect of adversarial attacks against these frameworks.

One of the first works on the vulnerability of DNN to adversarial examples was carried out by [10]. The box-constrained Limited memory approximation of Broyden-Fletcher-Goldfarb-Shanno (LBFGS) optimization algorithm was used to generate imperceptible alterations in the hand-written images in order to deceive the DNN. Although several attacks and defenses were subsequently proposed [4][5][6], these attacks were designed for the computer vision field in which the vulnerability was first discovered.

Lately, work on the effect of adversarial attacks against intrusion detection systems has been carried out. Wang [3] showed the effect of these attacks on intrusion detection systems using NSL-KDD dataset. [11] studied the impact of black boxes adversarial attacks on the performance of intrusion detection systems based on DNN. [12] investigated the robustness of Self-normalizing Neural Network (SNN) against adversarial attacks on IoT networks.

According to our review of the literature, there is no work on the effectiveness of adversarial training against adversarial attacks for deep learning-based intrusion detection systems, therefore this work is presented to cover this aspect.

C. Adversarial examples

Despite the fact that deep learning has made significant progress in a variety of areas, Szegedy *el al.*'s intriguing research [5] reveals that DNNs may not be as smart as they seem. They found that inserting small but carefully crafted perturbations into original images can lead to misclassification with even higher confidence. These crafted perturbations are small enough to be considered insignificant and imperceptible changes to humans. Methods of creating adversarial examples can be categorized according to two criteria: the target class and knowledge about the model under attack.

Adversarial examples' target: given a target class T different from the initial class $C^*(x) = I$ of an input x. An attacker seeks to find a slightly perturbed input x' very similar to x given a certain distance metric, yet the classifier assigns the class $C(x') = T$ to it. Thus, the **targeted adversarial attack** leads the DNN to misclassify the input as the class T desired by the attacker. As opposed to the **untargeted adversarial attack** where the objective is to find an imperceptibly modified input x' so that $C^*(x) \neq C(x')$ which is obviously less powerful than targeted attacks.

Knowledge concerning the model under attack: When the attacker has knowledge of everything related to the trained neural network model, including its gradients, it is a **"white box"** type attack. unlike **"black box"** type attacks where the attacker lacks knowledge of the model's gradients and has only access to the model's probability scores or, even harder, to the model's final decision. This is a common assumption for attacks on online ML services.

III. EXPERIMENTAL APPROACH

In this section, a state-of-the-art intrusion detection system based on deep learning is built to study the effectiveness of adversarial attacks. We focus on untargeted "white box" type evasion attacks, i.e., the attacker has prior knowledge of the internal architecture of the DNN used for detection and carries out his attacks during the prediction process in order to lead the system into misdetection. Subsequently, adversarial training [4] [6] is thoroughly assessed as a defense against adversarial attacks by mixing adversarial samples with clean training data during the training process to enhance the robustness of the DNN against these attacks.

A. NSL-KDD Dataset

As one of the most commonly utilized datasets for evaluating the performance of an intrusion detection system, NSL-KDD dataset -which was released in 2009 [13]- is an enhancement of the KDD CUP'99 dataset that suffers from two major drawbacks: a huge amount of redundant records and the bias of classifiers towards frequent records. NSL-KDD addressed the two issues by removing redundant records and rebalancing the dataset classes, thereby enabling comparative analysis of different ML algorithms.

This dataset covers several attacks organized into four classes according to their nature: denial of service (DoS) attacks, probe attacks (Probe), root-to-local (R2L) attacks, and user-to-root (U2R) attacks. The records in the NSL-KDD dataset have 41 features in addition to a class label. These features are grouped into three categories: basic features, content features, and traffic features. For the experimental part, we use KDDTrain+, which contains 125973 records, as follows: 80% of the records are training data and 20% are test data. Table I provides a summary of the data.

TABLE I. DIFFERENT CLASSES OF THE DATASET.

	Normal	DoS	Probe	R2L	U2R
Training data	53875	36742	9325	796	42
Test data	13468	9185	2331	199	10

B. Preprocessing

The preprocessing of the NSL-KDD dataset involves two steps: numericalization and standardization. Neural networks are unable to handle categorical values directly. Numericalization is the process of transforming these categorical values into numerical values. The features that contain categorical values in this dataset are "protocol_type", "service" and "flag". Standardization is an important step to prevent the neural network from malfunctioning because of large differences between features' ranges. That is why we transform each feature into standard normal distribution. In this paper, we focus on binary classification; therefore we qualify all attack records as "anomaly" and normal traffic as "normal". We use one-hot encoding to transform the class labels into numerical values.

C. Building deep learning-based IDS

In order to detect intrusions, a deep binary neural network with two hidden layers, each containing 512 hidden units, is implemented using TensorFlow [14]. Rectified Linear Unit (ReLU) is used as an activation function within each hidden unit so as to introduce non-linearity in these neurons' output. Following each hidden layer, a dropout layer with a dropout rate of 0.2 is employed to prevent Neural Networks from over-fitting. ADAM is set as an optimization algorithm and "categorical_crossentropy" as a loss function to be minimized. softmax layer is added at the end to convert the logits into a normalized probability distribution. the class with the highest probability is considered as the predicted class.

D. Generating adversarial samples

We use Adversarial Robustness Toolbox (ART) [15] to implement adversarial attacks as well as the adversarial training. ART is an open-source python library for ML security developed by the International Business Machines corporation (IBM).

The generation of adversarial samples can be explained in a simple way. One can consider it as the inverse process of gradient descent where, given a fixed input data x and its label y, the goal is to find the model parameters θ that minimize the loss function J. Now, to generate an adversarial sample x', we proceed inversely, given fixed model parameters θ, we differentiate the loss function J with respect to the input data x in order to find a sample x' - close to x - that maximizes the loss function J. FGSM [4] uses a specific factor ϵ to control the magnitude of the introduced perturbation where $\|x' - x\| < \epsilon$. The ϵ factor can be considered as the attack strength or the upper limit of the distortion amount. The adversarial sample x' is then generated as follows:

$$x' = x + \epsilon \nabla J_x(x, y, \theta) \tag{3}$$

BIM [5] is another attack and is basically an iterative extension of the FGSM applying the attack repeatedly. Similar to BIM, another iterative version of the FGSM is PGD [6]. However, unlike BIM, the PGD is relaunched at each iteration of the attack from many points on the ϵ-norm ball around the original input.

E. Adversarial training

The idea behind adversarial training is to inject adversarial examples with their correct labels into the training data so that the model learns how to handle them. To do this, we use the PGD attack to generate adversarial samples before mixing them with the training data set. Here, we want to study two parameters of this defense: first, the effect of attack strength ϵ used to generate adversarial samples for the training, let's call it $\epsilon_{defense}$ to avoid confusion with the strength of adversarial attack ϵ_{attack} in the attack phase. Second, the proportion of adversarial training samples compared to clean training samples in the training data.

IV. EXPERIMENTAL RESULTS

In this section, we first evaluate the effect of adversarial attacks on a deep learning-based intrusion detection system. then, in the second part, we examine the effectiveness of adversarial training as a means of making the system more robust against these attacks. we conclude this section by discussing and analyzing the results obtained.

A. Effect of adversarial attacks on deep learning-based IDS

After training our DNN model, we test its accuracy (the proportion of correct predictions among the total number of cases examined) on unmodified test data. The model gives an accuracy of 99.61%, we then proceed to generate adversarial test data using FGSM, BIM, and PGD respectively. For each attack, the experiment is repeated, intensifying the attack by increasing ϵ value each time. Figure 1 shows that all three attacks deteriorate significantly the performance of the intrusion detection system. The FGSM attack lowers the accuracy of the system from 99.61% to 14.13%, while the BIM and PGD attacks decrease it further to 8.85%.

This demonstrates that, with sufficient distortion, adversarial attacks are able to defeat intrusion detection systems based on DNNs and lead them into misdetection.

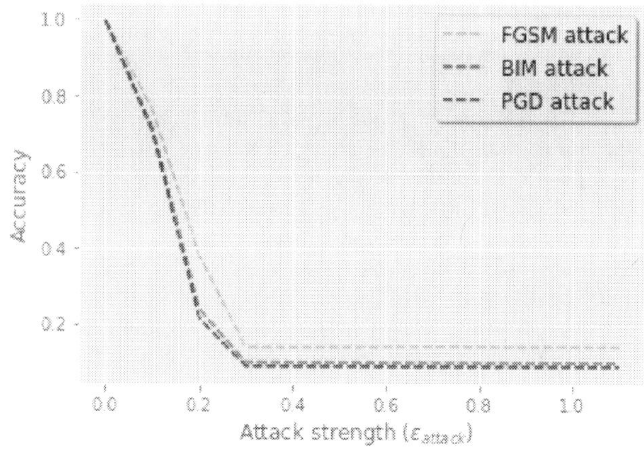

Figure 1. Effect of adversarial attacks on deep learning-based intrusion detection system.

B. Adversarial training effect

As mentioned in Section III-E, we examine two parameters of adversarial training: 1) $\epsilon_{defense}$ which represents the attack force used to generate adversarial training samples that are mixed with clean training samples. 2) the percentage of adversarial training samples, compared to clean training samples, in the training data. Note that all the adversarial examples used are generated via the PGD attack.

We begin by setting the percentage of adversarial training samples in the training data to 30%, giving a fixed value of $\epsilon_{defense}$. After training the model with this mixed training data, we apply PGD attack by increasing the value of ϵ_{attack} each time. We repeat the experiment by increasing the value of $\epsilon_{defense}$ used for adversarial training as shown in Figure 2(a). The whole process is repeated by setting the percentage of adversarial training samples to 30%, 50%, 70%, and 90% respectively.

Figure 2 illustrates that compared to using only clean training data, adversarial training improves the robustness of the intrusion detection system against adversarial attacks. Although with sufficient attack force, the accuracy of the detector decreases considerably. We also note that increasing strength of the adversarial examples $\epsilon_{defense}$ used for the training helps to improve the robustness of the detector to some extent, making it more difficult for the attacker to create adversarial samples with a small distortion that can mislead the intrusion detection system. The same cannot be said for the impact of the percentage of adversarial training examples on the robustness of the intrusion detection system because while for $\epsilon_{defense} = 0.7$, higher percentages improved the robustness of the detector against adversarial attacks as shown in Figure 3, this improvement is not observed for the other values of $\epsilon_{defense}$. Thus, it is safe to say that the percentage of adversarial training examples doesn't have a direct link to the robustness of the intrusion detection system using adversarial training. This could be explained by the fact that the added dropout layers are designed to reduce overfitting effect on DNN, so as long as the model is fed with enough adversarial samples in the training phase, its performance won't change much by adding data with similar information.

Another important aspect is the effect of adversarial training on the performance of the intrusion detection system when tested on clean test data. While results of the previous experiments indicate that adversarial training increases the robustness of deep learning-based intrusion detection systems, Figure 4 shows that adversarial training slightly decreases the accuracy of the detector when tested on clean test data. This indicates that there is a trade-off between robustness and accuracy. The decrease in accuracy of the intrusion detection system on clean test data could be explained by the fact that as the model is trained with adversarial samples, its decision boundary would change in comparison to clean data training.

From a practical point of view, given malicious network traffic, such as HTTP traffic that wants to connect to bad URLs, such as command and control servers, the attacker can use adversarial generation techniques to transform this malicious network traffic into normal traffic for the intrusion detection system while maintaining its maliciousness, for example by adding small amounts of specially crafted data to the network traffic as padding. This allows the attacker to mislead the intrusion detection system. Adversarial training, on the other hand, is a defensive technique. It seeks to make the attacker's task more difficult by making small distortions insufficient to bypass the intrusion detection system.

V. Conclusion and Future Work

In conclusion, adversarial attacks are a real threat to intrusion detection systems based on deep learning. By generating samples using adversarial attacks, an attacker can lead the system to misdetection and, given sufficient attack strength, the performance of the intrusion detection system can deteriorate significantly. As a defense against such attacks, the adversarial training was examined in depth. The results show that this method can improve to some extent the robustness of deep learning-based intrusion detection systems. However, it comes with a trade-off of slightly decreasing detector accuracy on unattacked network traffic. An interesting future work would be to propose new defense mechanisms against adversarial attacks by exploring uncertainty handling techniques.

References

[1] J. Kevric, S. Jukic, and A. Subasi, "An effective combining classifier approach using tree algorithms for network intrusion detection," Neural Computing and Applications, vol. 28, no. 1, 2017, pp. 1051–1058.

[2] I. Debicha, T. Debatty, W. Mees, and J.-M. Dricot, "Efficient intrusion detection using evidence theory," in INTERNET 2020 : The Twelfth International Conference on Evolving Internet, 2020, pp. 28–32.

[3] Z. Wang, "Deep learning-based intrusion detection with adversaries," IEEE Access, vol. 6, 2018, pp. 38 367–38 384.

[4] I. J. Goodfellow, J. Shlens, and C. Szegedy, "Explaining and harnessing adversarial examples," arXiv preprint arXiv:1412.6572, 2014.

[5] A. Kurakin, I. Goodfellow, and S. Bengio, "Adversarial examples in the physical world," arXiv preprint arXiv:1607.02533, 2016.

[6] A. Madry, A. Makelov, L. Schmidt, D. Tsipras, and A. Vladu, "Towards deep learning models resistant to adversarial attacks," arXiv preprint arXiv:1706.06083, 2017.

[7] A. Diro and N. Chilamkurti, "Leveraging lstm networks for attack detection in fog-to-things communications," IEEE Communications Magazine, vol. 56, no. 9, 2018, pp. 124–130.

[8] R. Vinayakumar, M. Alazab, K. Soman, P. Poornachandran, A. Al-Nemrat, and S. Venkatraman, "Deep learning approach for intelligent intrusion detection system," IEEE Access, vol. 7, 2019, pp. 41 525–41 550.

[9] Y. Zeng, H. Gu, W. Wei, and Y. Guo, "$deep - full - range$: A deep learning based network encrypted traffic classification and intrusion detection framework," IEEE Access, vol. 7, 2019, pp. 45 182–45 190.

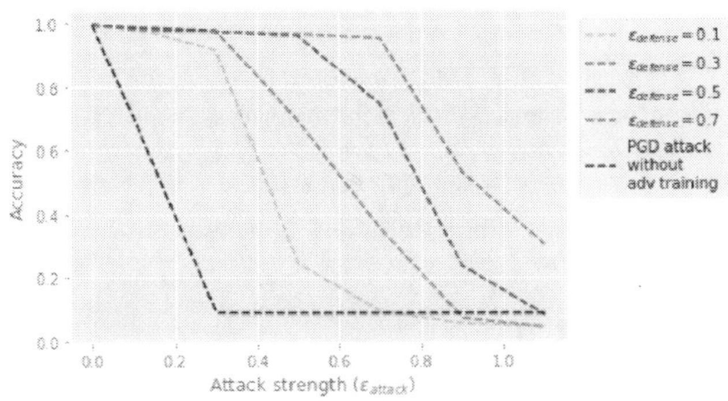

(a) Percentage of adversarial training samples in the training data = 30%

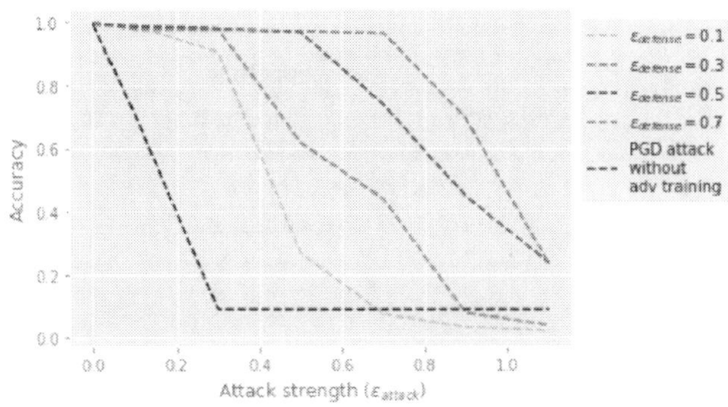

(b) Percentage of adversarial training samples in the training data = 50%

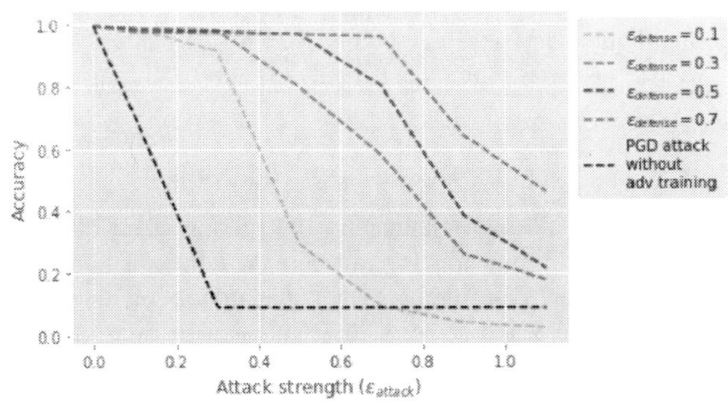

(c) Percentage of adversarial training samples in the training data = 70%

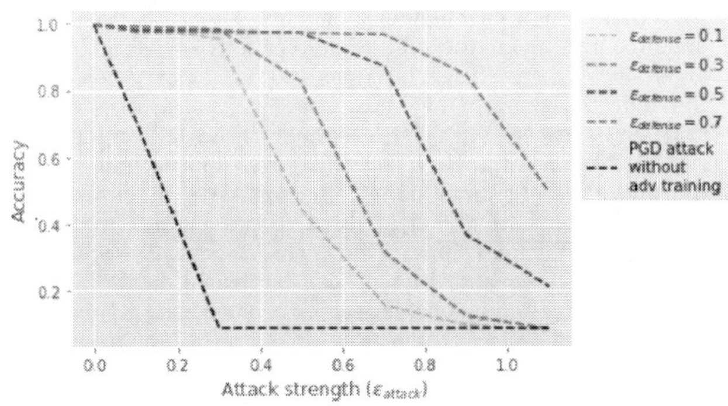

(d) Percentage of adversarial training samples in the training data = 90%

Figure 2. Effect of adversarial training on the robustness of deep learning-based intrusion detection system

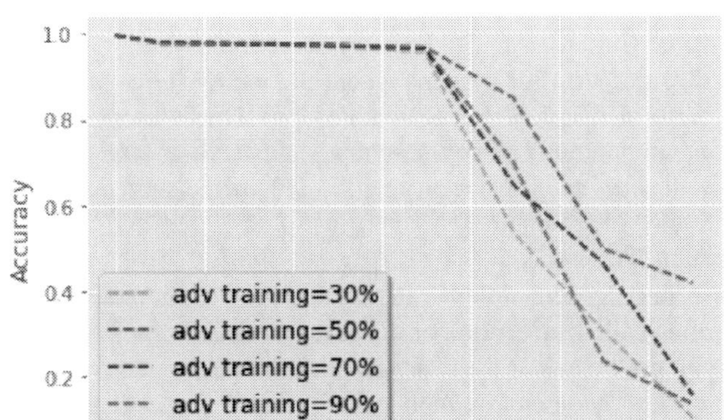

Figure 3. Effect of the percentage of adversarial training samples in the training data, $\epsilon_{defense} = 0.7$.

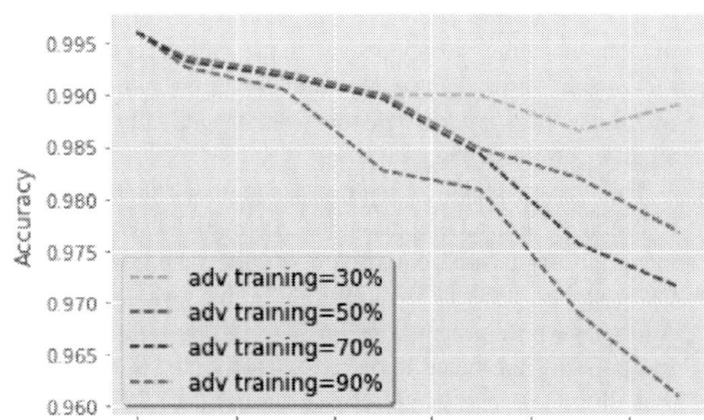

Figure 4. Effect of adversarial training on the performance of the intrusion detection system on clean test data.

[10] C. Szegedy, W. Zaremba, I. Sutskever, J. Bruna, D. Erhan, I. Goodfellow, and R. Fergus, "Intriguing properties of neural networks," arXiv preprint arXiv:1312.6199, 2013.

[11] K. Yang, J. Liu, C. Zhang, and Y. Fang, "Adversarial examples against the deep learning based network intrusion detection systems," in MILCOM 2018-2018 IEEE Military Communications Conference (MILCOM). IEEE, 2018, pp. 559–564.

[12] O. Ibitoye, O. Shafiq, and A. Matrawy, "Analyzing adversarial attacks against deep learning for intrusion detection in iot networks," in 2019 IEEE Global Communications Conference (GLOBECOM). IEEE, 2019, pp. 1–6.

[13] M. Tavallaee, E. Bagheri, W. Lu, and A. A. Ghorbani, "A detailed analysis of the kdd cup 99 data set," in 2009 IEEE symposium on computational intelligence for security and defense applications. IEEE, 2009, pp. 1–6.

[14] "Tensorflow," https://www.tensorflow.org/ , retrieved: March, 2021.

[15] M.-I. Nicolae, M. Sinn, M. N. Tran, B. Buesser, A. Rawat, M. Wistuba, V. Zantedeschi, N. Baracaldo, B. Chen, H. Ludwig et al., "Adversarial robustness toolbox v1. 0.0," arXiv preprint arXiv:1807.01069, 2018.

Ethical Dynamics of Autonomous Weapon Systems

Marcus Frølich
Department of Science and Industrial Systems
University of South-Eastern Norway
Kongsberg, Norway
e-mail: 218867@student.usn.no

Mo Mansouri
Department of Science and Industrial Systems
University of South-Eastern Norway
Kongsberg, Norway
e-mail: mo.mansouri@usn.no

***Abstract*—Introducing an Autonomous Weapon System (AWS) to warfighting has a multitude of intertwined military and civilian consequences. As we are in the early phase of this shift towards autonomy, we can still influence development and legislation. That makes such investigations valuable. Much has been written and debated about the ethical implications of AWS, but little about how these ethical questions interact. This paper models the ethical dynamics of AWS, using a causal loop diagram that shows causal links between topics related to military use and civilian acceptance. Using this novel approach to describe the ethical implications of introducing AWS, otherwise hard-to-find interactions are highlighted. Based on this model, two leverage points and their effects are discussed: feedback on soldier infractions and live/recorded battlefield data.**

***Index Terms*—autonomous weapon system, ethical dynamics, causal loop diagram, systems thinking, systems engineering**

I. Introduction

An Autonomous Weapon System (AWS) is a system that can select and engage targets without further intervention by a human operator [1]. They represent both the present and future of modern warfare. With them comes both advantages and a wide range of new challenges, especially concerning the ethics of war. It is the strong belief of the authors that AWS will increase in variety, autonomy, and capability, without wanting to take a position on whether this is ethically, morally, or legally correct or not.

This paper seeks to highlight some of the most relevant advantages and challenges with AWS to have a more well-informed discussion, comprising a wide range of contexts for the systems. It will also highlight some leverage points and solutions where potential downsides can be limited. However, this paper is not meant to be an exhaustive list of all arguments that illuminate every side of the discussion.

When the term AWS is used throughout this paper, there is never a particular weapon system in mind, but the broader sense of all physical autonomous weapon systems. This can be autonomous drones, autonomous patrolling vehicles, stationary mounted weapon stations able to autonomously detect and engage targets, etc. It does, however, not include the cyberspace domain.

To spark a well-informed discussion on the ethical dynamics, this paper is structured as follows: Section II describes the 'human and the loop' terms with some discussion on challenges with them, Section III gives an introduction to how AWS is entering the battlespace, Section IV gives a brief overview of where the future of AWS is heading, Section V describes categories and questions of legality for AWS, Section VI introduces a causal loop diagram to enable discussions on the dynamics for AWS acceptance and use, while Section VII highlights some leverage points, Section VIII discusses some future research topics, and finally, Section IX concludes the paper.

II. Human and the Loop

Some of the most frequently used terms when discussing AWS are the terms relating to where the human is in the loop. Following are descriptions of how the authors see these terms relate to AWS and some of the challenges in using them.

Human-in-the-loop

When robots can select targets and deliver force only with human command, we say the human is *in* the loop. Removing the human would limit the functionality of the robot.

Some argue that the term is very ambiguous as the human will always be somewhere in the loop, without necessarily specifying where [2]. For this reason, the authors argue to save the term for systems where the main actions will not be performed unless it has human input. One example is when an autonomous system can find and track a target, but the action of 'pulling the trigger' is left to the human operator. Such border control systems in South-Korea and Israel are later discussed.

Since systems in this category require human input, they are often called supervised or in some cases semi-autonomous, but can not be called truly autonomous, hence not covered by the term *autonomous* weapon system. Semi-autonomous weapon systems can, however, also be that a human operator selects a target that is engaged autonomously [1].

Human-out-of-the-loop

In the opposite case, the human is said to be *out* of the loop when the system can perform all its tasks without human input.

For an AWS, this means it can autonomously both select and engage a target without any human interaction, like the later described air defense systems that can autonomously detect and engage incoming air targets. This is full autonomy and is often referred to as an unsupervised system.

Human-on-the-loop

The middle ground is when the human is *on* the loop, meaning the system can operate autonomously under the oversight of a human operator who can override its actions.

An issue with this term that can make it considered de-facto 'out-of-the-loop' is when a human is given only a fraction of a second to make a veto decision [3] or the system lacks adequate or sufficient human supervision [4].

At the same time, human soldiers already have to make snap judgments in the field under highly demanding constraints, and often with limited situational awareness [3].

A risk when overseeing autonomous systems is the 'automation bias', the tendency to trust automated systems over own judgments, even when provided evidence that the system is unreliable or wrong [5]. We might attribute more capabilities to an AWS than it truly has [2].

III. Entry of Autonomous Weapon Systems

Depending on the cultural background, 'killer robots' like from the movie Terminator [6] might be the association of an AWS. The first appearance of the term 'robot' was in 'R.U.R. (Rossum's Universal Robots)' by Czech writer Karel Capek in 1921 [7]. Since then, the idea of highly intelligent robots taking over the world has inspired popular culture. Autonomous systems capable of applying lethal force are already a reality, albeit not in the dystopian sense some are envisioning.

Current systems include the Israeli 'Iron Dome' system at the Gaza border, 'CRAM (Counter Rocket Artillery Mortar)' in Baghdad [7], and the Norwegian made 'NASAM' system deployed by, amongst other places, the White House in Washington D.C. These are all air defense systems capable of autonomously taking down incoming air targets.

Other systems are targeted at humans. Samsung SGR-A1 is a South-Korean system deployed at the demilitarized zone towards North-Korea, able to recognize human shapes and command them to stop and surrender [4]. Israel also has a system at the Gaza border with automated kill zones [8]. Both systems are currently depending on a human in the loop to apply lethal force, but reports confirm that in both cases they have the capability to deliver lethal force without human input [8].

A highly successful system is the teleoperated system used in Afghanistan by both the American Army and its allies. These are weapon systems that are operated by a human soldier, but have additional capabilities, such as keeping the aim of the weapon stably on the target found by the operator, even if the system is mounted on a moving vehicle. Some see these systems as an extension of the soldier, thus not autonomous by themselves [9]. It is easy to envision a future where human input is no longer needed.

The now-retired American remotely piloted aircraft Predator sparked discussions about modern warfare where the operator no longer need to be physically present at the place where the action takes place. As Peter Singer, military expert and author, stated in an interview with E&E: "[...] 20 minutes after being 'at war' you're sitting at the dinner table talking to your kids about their homework" [7]. The successor of this system is Reaper, a remotely piloted aircraft that also includes autonomous capabilities.

IV. Future of Autonomous Weapon Systems

The U.S. Army Research Office has founded research into an algorithm that can be used to rank the most valuable targets in a terrorist network [10]. One can foresee a system that connects this algorithm with the Reaper drone to automate a drone strike if the algorithm decides that killing is more ethical than capturing the target [3].

For now, the human remains in the loop, but there is almost inevitable that humans in many cases will be omitted from the loop. As discussed, this might even be the case for systems where humans are designed to be *on* the loop. According to Peter Singer in 2009 [7], Pentagon already back then had a research project called 'Taking Man Out of the Loop'. In 2007 there was a proposal for research by a US Army division stating that "[...] Fully autonomous engagement without human intervention should also be considered [...]" [8].

Some even predict a future where the humans are no longer fighting the wars, but withdraw from them completely and let the robots shoot it out [3][11].

V. Just War Theory

Just War Theory is the tradition and justification of how and why wars are fought [12]. To ensure a morally justifiable war, multiple criteria must be met. It is common to divide the evaluation into three groups: 'Jus ad bellum' (going to war), 'Jus in bello' (fighting a war), and 'Jus post bellum' (after a war). The three core principles of Just War Theory are discrimination, proportionality, and military necessity [4]. Discrimination means distinguishing between enemy combatants and noncombatants (civilians). Proportionality means that the harm is in balance with the gains of the action. Military necessity means that the end goal of the war is achieved through the least amount of harm.

Note that in this paper the term 'Just War Theory' will be used in the broadest sense to cover all aspects of a just war, including International Humanitarian Law, Rules of Engagement, and the Geneva and Hague Conventions.

Since concepts like autonomy, artificial intelligence, and robots are all general terms with no clear-cut definitions, there will likely not be one simple legal assessment we can all agree upon. Even if a country concludes that its development and use of AWS is in accordance with Just War Theory, others might argue against it.

In the aftermath of a war, historians can generally agree on who was the attacker and defender. During the war, both sides will always declare they have an ethically justifiable cause to enter the war. When evaluating tactics during a war, the two sides will also disagree on, e.g., what are mistakes and what are deliberate actions. Although both attack and defense can be just, deploying AWS for defensive strategies is generally easier justifiable.

Regardless of this, humanity is best served with systems that answer to Just War Theory to the biggest possible extent. That is why it is important to discuss compliance in more contexts than purely to define the legality of a particular AWS.

Jus ad bellum

In the case of justification for going to war, there is generally one major concern with AWS that is highlighted: lowering the threshold of entry to war. AWS generally means less political risk. This lowers the barriers in entering conflict without enough forethought and without exhausting nonviolent options, thus contradicting 'Jus ad bellum' and potentially making it unethical [2][8][9][13]. Some even argue that 'risk-free war' might put the civilian population at increased risk from terrorist attacks at home and abroad, by making terrorism the only way to fight back [14].

A reason why AWS is seen to give less political risk is what is often referred to as the 'Dover test' [9]. It has its name from the Dover Air Force Base in Delaware, the base where soldiers are returned from the front line in flag-draped coffins. The 'test' determines how much war casualties affect the electoral chances of the sitting political administration. This has been a major inhibitor of military action by the US since the Vietnam War [9].

The argument of AWS lowering the threshold of entry to war is typical for any significant technological advance in weaponry and tactics [8]. Some argue this makes it not worth discussing, especially when evaluating the legality of AWS. The authors believe it is nevertheless important to discuss how to create a system that raises this threshold, as it has both legal and ethical implications.

Jus in bello

It is a principle under 'Jus in bello' that someone can be held responsible for deaths and infractions that occur in the course of war [8][9]. A human soldier can behave unethically or make errors, but can be held accountable for it. For an AWS is it more unclear, as neither the system's designer, developer, maintainer, nor the military officer who deployed the AWS had any intent to cause a crime [4]. It would be unfair, and hence unjust, to hold, e.g. the commanding officer of the AWS entirely responsible for actions over which he or she had no control, both to the commander and any resulting causalities [4][8]. This lack of clear responsibility for possible war crimes is often referred to as the 'accountability gap' [4], and can make AWS unethical.

As Lin is quoted in Defence Robotics [2]: "If a human orders a robot to storm a hideout and shoot the insurgents inside, but the robot detects mostly children and women, what should it do? [...] with potentially greater situational awareness, a robot could have reason to refuse". The principle of responsibility includes the consequences when obeying orders that are known to be immoral [8]. At the same time, do human soldiers have sufficient information about the situation to determine if the order is morally correct? The capability of an AWS to process large amounts of data might give it an advantage over human soldiers in evaluating the greater moral implications of an order [11].

Some see the problem of discrimination as the most difficult aspect of AWS [8]. Failing this key principle can be seen as a reason alone to ban such systems. Current pattern-recognition technologies can discriminate between civilians and uniform-wearing soldiers based on images [4]. This might lead the enemy to cease wearing uniforms, thus increasing the risk for civilians. The authors believe that the problem of discrimination is a technological issue that will eventually be solved for AWS, at least to a level that outperforms humans. In the meantime, some argue a ban is correct, equivalent to the ban on antipersonnel landmines that does not take into account a hypothetical future improvement of the equipment [4][8].

A middle ground might be found that avoids a complete ban, while the technological development and discussions on discrimination are still not settled. An AWS could be made to only identify and target weapons and weapon systems, not the individual(s) manning them ("target the bow or arrow, not the archer" [8]). By disallowing AWS to select and engage humans as targets, the limit is at their capability of initiating a kill order [1][2][8].

Jus post bellum

Establishing truce and lasting peace should be the goal of any war. This requires that the different parties see the other as a serious partner, despite the differences. A potential issue with the introduction of AWS is if it leads to a 'moral deskilling' [3], later discussed in Section VII-A. This can make it harder to secure meaningful peace.

VI. Causal Loop Diagram

The dynamics of how the general public sees AWS and whether it is accepted or not is complex. To help comprehend the various aspects that contribute to the varying use and acceptance, a causal loop diagram is created in Figure 1. The development of the diagram is based on literature research.

An arrow indicates interrelation between nodes. When two nodes change in the same direction, the causal link is noted positive ('+'). The opposite direction is noted negative ('-'). Closed cycles in the diagram can be either positive reinforcing ('R') or balanced ('B'). Delays are noted with crossed-out links. Nodes that are colored were found in the literature to be the most important nodes. The two green arrows will be discussed in further detail in Section VII.

When evaluating if a causal link is positive or negative, the context is important. One can compare military strategy, tactics, and operation. What is found as a positive link for e.g. strategy, might contribute negatively at the tactical level.

The diagram is simplified by putting the use and acceptance of AWS together, based on an assumption that they are proportional and directly intertwined. It is the use of AWS that the general public accepts, and the politicians approve

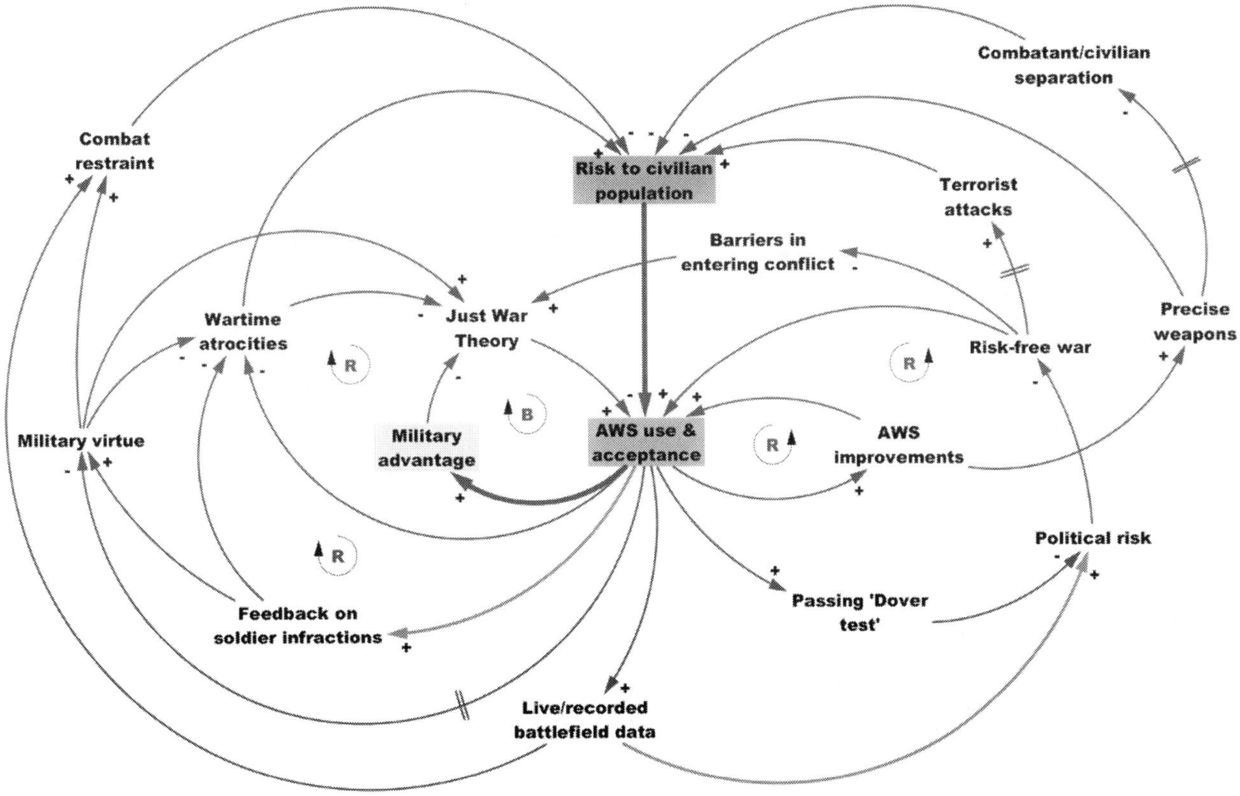

Fig. 1. Causal loop diagram, military use and civilian acceptance for AWS.

the development and use based on acceptance in the general public.

To model the dynamics, the most important nodes and causal links are included based on their contribution to the ethical dynamics. In order to ease discussions by ensuring better agreement on the meaning of the nodes, they are briefly described below. Most of them are discussed in further details in other sections of this paper.

Military advantage

The main reason for the military to push for the development and deployment of AWS is the military advantage they bring to the battlefield.

Risk to civilian population

The main concern with the introduction of AWS is the potential risk it may have to the civilian population, on both sides of the war.

Feedback on soldier infractions

An AWS may objectively assess and report soldier infractions from the battlefield.

Live/recorded battlefield data

An AWS may increase the amount and quality of data received from the battlefield, e.g. video streams.

Military virtue

Military virtue such as courage, integrity, honor, and compassion is deeply embedded in the human soldiers, but may both be reduced in humans soldiers that are removed from the battlefield and hard to embed into AWS.

Combat restrain

Combat restraint ensures the least amount of force necessary is used to reach a goal.

Wartime atrocities

A grim fact of wars is the occasional atrocities, an important node to keep an eye on.

Just War Theory

Used in this paper as a collective term for all laws, regulations, and ethical guidelines governing a just war.

Passing 'Dover test'

Refers to the number of war causalities and how this affects the dynamics.

Political risk

The political decisions of using military force come with a risk of upsetting the general public, i.e. voters.

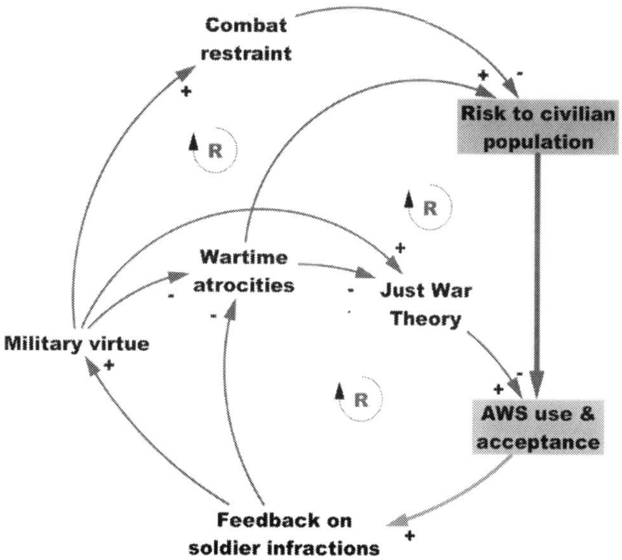

Fig. 2. Causal loop diagram, focus on 'Feedback on soldier infractions'.

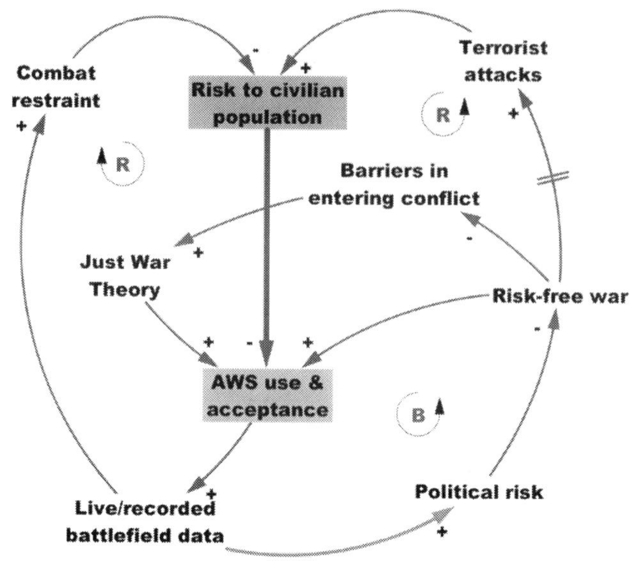

Fig. 3. Causal loop diagram, focus on 'Live/recorded battlefield data'.

Risk-free war

The concept of going to war without having to fear the consequences.

Barriers in entering conflict

There are always arguments for and against going to war. The threshold for when a war decision is taken is important.

Terrorist attacks

An opponent may resort to terror as part of warfighting, both abroad and at home.

AWS improvements

As experience is gained and general technology advances, the AWS will become improved.

Precise weapons

A property of AWS that is generally seen as superior to humans, is its precision on the battlefield.

Combatant/civilian separation

The (visually) clear differences between a combatant and a civilian.

VII. Leverage Points

An important reason to model the dynamics of a system with a causal loop diagram is to identify potential leverage points [15]. These are points where a small shift can have a big impact. Following are two of the leverage points found when analyzing the causal loop diagram in Figure 1.

A. Feedback on Soldier Infractions

The positive causal link to the node 'Feedback on soldier infractions' seems to be a key link. All the consequences from this link are isolated in Figure 2. It symbolizes a chance to use the AWS for objective and unbiased evaluations concerning the alignment of soldiers' habits and decision patterns with norms of military honor, courage, and restraint [3][8].

This increase in feedback may lead to reduced soldier infractions and wartime atrocities, as there is a constant awareness that such events will be reported [8].

Military virtue, such as courage, integrity, honor, and compassion is crucial to help fight a just war [3]. When each part in a war sees the other as a professional actor with honor and a moral purpose, it can motivate restraint. It also helps the soldiers to keep their moral connection with society. During the war's aftermath, military virtue helps secure meaningful peace between the parties. Having feedback on soldier infractions will help to keep the focus on, and maintain the credibility of, both the human soldier's and AWS's military virtue.

There are already suggestions for architectures with ethical governor, ethical behavioral control, and ethical adaptor and a responsibility advisor [8]. There is also research into 'Artificial moral intelligence' [3]. These can become tools that help AWS evaluate ethics and morale.

A great concern of Vallor [3] is that the introduction of AWS will have a negative impact on military virtue. If moral decisions during a war are performed by pre-programmed AWSs and not cultivated by humans in the chain of command, it can lead to a 'moral deskilling' of the military. To maintain such cultivation and expertise on moral virtue, repeated and habitual practice is essential.

As the extract in Figure 2 shows, all the loops created by the 'feedback' link are positive reinforcing loops. Thus, from the arguments presented in this paper, an increase in feedback will increase the use and acceptance of AWS. At the same time, when seen isolated, it has no negative effects on the other nodes leading back to 'AWS use & acceptance'.

One could argue that by knowing that an introduction of AWS will increase feedback on soldier infractions, this will in and of itself increase the acceptance of AWS from the general public. This will create an additional positive feedback loop. At the same time, soldiers might have a negative attitude towards a system constantly evaluating them.

B. Live/Recorded Battlefield Data

AWSs rely on a constant stream of data to take actions on the battlefield. Some of this data is processed internally on the AWS, while some will be transferred back to an operator. For instance, a drone will usually return a video stream, whether it operates fully autonomous or with a human operator or supervisor. An advantage of all the gathered data is that AWSs can rapidly share this and help improve decision-making [11].

Much like the potential for a dedicated system giving feedback on soldier infractions, knowing that the AWS will live stream and record battlefield data will restrain human operators, AWS developers, and chiefs of command from deploying fully autonomous systems. There already exists procedures to record data from weapon systems and to review this internally in the case of special battlefield incidents.

As depicted in Figure 3, the big leverage point lies in ensuring that this data is not only kept within the ranks of the military, but becomes publicly available. This way, it increases the political risk of using AWS in an unethical manner.

With an increase in political risk, it creates a balanced loop that helps avoid an uncontrolled escalation of unethical AWS use. The importance of this can be seen by studying the Vietnam War, often referred to as the "first televised war" [16]. During the middle of the war, the number of reporters grew tremendously, bringing all of the war's brutality home to the living rooms of the American public. Although we have become more custom to it, live and recorded video and other data from the battlefield will likely lead to an increased aversion to war by the general public [8].

No military general is likely to allow live streaming of all data from war, as this can reveal military secrets and give up military-strategic advantages. Journalists already have "freedom of information" laws that guarantee access to government documents. Similar rights of access by journalists could be expanded. The technicalities of how such data can be shared are no further discussed herein.

An example of the importance and ramification of sharing video footage is the July 12th, 2007 Baghdad airstrike, where two US Army helicopters launched air-to-ground attacks on a group of people, including civilians and reporters. The crew was heard laughing at some of the causalities. This video was not shared by the military, but leaked to the whistleblower website WikiLeaks by former US Army soldier Chelsea Manning [17].

VIII. Further Research

Expanding the causal loop diagram may make it harder to use as a discussion tool, but could help find more leverage points. For example, by finding more ways to influence the barriers in entering conflict and combat restraint, or to discover further negative causal links which must be offset.

Qualitative analysis of the causal loop diagram is given. Further detailing of the model can also enable quantitative evaluations. Computer simulations can, for example, be useful both to quantify and visualize how an effect on one node or link changes the whole dynamics of the model.

For a war with AWS to be just, according to the principle of 'Jus in bello', someone needs to be accountable for the actions of the AWS. What role this person has and how distributed the responsibility is may influence the ethical dynamics.

If a restriction is set on AWS to not target humans, how will this alter the dynamics? Instead of only analyzing how the flow in the causal loop diagram change, it might make more sense to develop separate diagrams for different levels of restrictions on AWS.

Further research should be done on decision support systems with prediction models that can judge when, how, and under what constraints it is ethical to deploy AWS. Some research into tools for evaluating ethics and morale is already mentioned [3][8].

Section II categorized AWSs into human-in-the-loop, human-out-of-the-loop, and human-on-the-loop. When analyzing ethical issues, it would be beneficial to have a much deeper classification tree.

Whether a side of the war is seen as the attacker or defender, aggressor or retaliator, will greatly affect the evaluation of ethics. For AWS, an autonomous border patrol system deployed on one's homeland is likely to have more acceptance than, e.g., a drone flying over foreign soil. Adding this dimension of context to the ethical dynamics of AWS will likely be useful.

Ethical dynamics that change depending on the context are important to clarify. For example, by investigating the three abstraction levels of military strategy, tactics, and operation. It should be investigated how a change in viewpoint might affect the causal loop.

IX. Conclusion

In this paper, the authors pursued to model the ethical dynamics of autonomous weapon systems, and identify leverage points and mitigations to dampen some of the challenges.

Analyzing the proposed model proved successful in finding positive contributors to AWS acceptance and maintained ethics. One suggestion was to introduce and embed systems to give feedback on soldier infractions, and another was to find ways to ensure that the public gets access to some of the data collected by the AWS on the battlefield. The latter was demonstrated to introduce both a positive balancing force into the dynamics and reinforce some desired effects.

REFERENCES

[1] United States Department of Defense, "Department of Defense Directive 3000.09: Autonomy in Weapon Systems, November 21, 2012," Homel. Secur. Digit. Libr., 2012.

[2] S. Davies, "Just War," Eng. Technol., vol. 6, no. 8, pp. 38–40, Sep. 2011, doi: 10.1049/et.2011.0802.

[3] S. Vallor, "The future of military virtue: Autonomous systems and the moral deskilling of the military," Int. Conf. Cyber Conflict, CYCON, 2013.

[4] A. Guersenzvaig, "Autonomous Weapon Systems: Failing the Principle of Discrimination," IEEE Technol. Soc. Mag., vol. 37, no. 1, pp. 55–61, Mar. 2018, doi: 10.1109/MTS.2018.2795119.

[5] P. M. Asaro, "Modeling the moral user," IEEE Technol. Soc. Mag., vol. 28, no. 1, pp. 20–24, 2009, doi: 10.1109/MTS.2009.931863.

[6] "Terminator (1984)," IMDB. https://www.imdb.com/title/tt0088247 (accessed Mar. 10, 2021).

[7] S. Davies, "It's war - but not as we know it [autonomous military robotics]," Eng. Technol., vol. 4, no. 9, pp. 40–43, May 2009, doi: 10.1049/et.2009.0907.

[8] R. C. Arkin, "Governing lethal behavior: Embedding ethics in a hybrid deliberative/reactive robot architecture part I: Motivation and philosophy," in Proceedings of the 3rd international conference on Human robot interaction - HRI '08, 2008, vol. 171, no. 1, p. 121, doi: 10.1145/1349822.1349839.

[9] N. Sharkey, "Cassandra or False Prophet of Doom: AI Robots and War," IEEE Intell. Syst., vol. 23, no. 4, pp. 14–17, Jul. 2008, doi: 10.1109/MIS.2008.60.

[10] D. Callahan, P. Shakarian, J. Nielsen, and A. N. Johnson, "Shaping operations to attack robust terror networks," Proc. 2012 ASE Int. Conf. Soc. Informatics, Soc. 2012, pp. 13–18, 2012, doi: 10.1109/SocialInformatics.2012.22.

[11] J. Khurshid and Hong Bing-rong, "Military robots - a glimpse from today and tomorrow," in ICARCV 2004 8th Control, Automation, Robotics and Vision Conference, 2004., 2004, vol. 1, no. December, pp. 771–777, doi: 10.1109/ICARCV.2004.1468925.

[12] "Just War Theory," Internet Encyclopedia of Philosophy. https://iep.utm.edu/justwar (accessed Mar. 10, 2021).

[13] P. M. Asaro, "How just could a robot war be?," Front. Artif. Intell. Appl., vol. 175, no. 1, pp. 50–64, 2008.

[14] P. W. Kahn, "The Paradox of Riskless Warfare," Philos. Public Policy Q., vol. 22, no. 3, pp. 1–24, 2002.

[15] R. Edson, "Systems thinking. Applied. A primer," Asyst Inst., 2008.

[16] R. H. Spector, "The Vietnam War and the media," Britannica. https://www.britannica.com/topic/The-Vietnam-War-and-the-media-2051426 (accessed Mar. 10, 2021).

[17] "Collateral Murder, 5 Apr 2010," WikiLeaks. https://wikileaks.org/wiki/Collateral_Murder,_5_Apr_2010 (accessed Mar. 10, 2021).

Application of System Thinking in Developing of the Public Transportation Network in Norway

Ebrahim Qaredaghi
Department of Science and Industry Systems
University of South-Eastern Norway
Kongsberg, Norway
Email: qaredaghi@gmail.com

Mo Mansouri
Professor at Department of Science and Industry Systems
University of South-Eastern Norway
Kongsberg, Norway
Email: mo.mansouri@usn.no

Abstract—**Public transportation systems have always provided important services to people. People or customers, as the main stakeholders, need available, fast and reasonably priced transportation systems. However, developing the public transportation system, on one hand, needs educated people to run and update the system based on the new technologies, and, on the other hand, needs to cover environmental agencies' requirements. Global warming as the main concern of environmental agencies has forced the public transportation system to control the greenhouse gas emission and find environmentally friendly solutions for public transportation networks. It is, therefore, important to not just think about the development of the public transportation network, but also consider other stakeholders' requirements as well. In this paper, the authors apply the "system thinking" approach to understand the stakeholders' requirements and how to have a public transportation system that respects all stakeholders' requirements. By using the systemigram method, we model the public transportation network in Norway, and analyze where we could affect the problems of its development.**

Keywords-system thinking; public transportation system; systemigram; system context diagram.

I. Introduction

Developing public transportation networks starts when people need to have an available system near their homes to cover daily basis requirements. It could be access to their workplace, shopping malls, their children's school and so on. The network development could be based on the other stakeholders request as well. However, developing the public transportation system is not just to build roads or rail tracks or physical development, it could be an update based on the new technologies, and it has its complexity both technically and environmentally.

In this paper, the authors applied a system thinking approach to analyze the existing public transportation system and how the stakeholders' requirements affect the development of it. The authors tried to study the current system to investigate different stakeholders, their roles, and requirements as well. Moreover, the authors tried to explore all the stakeholders, their interests, and look at the external influences that have evolved the problem to its existing state. Next, the systemigram method was implemented to obtain an understanding of what influences the issues and development of the system, and finally, the concept of openness [1] is applied to the systemigram in order to understand what part of the problem of the network development can be addressed.

The case. In this paper, the development of the public transportation network is followed. The public transportation system organization starts network development as a direct response to the stakeholders' requirement or their need for a new facility. This requirement is given to the organization in order to develop the existing network or build a new network. The organization should consider several solutions, and choose the feasible one in terms of cost, being environmentally friendly, and being compatible with the new technologies.

System (organization) of research. The system being targeted for this research is an organization that works under the supervision of the Public Transport and Communication Ministry. In other words, the organization works in the private sector and the government is one of the main stakeholders to ask directly or indirectly the organization for network development. The authors have conducted the research within a Norwegian transportation system.

II. Background

There are several definitions of system thinking in the literatures. According to INCOSE (International Council on Systems Engineering), *"system thinking is a way of thinking use to address the complex and uncertain real-world situations with emphasis on interconnected technical and social entities which are hierarchically organized producing emergent behavior"*. In addition, system thinking can be defined as a method to a problem or issue that considers how elements within the whole system interact and operate over its lifecycle, and how to optimize the design, implementation, and evaluation [2]. Haraldsen [3] defined system thinking as the *"science that deals with the organization of logic and integration of disciplines for understanding patterns and relations of complex problems. System thinking is also known as principles of organization or theory of self-organization and the way of using it involves "systemic" or "holistic thinking". It is a science based on understanding connections and relations between seemingly isolated things"*. He stated that, in general terms, system thinking is both the science of structuring the logic, the mental modelling, asking relevant questions, and practical applications through System Analysis and System Dynamics. As can be seen in Figure 1, system thinking embeds two concepts, System Analysis (SA) and System Dynamic (SD). System analysis involves group modeling, where the initial questions of the problem can be asked, and a mental model structure can be created by using Causal Loop Diagrams, to reflect that problem. However, the system dynamics is a mathematical recreation of our mental models to deals with and numerical analysis and understanding uncertainty of the practical representation in the developed mathematical model.

For defining the system openness, we define three boundaries for the system. Control, Influence or transactional environment and appreciate. Control is for the item of the system we could control to some extent. Influence is for items, we only influence and cannot control, and appreciate is for the environment the system operates in [4].

Systemigram is a system thinking tool whose evaluation may be recognized in three phases. First, its development as a structure of visual language. In this phase, the development of the technique focuses on the graphical portrayal of a structured pose. Second, its development as a procedure for business architecture. It is vital to emphasize that systemigram is not an architecture itself, but rather it can provide an inactive and simple environment for comparing and aligning business architectures. The last phase is its modification as a grateful learning system. The systemigram's writer creates a storyboard using carefully selected scenes which are subnets of the systemigram [5].

III. THE PROBLEM CONTEXT

In order to define the context for the problem, first we need to study and define the System Of Interest (SOI). In the following, we present the system of interest definition.

A. The System Of Interest For Development

The public transportation in Norway is the SOI in this paper. The main purpose of the public transportation is to provide transportation vehicles and networks for people who want to use them daily. Several parameters are necessary for customers or people as the main stakeholder, such as price, access to transportation vehicles, roads, and its network, being environmentally friendly etc. In order to cover these requirements, there are many other systems, and infrastructures which should cooperate with the SOI. The public transportation system in Norway consists of rail transportation, road transportation, water transportations, and aviation transportation. Trains, trams, subway count as rail public transportation system. Taxis, busses and minibuses are road public transportation systems, and ferry is the water public transportation system. The authors of this article do not count aviation transportation since they are not used as daily purposes. However, trains are public transportation because many people take them every day from their hometown to workplace. Basically, all the mentioned transportation services can be found in the big cities like Oslo. However, for small cities, we have some of them.

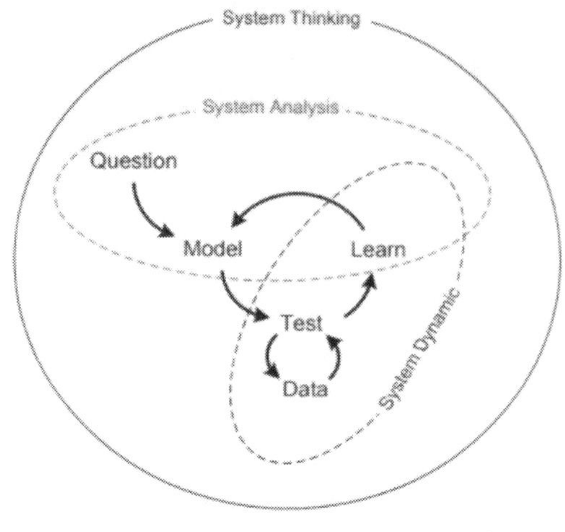

Figure 1. System thinking definition diagram [3]

The two popular public transportation vehicles among people are electrical scooters and electrical bicycles these days. Normally, people are using them inside the cities for short-distance travel. To use them, it is necessary to install an Application (App) on the phone and scan a barcode that is on the vehicles. The payment is based on the time and is very reasonable. The municipalities of the cities have also provided enough parking slots for electrical bicycles. There are several operators that provide electrical scooters, and services as well. However, safety, lower speeds, a campaign to get users to be more considerate, and better parking facilities, are among measures discussed these days to address this new business's issue in municipalities. Since it is necessary to implement the new rules for using them in cities, the writers of this article considered these two new public transportations systems as the new technology and did not consider them as the main and common public transportation system in Norway.

B. The System Boundaries-Developing Context

Figure 2 presents the system boundaries for development context. The public transportation organization is in the inner circle. We can control it, and the team and organization that is responsible for network development is in this circle. Environment, particularly CO_2 emission, sub-contractors included maintenance contractor, education system (schools, universities), and business such as, shopping malls, restaurants, companies can be developed, and are influenced by the public transport network development system. Other items that are in the boundary include people, political decisions, new technologies, and government. These are items which we cannot influence and we should appreciate.

C. Stakeholders Context Diagram

After the SOI explanation and system boundaries, we can define the stakeholders and their main interests. Figure 3 illustrates the high-level stockholders. The main stakeholder is represented by the people or customers who are using the public transportation system. Since in Norway, people pay a

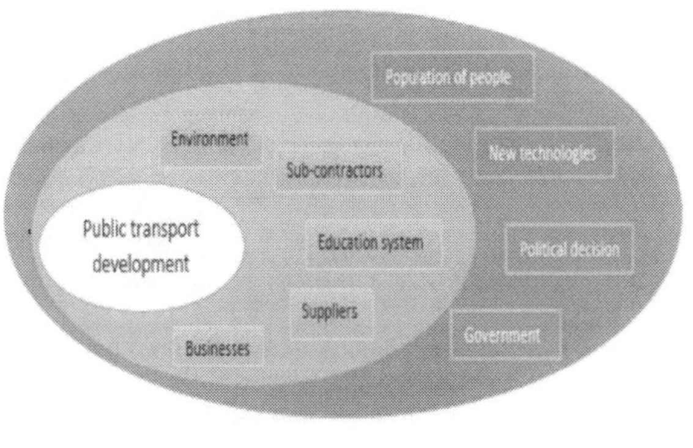

Figure 2. System boundaries in development context

high amount of tax from their salaries, they expect high-quality services in terms of new and comfortable facilities in public transportation vehicles, roads, and infrastructures. In addition, Norway is a relatively expensive country compared to the other European countries, and price is the main concern of the people for receiving services from public transportation system. Developing new methods of transportation could be an option to tackle the expensive transportation system.

On the left side of the interest map, we have people who have an interest in the public transportation system with yellow color in Figure 3. People or customers, tourists, politicians, private owners of lands, people who are working as staff or clerks for public transportation organization are in this category. Customers, tourists and clerks are willing to have a developed transportation system, while owners of land who should sell their land to government do not want it. In order to solve lands' owner issue, either the government should pay good money for it or change the network root. For both solutions, the organization should spend money to tackle these issues.

On the right side of the interest map, there are organizations that have an interest in the SOI with green color in Figure 3. Government, environmental agencies, banks, and legal regulation organizations are these organizations. By developing the public transportation, all these organizations or institutes receive a benefit. The government could get people satisfactions by developing the public transportation system. Environmental agencies should set some rules for transportation system organization to control the greenhouses gas emissions and pollutants based on their criteria and limitations. Banks could provide the loan for SOI, and could also receive interest. The legal organization authorities could set some urban rules for public transportation organization such as, parking places, speed limit etc.

At the bottom of the interest map, we can see the rest of the stakeholders with orange color in Figure 3. These stakeholders are IT and ICT companies, neighbor countries, suppliers or manufacturers, maintenance companies, and the new businesses or markets.

All these stakeholders have connection with the public transportation system directly or indirectly. IT companies need to provide the App(s) and Internet infrastructures to keep updating the business based on the new technologies and communication services. Neighbor countries could develop their transportation network to Norwegian transportation network easily. Manufacturer or suppliers and maintenance companies or subcontractors could earn money from the public transportation development. They could hire more people and expand their businesses. In addition, new markets or business such as, electrical scooters and electrical bicycles, could be developed as well as existing public transportation to expand the network.

IV. THE PARIS AGREEMENT

In 2016, there was an international agreement called the Paris agreement to control global warming. This agreement is an agreement within the United Nations Framework Convention on Climate Change (UNFCCC) to prevent dangerous anthropogenic interference with the climate change. This agreement gives the long-term temperature aim

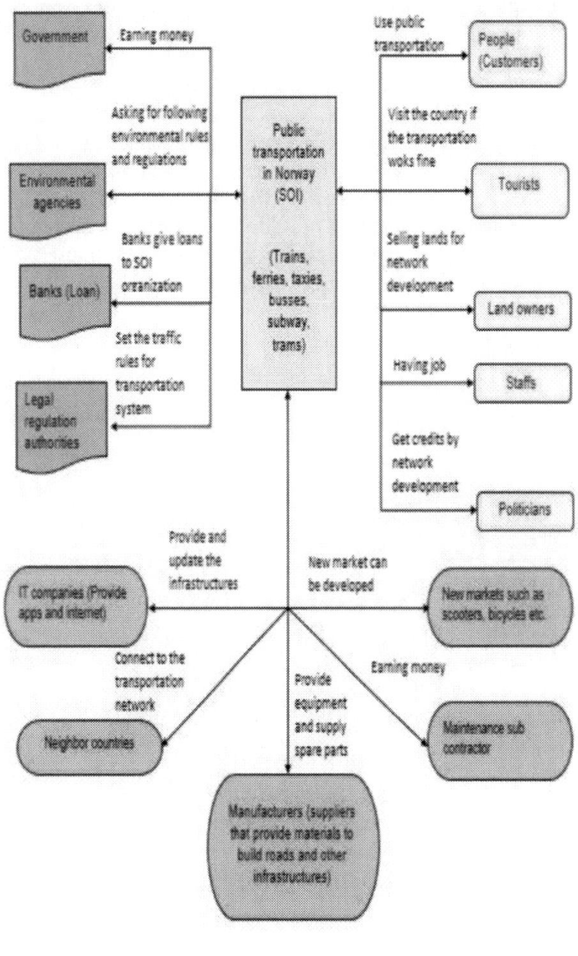

Figure 3. Stakeholders' interest map

holding the increase in the global average temperature to below 2 °C above pre-industrial levels and to follow efforts to restrict the temperature increase to 1.5 °C above pre-industrial levels, recognizing that this would reduce the risks and effects of climate change pointedly [6]. The countries involved in this agreement have tried to find solutions to control and mitigate global warming. Norway, as one of the European countries involved this agreement, has tried to play a role by developing green industries and applying a green energy mindset in all aspects of industries, as well as transportation. Therefore, using renewable fuels instead of fossil fuels was part of the Norwegian public transportation development plans. In order to follow this plan, the suppliers need to develop new technologies and update the current fuel consumption system in the public transportation systems which cost them as well. As mentioned before, the electrical scooters and electrical bicycles are new technologies to mitigate the greenhouse gas emissions as well.

V. THE SYSTEMIGRAM

Following the stakeholders' interest maps, we developed the systemigram to visually represent the problem. Figure 4 illustrates the systemigram for the whole system of interest.

A. The Mainstay – The Purpose of the System Development

Figure 5 shows the mainstay of the system. We can read the story as "*Public transportation organization shall develop the new transportation network and system to cover environmental criteria to provide accessible transportation services to tackle customer requirements.*" The mainstay is the path for how the public transportation systems develop from where they are today to where they should be in the future.

B. The Other Parameters

Figure 6 presents the agencies that set sorts of rules and centers communicate directly, and control the developing system. The environment quality center sets environmental regulations to ensure that greenhouse gas emissions is under the criteria, and the public transportation system is working properly. This center will communicate with the organization to ask them to make a change in their system and modify it to cover the environmental criteria in case of any deviation from the regulations.

The traffic control center is responsible to monitor the public transportation traffic. This center is also communicating with the organization if there are issues that could be solved by public transportation cooperation. Basically, this center either receives a report from public transportations, or checks the transportation system itself and if there is an issue that could be managed by the organization, they will contact the organization. Normally, the issues discussed with the public transportation organization first, and if they could manage it, they will cooperate. The issues that could be tackled, such as traffic jams, the design of the public transportation system network, and improvement of the transportation network can be discussed with the traffic control system.

The legal regulation authority is responsible to set the driving rules such as, speeding control, parking zones, road pricing, road taxes etc. This center will impose rules to the new public transportation network, and the existing network. In addition, this legal regulation authority regularly controls the transportation system to find out if there is any need for improvement of the network. Basically, government asks this organization to set these rules and impose to the transportation system.

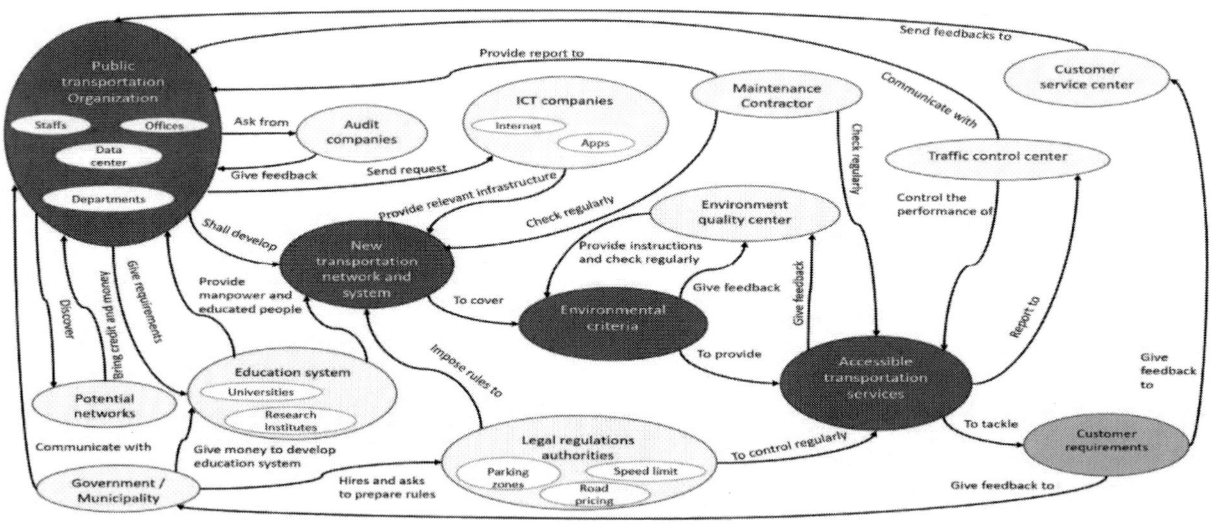

Figure 4. Systemigram

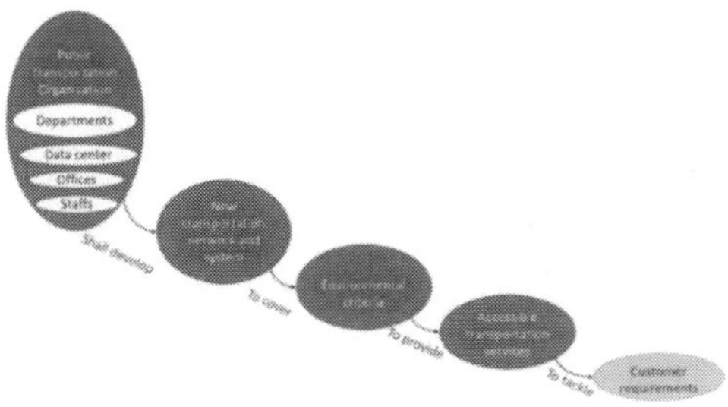

Figure 5. The mainstay

Figure 7 shows the subsystems and sub-contractors. The education system, the potential market, ICT (Information and Communications Technology) companies, audit (third party) company, and maintenance contractor are listed in this group. These subsystems and sub-contractors either support the system or the system gets influenced by them.

Education systems play a significant role in the public transportation development. On one hand, the education system receive money from the government to increase the education quality, and, on the other hand, they have a close relationship with the transportation organization to keep the education system updated, and if necessary, start to research and find a solution about the possibilities to increase the efficiency of public transportation system. As an output of

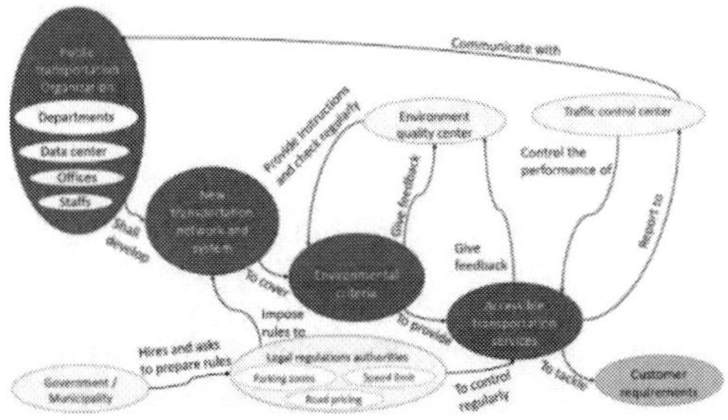

Figure 6. The regulation agencies

the education system, either they perform the research based on the public transportation system order or they provide educated people to help the transportation organization with their knowledge. The education system keeps itself updated and supply the manpower for the public transportation organization by providing and updating the education courses. The main goal of the education system is to support the public transportation system and increase its efficiency.

The potential market is referred to new markets and technologies that could improve the public transportation network services. Since the potential market and new technologies are underdeveloped, they try to find how to impact the SOI.

As mentioned earlier, the electrical scooters and electrical bicycles are the new technologies that could help the current public transportation system. In addition, the SOI has several departments and they can study the new markets and possibilities. The studies could be about the new roots and finding new networks.

The main responsibility of the ICT companies is to keep the SOI updated in terms of online services such as, Apps and available internet networks. Nowadays, customers buy online tickets, and it is important for them to know the schedule of the public transportations as well. In this regard, Norway is one of the countries that online information and tickets are available for customers, and customers need to receive accurate information in time. It is therefore important for customers to have accessible information in time to plan based on them. The SOI, basically, order to ICT companies what they need, and the ICT companies are responsible to develop the online infrastructures.

Another subsystem that supports public transportation organization is the audit companies. The audit companies perform audits based on the standards to issue certificates. Besides, they perform audits to show the transportation system organization's possible improvement areas. Since the audit companies are external companies, they do not hide the system management negative points and organizations can trust their advice in order to improve the system.

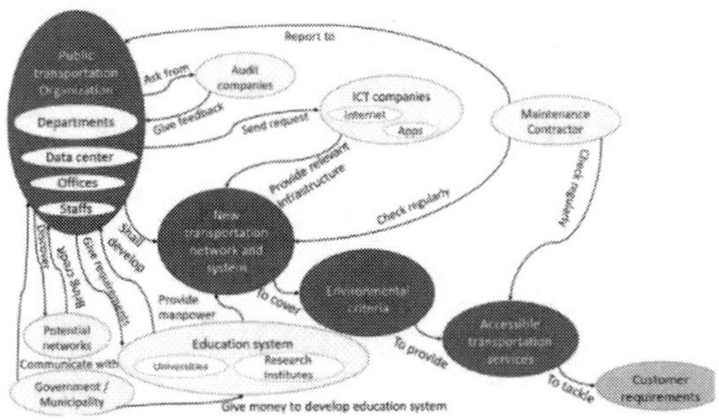

Figure 7. The subsystems and sub-contractors

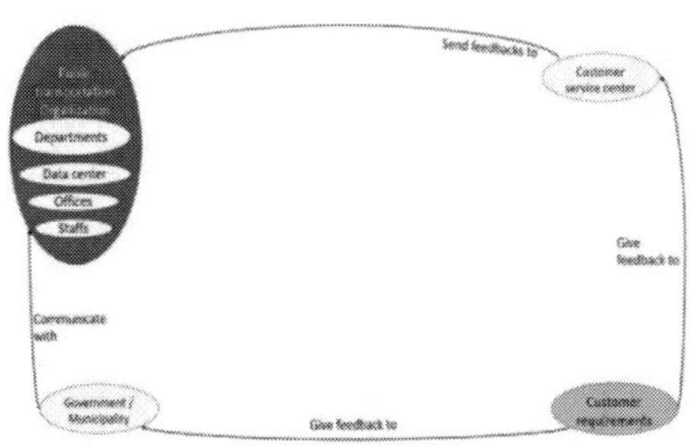

Figure 8. The customer service

The main responsibility of the maintenance contractors is to fix any damage or possible damage. Unlike ICT companies that are trying to support online services, the maintenance companies provide physical services and they are much bigger than ICT companies in terms of the staff and hardware facilities. The maintenance companies have plans and schedules to give SOI services. So, it is very vital for customers and SOI to receive high-quality services from the maintenance subcontractors based on educated and experienced staff.

Figure 8 illustrates the customer service of the SOI. As can be seen from this figure, there are two options for customers to give feedback to the SOI. One possibility is to contact the customer service centers and provide their feedback to them. This could be by calling or even by sending emails. Even some centers have their online questionnaire forms to receive feedback from customers. Another method or way is to contact to government. The customers can provide their feedback to the government through political parties. This method takes more time compared to another way and customers normally use this method if they are not satisfied with the SOI at all, and the consequence of this method could change the whole system.

VI. How To Tackle The Problem

We used the systemigram to analyze the system of interest and to have a good visual representation of all the factors and forces that can play a role in our system. In order to analyze the system better, we will use the openness principle of the systemigram to analyze where the system interest can influence other forces and where the system of interest can be influenced by the other forces.

Figure 9 presents the openness principle to the systemigram and we categorized the systemigram the nodes into control with green color, influence with purple color and appreciate with red color. Following is the brief explanation of each of them.

A. Control

As Figure 9 shows, the important nodes that can be controlled to develop public transportation systems are technical factors. In other words, ICT companies and maintenance sub-contractors are the most important subsystems for controlling the SOI. Basically, ICT companies and maintenance companies receive orders from the public transportation organization to develop the public transportation system.

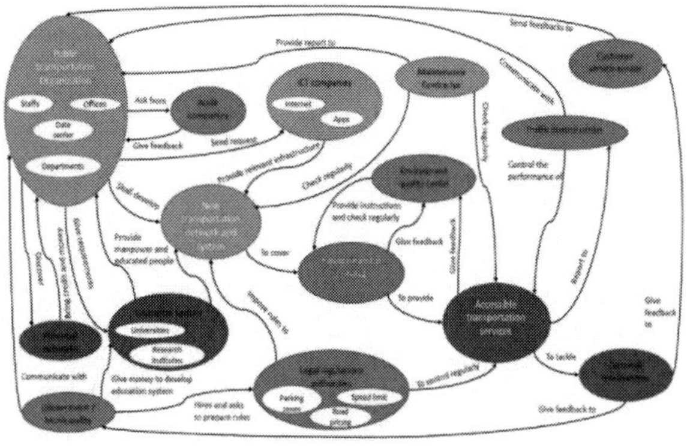

Figure 9. The openness principle

B. Influence

The most important nodes that can be influenced in the influence category are customer requests and the SOI itself. These two nodes are important since the aim of the development of the public transportation system is to cover the customer requirements. On the other hand, by developing the public transportation system the organization can be influenced as well.

C. Appreciate

Many nodes in Figure 9 are categorized as appreciate nodes. These nodes cannot be controlled or influenced and as we can see clearly the legislation organizations such as, environmental quality control center and traffic control center are in this group. The main nodes as can be seen are the government, environment quality control center, legal regulation authority, and the traffic control center. One of the main concerns during the developing public transportation system is to cover the environment quality control criteria based on the Paris agreement. The environmental quality center is the most important center among other nodes in the appreciate group.

Based on the openness principle of the systemigram and analyzing of the systemigram, we could say that the main factor to have a successful development of the public transportation is first to analyze and understand the customer requirements. The customer requirements for having a public transportation network consist of ticket price, accessible public transportation system, comfortable, and environmentally friendly services. The next step is to start a technical study of the possible networks and select the feasible one among other options in the public transportation system development organization. The next step is to influence the items that development the organization can do. The next step is to cover the rules and standards which are sets by the legislation agencies and authorities such as, traffic control agencies, legal regulation authorities in the design and in the construction phase of the development, and the final step is to control the items that can be controlled by the development system. Basically, the factors and aspects that could be controlled are technical factors.

VII. Conclusion and Further Work

Public transportation plays a significant role in the daily life of the people. It is, therefore, important to cover, and plan based on the stakeholder's requirements. Normally, the customers require for public transportation development. They are expecting a high quality of the services. In order to analyze the stakeholders' requirements, in this paper, we used the application of the system thinking. Specifically, we used the systemigram method and principle of the openness to analyzing the necessary factors to develop the public transportation system.

Systemigram is a useful method in order to analyze the system. This method also gives the visual presentation of the system and the connection between the factors. By applying the openness principle, we could analyze and tackle the problem and provide the solution for the issue step by step. There are several stakeholders that are involved in the public transportation development. The government, people, and education system play a significant role among stakeholders. The environmental quality center sets the rules and regulations in order to control the greenhouse gas emission and find the environmentally friendly solutions for public transportation system development.

REFERENCES

[1] J. Gharajedaghi, Systems thinking: Managing chaos and complexity: A platform for designing business architecture. Elsevier, 2011.

[2] B. A. Addae and Z. Ling, "Acculturation of systems thinking for requirements need analysis for smart energy city development: A case study in Accra," International Journal of Management, Information Technology and Engineering, pp. 9-20, 2018.

[3] H. V. Haraldsson, Introduction to system thinking and causal loop diagrams. Department of Chemical Engineering, Lund University, 2004.

[4] S. Engen, M. Mansouri, and G. Muller, "Application of system thinking to frame the problem in a subsea development projects with high-level business requirements," in SoSE, 2019, pp. 81-86.

[5] C. D. Blair, J. T. Boardman, and B. J. Sauser, "Communicating strategic intent with systemigrams: Application to the network-enabled challenge," Systems Engineering, vol. 10, no. 4, pp. 309-322, 2007.

[6] C.-F. Schleussner et al., "Science and policy characteristics of the Paris Agreement temperature goal," Nature Climate Change, vol. 6, no. 9, pp. 827-835, 2016/09/01 2016, doi: 10.1038/nclimate3096.

Systems Thinking in the Zero Emission Solution for Railway Diesel Locomotive

A Case Study for Battery Train with Partial Electrification from Norwegian Railway Sector

Hawar Said
University of South-Eastern Norway
Kongsberg, Norway
hawar19@gmail.com

Mo Mansouri
University of South-Eastern Norway
Kongsberg, Norway
mo.mansouri@usn.no

Abstract— **This paper seeks to understand the Zero Emission solution that the Norwegian Railways Directorate adopted in its 2019 report. The report presented the battery with partial electrification as an ideal solution for achieving the government's goals of reaching Zero Emission. Using the battery as a replacement for diesel engines is a new technology in Norway. The newly proposed technology for use in the railway sector is a new challenge and raises many questions about its suitability to operate on the Norwegian railway. In this paper, we applied the concept of Systems Thinking methodology. We applied this methodology to get deeper understanding of the system and its boundaries. Understanding the issues could be of influence now or in the future, as well as identifying and defining the stakeholders and understanding their needs. The tools we used in this paper are: applying Cynefin framework to sort the set of issues that managers face in five contexts, applying Openness (context diagram) to manage the chaos and complexity by understanding the context of its environment, applying CATOWE analysis to understand the stakeholder perspective and the impact of the issues, applying WHY question to understand why the actors do what they do, applying Systemigram to understand and model the system of interest and also to visualize the representation of the system structure, & applying Leverage points to identify places in the system that a small force change can cause a large effect in system behavior.**

Keywords— Systems Thinking; Battery Train; CATOWE; Openness of system; Leverage points; Systemigram; Zero Emission; Systems Engineering.

I. INTRUDUCTION

A. Understanding the new technology

This paper discusses many factors that have impact on systems and their environment by applying System Thinking. This will help us to increase the understanding of the internal and external requirements of the new technology. The early understanding of the demands of the desired system are also mentioned in the system engineering handbook [4] and defined as a factor for developing and improving the systems.

Using the battery train as a new solution in the Norway Railway System will increase the uncertainty and make the boundary unambiguous. In this project, it would be difficult to predict the issues caused by interaction of the human – machine and the environment. We need to understand the system type to predict the possible issues that can face our system. This new technology requires more analyzing and studies to improve their performance and to ensure the operational safety in the Norwegian Railway Sector.

The Cynefin framework identified five contexts, as introduced by Snowden and Boone [2]. The framework offers the decision makers five contexts to demonstrate the differentiation among them by showing the nature of the relationship between cause and effect, as shown in Figure 1.

The Cynefin framework will help the management of an organization to select the right context and involve the right stakeholders to make a proper decision.

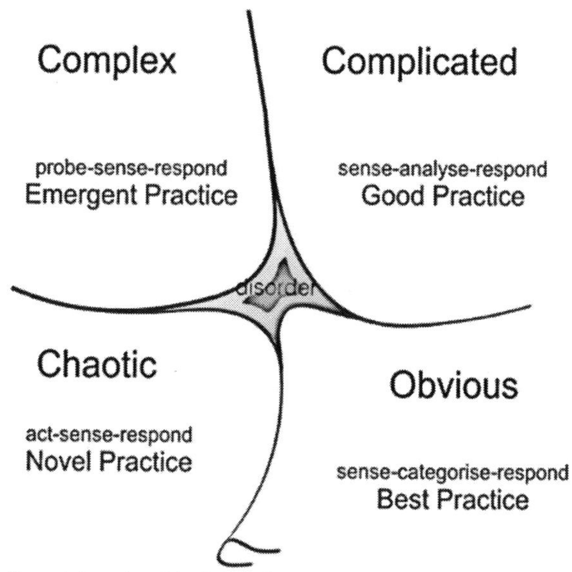

Figure 1. Domains of the Cynefin framework; the dark domain in the center is disorder.

Figure 1 shows the five-decision making contexts, namely: obvious, complicated, complex, chaotic, and disorder (the actual context is not known), in order to aid or help the managers to make sense of a situation. Cause and effect on the new battery train system have no answers and cannot be deduced, unless in retrospect. "*Instructive patterns ... can emerge,*" write Snowden and Boone, "*if the leader conducts experiments that are safe to fail.*" Cynefin calls this process "*probe–sense–respond*" [2].

B. Battery Train - with partial electrification

This new technology is still under study and testing process in Norway. The National Directorate for Norway, using this solution, aims to reduce the CO_2 (Carbon dioxide) emission to the community and provide clean energy for the environment. "*This concept is compatible with today's technology and can therefore be used on the entire existing rail network,*" says the Railway Directorate.

Figure 2. Bombardier train

The train will become more stable, less noisy, will have less vibration and zero emissions after replacing the diesel engines with a battery-powered engine. This solution optimizes the energy efficiency and provides maximum safety. The batteries will be installed on the roofs of the locomotives. The batteries will supply the motors and the mount with the power necessary to control all moving parts.

Figures 2 and 3 illustrate a bombardier train which can travel at a maximum of 160 km/h for more than 7 hours without the need for additional impetus, such as diesel engines or electric power.

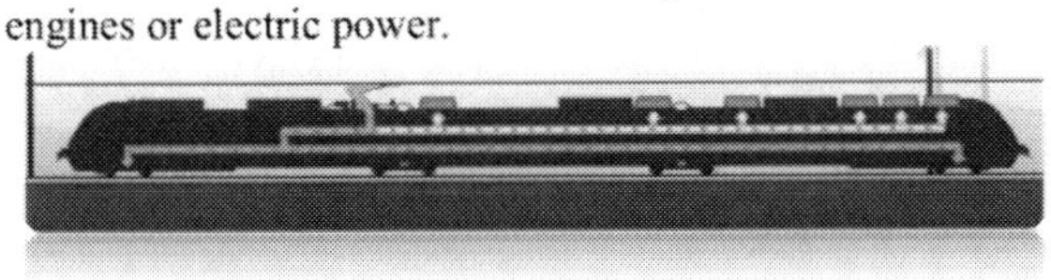

Figure 3. Recharging the battery for Bombardier train

The batteries can be recharged within 7-10 minutes and this is done by connecting the wattage to the batteries as they travel along the lines that have electrical power. Each battery has 5-8 years lifetime with daily operation.

II. Background

The Norwegian Government Transport Committee has requested the Railway Directorate to investigate the possibility of a test project with Zero Emissions Solutions for railway vehicles. The Norwegian National Railways Directorate Performed a study in 2019. The study was performed in partnership with Bane NOR SF (infrastructure manager) and Norske Tog AS (a train company) and Trains manufacturers [9]. The study was called The Null Emissions Solutions for Non-Electrified Railways (NULLFIB) [9].

The study suggested many alternatives to replace the fossil fuel with zero emission solutions for non-electrified stretches, considering best financial alternatives.
The options that have been selected were:

- Hydrogen
- Biogas
- Biodiesel
- Battery
- Battery operation with partial electrification

The study selected the battery with partial electrification as the most durable and robust alternative to replace the diesel engines because it would be expensive and require more international coordination to refill the other forms of fuel (hydrogen, biogas or biodiesel) in case of crossing borders. This solution will increase the socio-economic savings according to the National Railway Directorate "*A transition to zero-emission solutions will reduce the railway's carbon footprint, and will provide favorable socio-economic savings*".

III. Paper Method and Solution Challenge

The paper is based on outcomes from the National Directorate and Bane NOR infrastructure, and we applied qualitative research methods using reports and article outcomes observations and informal communication with suppliers. This paper applies the System Thinking methodology to provide the understanding of the solution.

The National Directorate collaborated with Norske Tog AS to provide battery-powered engines to their vehicles by using Bane NOR infrastructure to ensure the Zero Emission. All three actors (National Directorate, Norske AS & Bane NOR) have focused on the new technology, which is still unclear and unambiguous. The battery solution is new to the market and unknown for a lot of railway companies. The Norwegian government requires adopting the new solution with a high level of focus on Zero Emission to provide an operational and cost-effective rolling stock to the Norwegian community.

IV. Applying the General System Thinking (GST)

One of the challenging aspects is knowing the boundary of the systems and their environment. The formalization of systems thinking goes to Ludwig Von Bertalanffys formulation of the General System Theory in 1940, which states "*... an important means of controlling and instigating the transfer of principles from one field to another, and it will no longer be necessary to duplicate or triplicate the discovery of the same principle in different fields isolated from each other*" [7]. In his book, the author mentions that the characteristics of the complex will manifest as new or emergent. Further, he explains the system complexity by interfaces. The elements are interacting and they are open to interact with their environments. We can introduce the environments as variables or circumstances surrounding the system of interest and the interaction between the two is done through interfaces. Therefore, the system context and interaction with their environments is the major principle to provide an understanding of the Openness of the system.

A. Openness of Battery Train

Stephen G. Haines stated "*All systems have boundaries which separate them from their environments. The concept of boundaries helps us understand the distinction between open and closed systems. The relatively closed system has rigid, impenetrable boundaries; whereas the open system has permeable boundaries between itself and the broader environment.*" [10]. The battery train as a system has elements that interact with each other and with their environments, therefore, we can consider the system as an Open System.

J. Gharajeddaghi stated "*the controllable variables, the uncontrollable variables we can influence and the uncontrollable variables we cannot influence but will have to appreciate.*" [5]. The battery train has controllable variables that come to have influence within their environment and uncontrollable variables that have appreciating variables.

Figure 4 shows a context diagram of the battery-powered train and we can see the Openness of the battery-powered train. Figure 4 also shows the system boundary and the interaction between controllable and uncontrollable variables, on one side, and the system of interest, on the other side.

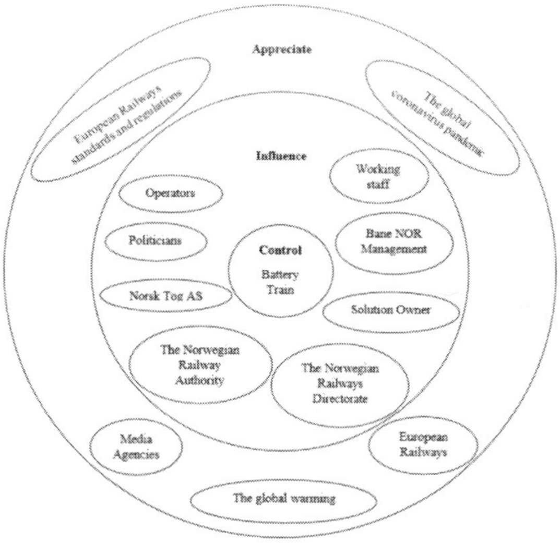

Figure 4. Openness Shows system boundary.

Openness consists of:

a) Control - refers to the system of interest

Battery-powered train

b) Influence - refers to the controllable variables that have influence within the system of interest environment

Operators can include railway companies such as VY or Cargo Net, The Norwegian Railway Authority, the Norwegian National Railways Directorate, staff working on the project, including managers and employees. The solution owner is the Government. Politicians that propose or create laws have power over the governmental strategies. Bane NOR SF Management wants to ensure good and safe solution for operators. Norske Tog AS wants to ensure good service to citizens.

c) Appreciate – Refers to the uncontrollable variables

The global coronavirus pandemic has a huge effect on CO_2 emissions. This abnormal situation caused CO_2 emissions cuts, maybe the largest fall we have seen. The global warming is another factor that is an uncontrollable variable. European railways companies can increase the emergence occurring. European railways standards and regulations have an effect on the Norwegian battery – powered train according to the operational conditions. Media Agencies will share the information of the new technology with the citizens to decrease the worry surrounding the new technology. They can provide feedback from the potential users to the working staff or to the competent authorities.

B. CATWOE and Variable behavior

We identified two groups of controlled and uncontrolled variables that affect the system. The uncontrolled variables are predictable and the system should be prepared for such an environment. The controlled variables are influenced by the system and have a significant effect on decision making. We will analyze the controlled variables behavior because the organizations can change the controlled variables, but cannot change the uncontrolled variables.

Figure 5 shows the CATWOE analysis from Bane NOR SF' viewpoint to ensure a better understanding of the system of interest.

	C.A.T.W.O.E ANALYSIS
C	Bane NOR SF
A	Operators, The Norwegian Railway Authority, The Norwegian National Railways Directorate, Working Staff, Solution Owner, Politicians, Bane NOR SF Management, Norske Tog AS, The global coronavirus pandemic staff, The global warming staff, European railways companies, European railways standards and regulations staff and Media Agencies
T	The need for the purpose of the new system is met by presenting, evaluating, and deciding upon the results from the National Railways Directorate study.
W	Increase the work safety and reduce the cost and CO_2 emission
O	Government
E	Must operate within the European and Norwegian Railways lows and regulations

Figure 5. CATWOE analysis.

C. Influencing the actors

The actors have a significant effect on the system and we need to understand why they do what they do. This effect can have an effective role in system transactional environment. Understanding the actors needs and their influence on the process makes the system more understandable and gives the decisions maker more confidence over their decisions. Those actors have influence on the systems output.

J. Gharajeddaghi stated "*Thereafter, to be an effective player, one has to move yet higher, to the level of understanding, and learn why they do what they do. The why question is the matter of purpose, that of choice*" [5]. We can gain knowledge by asking the why question. Figure 6 shows the actors and why they do what they do.

In the past years, the Norwegian railway sector and politicians with government support showed increased interest in environmental purity and reducing the sources of energy that are harmful to the environment. This supports the global organization trends such as the global warming and European Railway Management. The reduction of CO_2 will support global organization orientation and this project could have funding as an advantage.

The operators of the battery train are motivated by politicians and railway managers to replace the current trains with diesel engines by battery trains to ensure reducing the CO_2 and to participate in the railway activities to provide Zero Emission. Bane NOR SF is an agency that manages the railway infrastructure and has the responsibility for the safety of worker and the passengers. Norske Tog AS collaborated with Bane NOR SF while working on the first battery with partial electrification train as a pilot project within the Norwegian Railway infrastructure sector. The National Railway Directorate leads and supervises the project to ensure the performed work is within Norwegian laws and regulations. They will ensure a good communication with the regulation authority. The Norwegian Railway Authority will also provide guidance to ensure that the project is within Norwegian and international laws and to ensure sustainable and safe operation.

Actors	Why they do what they do
Operators	Provide feedback, test the new system, ensure it meets the purpose of CO_2 free
Politicians	Support the national and international community towards null emission
Working staff	Gain a better salary and experience. Collect and share information.
Owner	Lead, enable and accelerate the commercialization of the battery train.
Bane NOR SF	Ensure that the trains used on its railway lines are modern and safe.
Norske Tog	Owner of the train. Ensures the train is equipped with the new system as a pilot project. Provides the new technology to all operators.
Railway Directorate	Has the responsibility to develop new regulations and standards for the new system.
Railway Authority	Carries out supervision to ensure that companies in the rail industry operate in accordance with legal requirements regarding safety and security.

Figure 6. The actors and Why question.

The project manager will gain knowledge on the new system and how to deal with different situations the working staff could face. They ensure the staff has the necessary tools and the necessary documents to perform their work. The working staff also would gain work experience and probably better salary.

The Directorate study reports will probably take the uncontrolled variables into consideration and try to make them more predictable in order to position the battery train as a new solution to the market with high level of CO_2 reduction until getting the Zero Emission.

D. Systemigram

Sytemigram is derived from "Systemic Diagram" and provides a tool to help managers, working staff and project stakeholder to have a better understanding of the system concepts, processes, and events. This tool, through the diagram, allows the system to tell a story and catch shallow leverage points (Material & Processes) & deeper leverage points (Design & Intent).

The systemigram shows the interfaces, improves the communication and makes the stakeholders part of the decision-making. The systemigram was developed by John Boardman as a part of his approach to develop and provide the systems thinker with a conceptual modelling tool aligned with the soft systems method [8].

"*Integration is the word we use to introduce the subject matter of this chapter, which is systemic diagrams (referred to as systemigrams): what they are, how they are created, who would want to use them and why, and where they are headed as a decision-support tool, in our opinion*" [6]. Integration is the word that can be used to describe the Systemigram. Through the systemic diagram, we can define the system and how it interacts with the environment, define the different stakeholders and why they have interest, and express how they could be used to enable the system to achieve its goal effectively.

The systemigram in Figure 7 shows, from the top-left, the system of interest (battery train) and runs towards the purpose of the system, which is located down-right (Zero Emission). The battery train should be resilient in order to achieve its purpose by performing the system adaptability.

The elements of the system are classified into 5 groups with different colors. The selected groups are: Agencies (orange color), Physical Train (black color), Emission (green color), Infrastructure (gray color), and Financial influence (yellow color).

E. Leverage Points

The leverage point for any system has a significant effect over the entire system, where any small changes or modification can cause a large effect, as seen in Figure 7.

The Norwegian Railway Directorate has selected the battery train with partial electrification as a proper solution to the Norwegian Railway Sector. This will help the global effort to support zero emission. That means, the Government should provide the funding to the project. Adapting this solution means we should adapt laws, regulations, legislation, and commercial structure.

Applying the new battery on trains will make the transportation more cost effective and the load of the work for railway sector could be increased and cause new challenges to our system. D. H. Meadows stated "*Missing information flows is one of the most common causes of system malfunction. Adding or restoring information can be a powerful intervention, usually much easier and cheaper than rebuilding physical infrastructure*" [3].

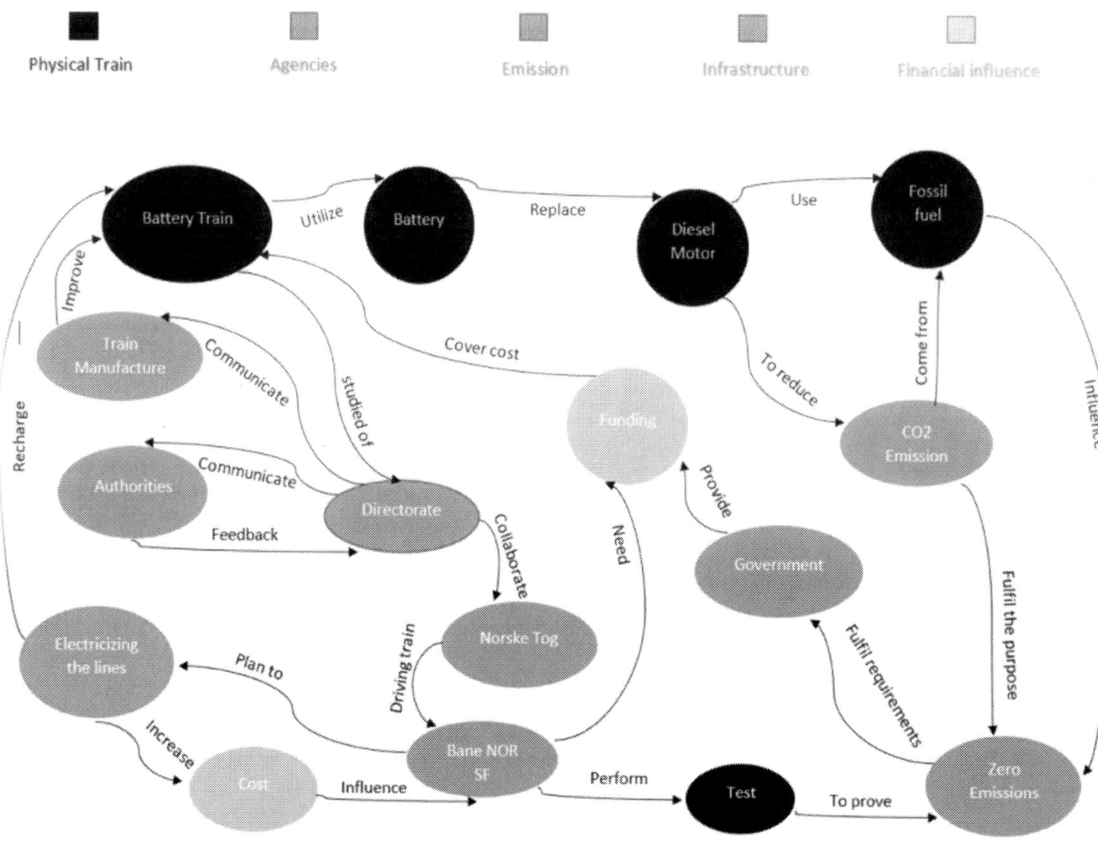

Figure 7. Systemigram for battery train

In Figure 7, we can see from the Systemigram how important the communications and feedback among Directorate Authorities and the train manufacturers is, in case modifications to satisfy the European and Norwegian railways are required. Therefore, the system should have a new method of communication and feedback for better response, such as putting the information on a website and giving access to the users, depending on their positions in the organization.

Additionally, Bane NOR SF must change the stretches to build new electrified stretches to enable recharging the new battery train. This will make the railway sector ready to receive more battery-operated trains that cover the entire Norway stretches. However, this will also cause an increase in the cost to Bane NOR, due to the need to build a new stretch.

One of the new impacts that could affect the new project is the Coronavirus global pandemic. The world has become increasingly isolated and the advice from experts goes against being in groups, which could further spread infection. Among the measures taken is to reduce the use of public vehicles, including locomotives. This approach may have a negative impact in terms of financing the project and in terms of continuing to implement it.

Another leverage point is how the new battery train influences human factors. The new technology will require a new type of working staff with a high education level. In addition, it requires a new type of data and IT systems to deal with it.

V. Conclusion and Recommendations

We need to rethink the design of the Norwegian Railway infrastructure and understand the impacts of the new technology on the cities. Rebuilding or building new lines to fit the new system will require resource, money, and time to perform the works.

The battery train is considered a railway solution for Zero Emission, but not as the only one. This solution will increase the awareness in the community and have a positive impact on the global environment in terms of global warming, noise, and clean air. However, at the same time, increasing fears of lack of clarity of the new technology system and the need to improve the quality of train service exist.

This paper has presented the new battery train technology of with partial electrification by using the Systems Thinking Methodology Framework. The purpose was to understand the complexity of the system, locate the system boundaries, identify and define the uncontrollable and controllable variables within the system environment, allocate the stakeholders and their roles, and visualizing the system through applying the Systemigram.

The paper used Openness to categories the system variables. Some of the variables can be controlled by actors categorized under Influence such as operators. Another group no one has control over are variables which are unpredictable, categorized under Appreciated, such as the global Coronavirus pandemic.

The paper used the WHY question technique to find out why different actors do what they do. This method helps the project managers to understand the expectation of stakeholders for this new system. In addition, CATOWE analysis is performed from the stakeholder viewpoint.

Using the Systemigram allowed us to see the system from a different and bigger point of view. This tool demonstrates the complex systems in a simple way and helps visualize the elements and their influence in the system. This tool makes the communication among different stakeholder easier and effective.

Further, we want to recommend Systems Thinking methodology to be used. It can be used in any field of Engineering research or analysis and many different areas of specialization. This methodology makes the system better understood by identifying its strengths and weaknesses and how the system elements are connected internally and externally. Also, it facilitates the process for developing and improving the system's outputs.

ACKNOWLEDGEMENT

This paper was based on the Norwegian Railway Directorate reports. The first authors' previous manager, senior technical advisor (Dag Aarsland) from the Norwegian National Railway Directorate was a part of the working staff for The Null Emissions Solutions for Non-Electrified Railways (NULLFIB). This gave the first author the inspiration to work on this topic and to apply the systems thinking methodology on the battery train with partial electrification solution. We would like to express our thanks to everyone who helped us in providing information to complete this paper.

REFERENCES

[1] B. Gray, "The Cynefin framework: Applying an understanding of complexity to medicine", December 2017.

[2] D. J. Snowden and M. E. Boone, "A Leader's Framework for Decision Making", 2007

[3] D. H. Meadow. Thinking in Systems. Chelsea Green Publishing Co., 2015

[4] INCOSE. Systems Engineering Handbook, 4thHoboken, New Jersey: Wiley, 2015

[5] J. Gharajedaghi, Managing Chaos and Complexity. Morgan Kaufmann Publishers In., 2011

[6] J. Boardman and B. Sauser, Systems Thinking, Coping with 21st Century Problems. Published January 29, 2008 by CRC Press.

[7] L. von Bertalanffy. 1968. General System Theory. published on March, 1976.

[8] M. L. Loper, "Modeling and Simulation in the Systems Engineering Life Cycle", 2015

[9] Norwegian Railway Directorate. Published 2019. NULLFIB Final Report.

[10] S. G. Haines, Strategic and System Thinking: The Winning Formula. Publisher: Systems Thinking Press, 2007.

Autonomous Network Provisioning for Digital Transformation Era

Intent oriented service provisioning assisted by Machine Learning

Taro Ogawa
IoT & Cloud Services Business Division
Hitachi, Ltd.
Tokyo, Japan
e-mail: taro.ogawa.tg@hitachi.com

Tomokazu Makino
IoT & Cloud Services Business Division
Hitachi, Ltd.
Tokyo, Japan
e-mail: tomokazu.makino.ax@hitachi.com

Kenji Arai
IoT & Cloud Services Business Division
Hitachi, Ltd.
Tokyo, Japan
e-mail: kenji.arai.jo@hitachi.com

Abstract— **Systems engineering, especially in requirements engineering, has become a more complex process because of the diversification in both application and infrastructure aspects. The needs of application users are diversifying industry by industry and are not easy to formulate in a conventional mass-optimization way. Infrastructure technologies are also evolving endlessly. Mitigating these complicated and changing gaps between the requirements and infrastructures should be crucial for the business process optimization in digital transformation. This contribution provides the machine learning assisted transformation of ambiguous user intents to network service specifications conforming to underlying network infrastructures. The proposed system utilizes ensemble learning with several decision-tree based algorithms stacked. The vertical-industry classification process is also implemented as a feature space reduction methodology to exploit each category's knowledge of domain experts. The preliminary evaluation of the prediction performance achieves an accuracy of around 80%.**

Keywords-service provisioning; intent-based networking; machine learning; digital transformation; vertical indutry.

I. Introduction

Digital Transformation as refinement in any business procedure context has become relevant for every industry: Industry 4.0 in manufacturing, autonomous cars in transportation, remote diagnosis, operations in medical care, etc.

Networking as an enabler for these systems advancements can not be a "one-size-fits-all" type solution, however. In other words, just the cloud-smartphone infrastructure is not sufficient for the wide range of requirements spectrum from various vertical industries. Manufacturing industries demand low-latency and high-availability, while some medical care facilities necessitate higher bandwidth for high-definition diagnostic image transfer, for example.

Since such diversification of networking requirements causes the customized networking-capability provisioning for each network service user, accurate comprehension of an individual's network service requirements must be essential. An accurate understanding of network service requirements, however, can not be straightforward because of the multifaceted business situations of users, as well as the diversification of technologies and available services in networking or cloud infrastructure.

Additionally, network service users may not be experts in networking technologies and just aim at their business operation efficiency. Usually, their requirements are expressed as various "intent" levels, namely, business-, service-, or resource-related ones [5]. Moreover, since each user's business situation will be changing dynamically, the intents themselves will also change swiftly.

Network service provisioning should be adapting to these circumstances, preferably in an autonomous manners, where Machine Learning technologies will come in.

Applying machine learning technologies to communication networks has been mainstream in research communities. However, almost all the efforts are focusing on network resource efficiencies [1]. Further, there has been hard to find case studies with communication networks composed of multiple technology- or administrative-domains infrastructures. Only several vision articles mentioned machine learning and artificial intelligence aspects on the network service provisioning, such as vertical industries or service orchestration related themes [2][3][4].

Our main contributions are:

- Presenting the overall procedure of network-service requirements engineering and provisioning for vertical industries.
- Introducing the machine learning architecture for network service requirements engineering, which transforms the user's ambiguous intents into a dedicated network service specification conforming to underlying network infrastructures.

- Initial experimental evaluation of the proposed architecture, combining with various industries' expert knowledge.

The rest of this paper is organized as follows. Section II describes conventional network provisioning procedures and problems related to the current diversified situations of application usage and infrastructure technologies. In Section III, a detailed description of the proposed system architecture with an ensemble learning approach is presented. Section IV provides the evaluation results of the proposed architecture for various vertical industries, including transportation, medical care, and e-commerce. Section V concludes the article with our considerations for future enhancements.

II. NETWORK SERVICE PROVISIONING

Usually, requirements engineering for network service provisioning has been relying on the knowledge of experts of each industry domain. The experienced domain experts interact with each user to derive the network service specifications from the user's intents, mainly business and service level ones. Although some rule-based approaches might be possible in the past business environments, the more advanced and expeditious ways must be necessary for the digital transformation era depicted above.

There will be more diversified network infrastructures, including mobile accesses (4G/5G/6G, WiFi6 and beyond, local- and private-cellular, CBRS, LPWA, etc.), metro accesses, core transport lease lines. There will also be more sophisticated cloud-based networking services, such as SD-WAN and intra-/inter-cloud networking gateway services. Cloud services are also expanding their capabilities, including edge and serverless computing.

Regarding these advancements in both technologies and services, the conventional network service provisioning with human experts might become impossible or inefficient at least. Without accommodating such networking environmental changes, network service users may lose their business opportunities.

However, the necessary procedure for domain experts should remain. Domain experts extract the generic networking requirements from the user's intents expressed by the user, although having said ambiguously. They could use their expert knowledge relating to the domain and the user's business situation. They also classify the requirements into functional and non-functional ones.

The extracted and inferred generic networking requirements are translated into network service specifications alining to the underlying network infrastructures. There might be many choices for selecting the underlying network services in the multiple domains for end-to-end network system configuration. The domain experts also utilize the cost or reliability performance knowledge for such selection.

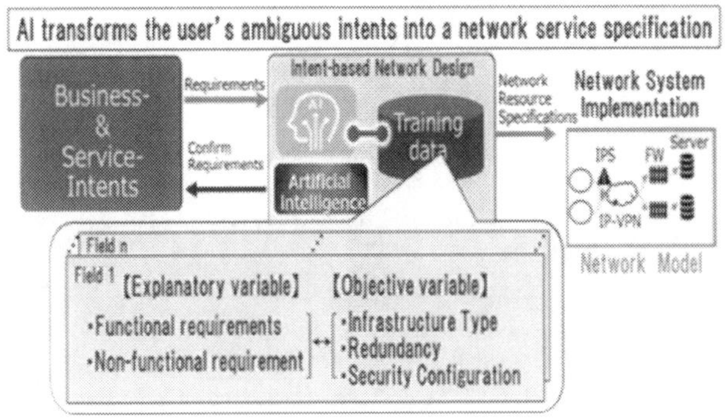

Figure 1. Proposed system workflow.

III. NETWORK REQUIREMENTS ENGINEERING AND MACHINE LEARNING

A. System Architecture

The proposed system workflow is depicted in Figure 1. The extractor accepts the corresponding user's intents via a graphical user interface (GUI). It also validates and preprocesses the input data into the appropriate network service requirements. The preprocessing procedure includes not only conventional operation, such as regularization but also pre-classification of the input feature space based on the industry-specific class structure relevant to the user concerned [6].

The analyzer then classifies the network service requirements with several types of machine learning methodology. It derives the candidates of the network configuration with machine learning performance indicators for each classified model.

B. Model-based engineering

The most critical part of the system is how to mitigate the gap between the user's intents and network service requirements sufficient to the configuration of the workable end-to-end network service composed by the various underlying network infrastructures.

The extractor functional capabilities are shown as a model-based engineering GUI. Figure 2 depicts a case of a smart-meter distribution network system.

The GUI provides two types of interface: a system model input part (left) and a topology input part (right). The former part accepts the system model, including the information related to network scalability, social impacts of failure (measured by some metric, such as resulted economic loss and affected population). The latter part obtains the parameters, such as the service category (a relevant vertical industry), types of the end system, and the connecting topology between the end systems. The extractor deduces the generic network service requirements, both functional, such as required bandwidth and non-functional, such as resiliency and availability.

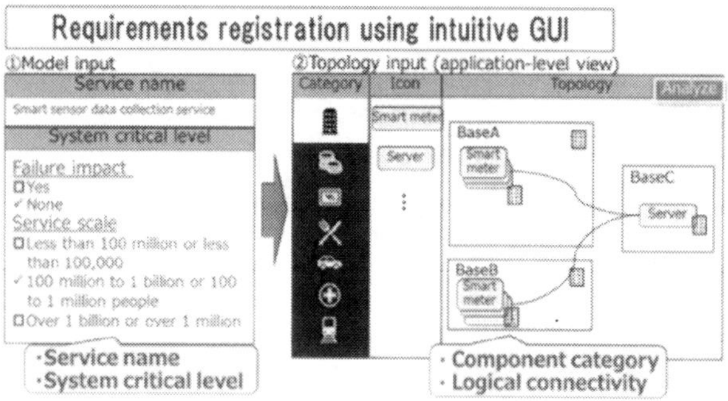

Figure 2. Model-based engineering GUI.

Currently, this extrapolation of network service requirements from the input intents is almost rule-based, with the conversion table for the relevant industry classification, which is expert-knowledge based.

C. Classifier

The generic network requirements transformed from the user's intents by the extractor are fed to the analyzer; its functional configuration is shown in Figure 3.

The analyzer predicts the appropriate network configuration for the user concerned utilizing the learned data accumulated through related industry cases' design and operation.

The diversification of business intents and technologies, however, makes the prediction difficult. The classifier optimization might not be straight forward like the usual machine learning process. We adopt a sort of ensemble learning approach and human intervention inside the prediction and selection pipeline to alleviate this issue.

D. Ensemble Learning and Confidence

Table I shows the consideration of classifier selection, comparing the techniques, such as Cosine Similarity, Support Vector Machine, and Random Forest, from the viewpoints of computation and accuracy. Considering the current problem space depicted in Figure 2, Random Forest can be concluded as a fundamental approach to the present purpose of classification from the comparison.

Furthermore, several tree-based techniques are stacked to achieve a broader range of application of this approach. Other than Random Forest, we apply Gradient Boosting Decision Tree (GBDT) and Light Gradient Boosting Machine (LightGBM). These classifiers are stacked and independently predict the optimized network configurations using the same learned data. The performance of the predictions is figured up as confidence of each classifier's prediction.

If the particular classifier's confidence exceeds the threshold set, the analyzer recommends the classifier's prediction. In case that none of the prediction confidence passes the threshold, the analyzer requests human interventions, and takes the human decisions as learning data. Even if the prediction exceeds the threshold, the analyzer provides each classifier's confidence to human considerations to enhance the learning process.

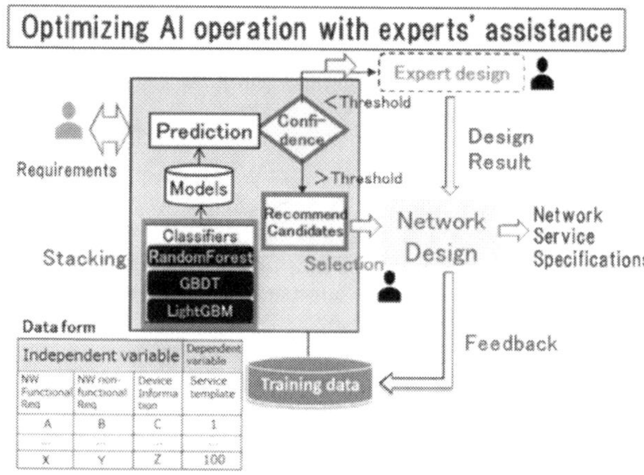

Figure 3. Architecture.

TABLE I. CLASSIFIERS COMPARISON

ML Method	Computational Complexity	Accuracy
Cosine Similarity	Low	Low
Support Vector Machine	High	Medium to high
Radom Forest	Medium	Medium to high
Stacking	Acceptable	High

E. Networking Components and Configuration Model

The derived generic network configuration should be translated to network service specifications for underlying infrastructures. Such an arrangement can be modelled by networking components and their setup as a system. Figure 4 depicts an example of the network model as a type of client-server system, which is the prevalent cloud system architecture. Figure 4 also includes the public networking apparatus, such as access and core.

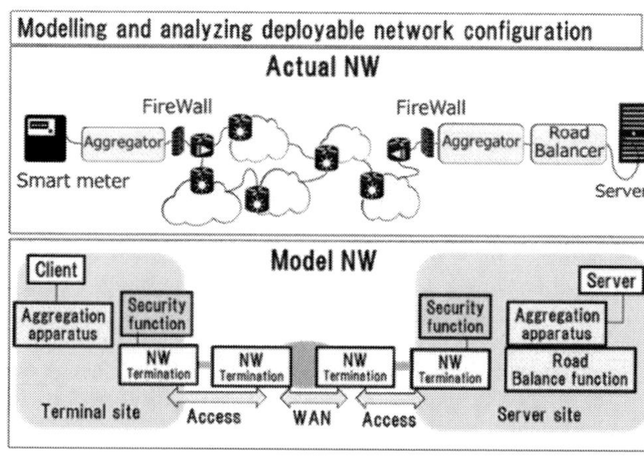

Figure 4. Network model.

The analyzer's output for the translation based on the network model is expressed as a parameter set up on a network template. The network template includes the network components to achieve the networking connectivities between the end systems and servers. An example of the template is depicted in Figure 5, including concentrators aggregating the signals from IoT devices (smart meters), middleboxes for security, load balancers at the server-side.

It also defines the access lines and WANs. Each networking components can have various capabilities depending on the networking service requirements. The capability ranges and examples of the networking components are also shown respectively in Figure 5.

F. Data representations and constraint

Appropriate networking configurations for various industry categories have been generated by each vertical industry's domain experts and validated through machine learning processes. These learned configurations are associated with the network templates as a network menu. An example of the network menu is shown in Figure 6.

The network menu also contains the restrictions for the combination of network components and configuration. For example, a smart factory network configuration requires real-time, low-latency, and availability. Connected cars necessitate edge computing capabilities in addition to that. High-definition image transfer should be essential for remote medical cares. These category-specific requirements can be accomplished through specific network configurations, and no versatile layout should be existing.

Figure 7 depicts the examples of the output of the network configuration for the smart-meter networking case.

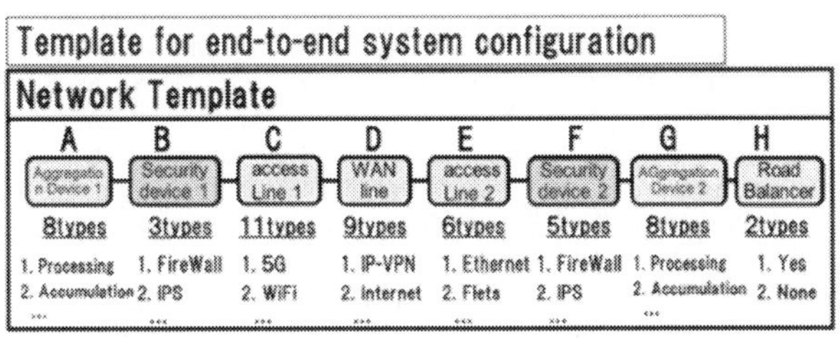

Figure 5. Network template example.

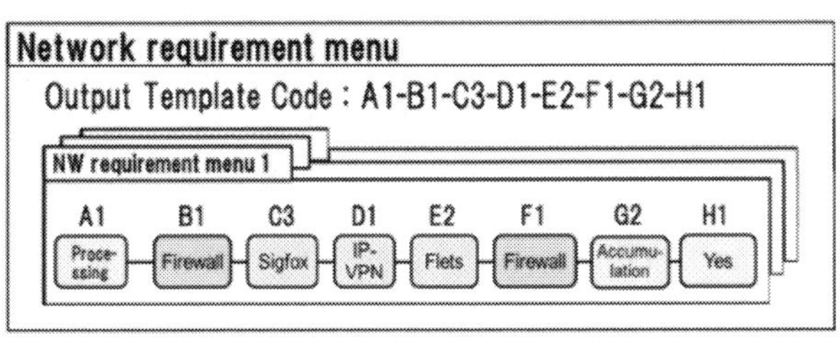

Figure 6. Network menu example.

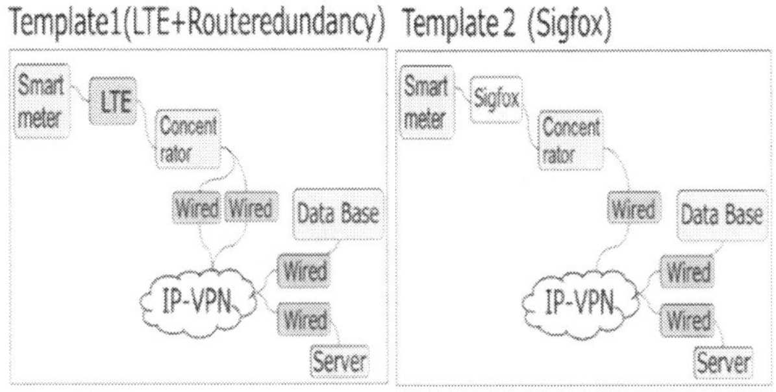

Figure 7. Examples of the outputs.

Two candidates for such a system are selected by the analyzer, one for LTE-based and another using Sigfox. The analyzer recommends the optimized one considering the various possibilities, including the cost related viewpoints.

IV. PERFORMANCE EVALUATION

Even though usual data-shortage problems for this investigation exist, the initial preliminary performance evaluation has been carried out. A base data set is generated to bootstrap the machine learning system through the procedure as follows.

Table II lists several reference sites of the actual use cases incorporated into the evaluation. 52 IoT related system configurations are picked up as basic patterns from the examples in these sites.

Furthermore, a data augmentation approach is deployed to generate more training data from the samples mentioned above. Some parameters, such as the number of end-devices or branches, can be varied in a reasonable range for each use case. It is to be noted that the parameters are not independent of each other but correlated, as depicted in Figure 8. Additionally, the correlation strength should differ parameter by parameters.

According to the industry categories, the generated data is pre-classified, such as transportation, medical care, and e-commerce.

An example result of the process with hold-out validation is shown in Table III. The accuracies of the classification for the categories are about 80%.

TABLE II. USE-CASE REFERENCE

Source	URL
MIC Japan	http://www.soumu.go.jp/main_sosiki/joho_tsusin/top/local_support/ict/index.html
Hitachi Lumada	https://www.hitachi.co.jp/products/it/lumada/usecase/index.html
KDDI	https://iot.kddi.com/cases/

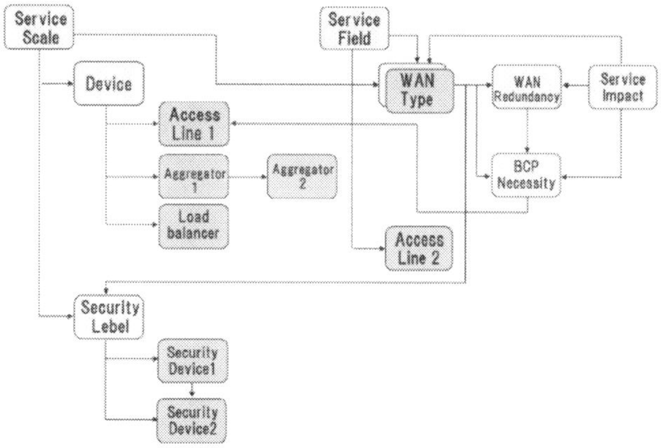

Figure 8. Correlation between the parameters.

TABLE III. EVALUATION RESULTS

Target Industry Category	Accuracy		
	Random Forest	GBDT	LightGBM
Smart city	0.837	0.876	0.855
Construction	0.799	0.858	0.828
Commerce	0.846	0.923	0.928
Manufacturing	0.835	0.877	0.869
Transportation	0.795	0.845	0.831

V. CONCLUSION

This contribution provides the machine learning assisted transformation of ambiguous user intents to network service specifications conforming to underlying network infrastructures. The proposed system utilizes ensemble learning with several decision-tree based algorithms stacked. The vertical-industry classification process is also implemented as a feature space reduction methodology to exploit each category's knowledge of domain experts. The preliminary evaluation of the prediction performance achieves about accuracy of around 80%.

Systems engineering in the digital transformation era, however, may have an intrinsic difficulty of ever-changing conditions, which causes situations of data shortage for the usual statistical machine learning approach. The proposed architecture utilizes not just conventional machine learning techniques but also domain-expert knowledge and other approaches like data augmentation and simulation.

Although the evaluated system is a preliminary one to bootstrap the proposed architecture, the approach should be essential in the diversified and accelerated digital transformation era.

Expanding the applicable industrial categories is a direction of future enhancements. Some hierarchical structure can exist composed of common features to every industry, specific characteristic to each sector, and individually segmented distinction of each user. Network model enrichment is also possible enhancements.

Finally, some standard organizations are starting activities related to service provisioning with machine intelligence [7][8]. The architecture and results presented here should contribute to the advancement in these standardizations.

ACKNOWLEDGEMENT

This work was conducted as a part of the project titled "Research and development for innovative AI network integrated infrastructure technologies (JPMI00316)", supported by the Ministry of Internal Affairs and Communications, Japan.

REFERENCES

[1] M. Morocho-Cayamcela, H. Lee, and W. Lim, "Machine learning for 5G/B5G mobile and wireless communications: potential, limitations, and future directions, " IEEE Access, vol. 7, pp. 137184-137206, 2019

[2] N. Kato, B. Mao, F. Tang, Y. Kawamoto, and J. Liu, "Ten challenges in advancing machine learning technologies toward 6G," IEEE Wireless Communications, vol. 27, No. 3, pp. 96–103, June 2020.

[3] X. Li et al., "Automating Vertical Services Deployments over the 5GT Platform," IEEE Communications Magazine, vol. 58, No. 7, pp. 44–50, July 2020.

[4] B. Spinnewyn, S. Latré, and J. F. Botero, "Service Orchestration in NFV-Based Traditional and Emerging Cloud Environments: State of the Art and Research Challenges," IEEE Communications Magazine, vol. 58, No.8, pp. 76–81, August 2020.

[5] TM Forum White Paper, "Autonomous Networks: Empowering digital transformation for smart societies and industries," Release 2, October 2020.

[6] Information-technology Promotion Agency Japan (IPA), "Non-Functional Requirements Grades Usage Guide [Description Manual]," April 2010.

[7] ITU-T Draft Recommendation Y.3178, "Functional framework of AI-based network service provisioning in future networks including IMT-2020," March 2021.

[8] TM Forum Insight, "Intent oriented customer engagement: understanding customer purpose," July 2020.